Flash™ *5 Cartooning*

W9-AHB-810

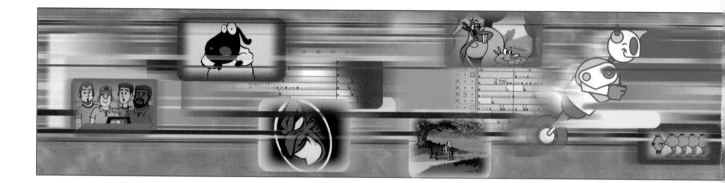

MARK CLARKSON

FLASH™ 5 CARTOONING

Hungry Minds™

New York, NY ▲ Cleveland, OH ◆ Indianapolis, IN ▼ Chicago, IL ◆ Foster City, CA ▲ San Francisco, CA

Flash™ 5 Cartooning

Published by
Hungry Minds, Inc.
909 Third Avenue
New York, NY 10022
www.hungryminds.com

Copyright © 2001 Hungry Minds, Inc. All rights reserved. No part of this book, including interior design, cover design, and icons, may be reproduced or transmitted in any form, by any means (electronic, photocopying, recording, or otherwise) without the prior written permission of the publisher.

ISBN: 0-7645-3547-1

Printed in the United States of America

10 9 8 7 6 5 4 3 2 1

1K/RT/QS/QR/FC

Distributed in the United States by Hungry Minds, Inc.

Distributed by CDG Books Canada Inc. for Canada; by Transworld Publishers Limited in the United Kingdom; by IDG Norge Books for Norway; by IDG Sweden Books for Sweden; by IDG Books Australia Publishing Corporation Pty. Ltd. for Australia and New Zealand; by TransQuest Publishers Pte Ltd. for Singapore, Malaysia, Thailand, Indonesia, and Hong Kong; by Gotop Information Inc. for Taiwan; by ICG Muse, Inc. for Japan; by Intersoft for South Africa; by Eyrolles for France; by International Thomson Publishing for Germany, Austria, and Switzerland; by Distribuidora Cuspide for Argentina; by LR International for Brazil; by Galileo Libros for Chile; by Ediciones ZETA S.C.R. Ltda. for Peru; by WS Computer Publishing Corporation, Inc., for the Philippines; by Contemporanea de Ediciones for Venezuela; by Express Computer Distributors for the Caribbean and West Indies; by Micronesia Media Distributor, Inc. for Micronesia; by Chips Computadoras S.A. de C.V. for Mexico; by Editorial Norma de Panama S.A. for Panama; by American Bookshops for Finland.

For general information on Hungry Minds' products and services please contact our Customer Care department within the U.S. at 800-762-2974, outside the U.S. at 317-572-3993 or fax 317-572-4002.

For sales inquiries and reseller information, including discounts, premium and bulk quantity sales, and foreign-language translations, please contact our Customer Care department at 800-434-3422, fax 317-572-4002 or write to Hungry Minds, Inc., Attn: Customer Care Department, 10475 Crosspoint Boulevard, Indianapolis, IN 46256.

For information on licensing foreign or domestic rights, please contact our Sub-Rights Customer Care department at 650-653-7098.

For information on using Hungry Minds' products and services in the classroom or for ordering examination copies, please contact our Educational Sales department at 800-434-2086 or fax 317-572-4005.

For press review copies, author interviews, or other publicity information, please contact our Public Relations department at 650-653-7000 or fax 650-653-7500.

For authorization to photocopy items for corporate, personal, or educational use, please contact Copyright Clearance Center, 222 Rosewood Drive, Danvers, MA 01923, or fax 978-750-4470.

Library of Congress Cataloging-in-Publication Data

Clarkson, Mark (Mark Alan), 1960-
  Flash 5 cartooning / Mark Clarkson.
    p. cm.
  Includes index.
  ISBN 0-7645-3547-1 (alk. paper)
  1. Computer animation. 2. Flash (Computer file) I. Title: Flash five cartooning. II. Title
TR897.7 .C545 2001
006.6'96--dc21

00-054156

LIMIT OF LIABILITY/DISCLAIMER OF WARRANTY: THE PUBLISHER AND AUTHOR HAVE USED THEIR BEST EFFORTS IN PREPARING THIS BOOK. THE PUBLISHER AND AUTHOR MAKE NO REPRESENTATIONS OR WARRANTIES WITH RESPECT TO THE ACCURACY OR COMPLETENESS OF THE CONTENTS OF THIS BOOK AND SPECIFICALLY DISCLAIM ANY IMPLIED WARRANTIES OF MERCHANTABILITY OR FITNESS FOR A PARTICULAR PURPOSE. THERE ARE NO WARRANTIES WHICH EXTEND BEYOND THE DESCRIPTIONS CONTAINED IN THIS PARAGRAPH. NO WARRANTY MAY BE CREATED OR EXTENDED BY SALES REPRESENTATIVES OR WRITTEN SALES MATERIALS. THE ACCURACY AND COMPLETENESS OF THE INFORMATION PROVIDED HEREIN AND THE OPINIONS STATED HEREIN ARE NOT GUARANTEED OR WARRANTED TO PRODUCE ANY PARTICULAR RESULTS, AND THE ADVICE AND STRATEGIES CONTAINED HEREIN MAY NOT BE SUITABLE FOR EVERY INDIVIDUAL. NEITHER THE PUBLISHER NOR AUTHOR SHALL BE LIABLE FOR ANY LOSS OF PROFIT OR ANY OTHER COMMERCIAL DAMAGES, INCLUDING BUT NOT LIMITED TO SPECIAL, INCIDENTAL, CONSEQUENTIAL, OR OTHER DAMAGES.

Trademarks: Hungry Minds and It's all possible! are trademarks or registered trademarks of Hungry Minds, Inc. All other trademarks are the property of their respective owners. Hungry Minds, Inc., is not associated with any product or vendor mentioned in this book.

is a trademark of
Hungry Minds, Inc.

To Pamela, light of my life.

PREFACE

Hiya. Welcome to *Flash 5 Cartooning*. This book is about animation.

Over the years, Flash has evolved into the number one tool for building sexy, animated Web sites. You know the ones: fly-out menus and little sparkles flying around the screen, chasing your mouse, while playing hi-fi music. Every element spins and jumps and sings a little song when your mouse passes over it. That's not the kind of animation I'm talking about.

I'm talking about cartoon animation: *Yogi Bear, Heckyl and Jeckyl, Tom and Jerry, Beavis and Butthead, Pinocchio, Mickey Mouse, Fritz the Cat, Bugs Bunny, Rocky and Bullwinkle*.

This book is about using Flash for making cartoons, for telling stories, for making people laugh. There are roughly 7,913 books on the market about Macromedia Flash. Many of these books are more comprehensive than the one you're holding in your hands. But this book is different: it focuses on Macromedia Flash 5 as a tool for cartooning and animation. It emphasizes Flash's ability to entertain and tell a story.

This book covers much of the same subject matter as any other book on Flash, but the material is presented in the context of cartooning. What sets it apart is the emphasis it gives to subjects that other Flash books don't cover, such as storyboards and scripts, squashing and stretching, walk cycles, and character design.

Flash 5 Cartooning is project-oriented. It covers various Flash tools and techniques, from basic drawing to complex interactivity, as they come up naturally in the process of making cartoons.

Flash 5 Cartooning is aimed at beginning to intermediate Flashers, but everyone is invited.

FLASH CARTOONING

A Flash cartoon can be a lot of things: it can be a familiar, linear comic book, or an online graphic novel with music and spoken dialogue; it can be an interactive "toy" like a dancing monkey or a frog in a blender; it can be an adventure game; it can be a traditional animated cartoon with wacky gags and talking animals; it can even be a commercial, broadcast-quality animation.

A Flash cartoon can be available worldwide the minute it's finished, and if it's good, it can be up on a major Internet Web site within a week, earning money.

You don't have to be a great artist to make Flash cartoons. My twelve-year-old daughter is a Flash cartoonist. Flash's drawing tools go a long way toward hiding any clumsiness with a virtual pencil. Drawing isn't even mandatory in Flash cartooning: the characters in Honkworm International, Inc.'s popular *Fishbar* series (`www.honkworm.com/ fishbar-series.htm`) are fashioned from digital photographs of dead fish and such.

A WIDE MARKET

Not all Flash cartoons are done purely for art's sake. You may harbor dreams of using Flash to turn your art into filthy lucre. Well, you can.

When I spoke recently to Cory Wynne, Senior Content Manager at AtomFilms, he said something that struck me: "Flash is driving online entertainment more than anything else." Web denizens watch around 100,000 short films every day at AtomFilms. AtomFilms is dedicated to all types of short films, but most of the films viewed are animation, and most of the animation viewed is in Flash. Overall, more than a third of all films viewed at AtomFilms are Flash cartoons — that translates into around 35,000 viewings a day.

And that's just at AtomFilms. Add in Hotwired's Animation Express, WildBrain.com, the Cartoon Network, and independent cartoonists' sites like JoeCartoon.com and Killfrog.com — not to mention the countless number of downloadable Flash cartoons that pass from desktop to desktop as e-mail attachments — and there's no telling how many times a day somebody, somewhere watches a Flash cartoon. But trust me, with a quarter of a billion Flash-equipped surfers cruising for entertainment, it's a lot. If you have talent, then there's a market for your Flash cartooning.

CAVEAT ANIMATOR

I've been fooling with Flash since way back in early 1995, which, in Internet time, corresponds roughly to the Pleistocene Epoch. This was back before Macromedia acquired the program, when it was still called FutureWave SmartSketch and had no animation capabilities at all.

ACTIONSCRIPT

Flash 5 includes a programming language called ActionScript, which is very, very similar to Java. This book covers ActionScripting, but only the easy stuff. If you're asking, "Hey, how do I make a little animation that plays while my movie loads?" Or, "How do I use buttons to jump from place to place in my animation?" then you'll find the answers here. If your questions run more along the lines of, "How do I integrate my Flash-based Web site with CGI shopping cart services?" or "How can I program a Flash version of Ms. Pacman?", then I must refer you to *Flash 5 Bible* (also published by Hungry Minds, Inc., formerly IDG Books Worldwide, Inc.) and other, more authoritative texts such as Bill Sanders' *Flash ActionScript f/x & Design* (Scottsdale, AZ: The Coriolis Group, 2000).

Despite my comparatively extensive amount of experience with Flash, I make no claims to be the best Flasher out there. I am not *the* authority on Flash ActionScripting. I'm not really *an* authority on Flash ActionScripting at all.

Nor am I the greatest Flash animator in the world—I'm not even ranked. I can't even draw very well. I'm not a natural artist, cartoonist, or animator. None of those skills comes especially easily to me. If I have an advantage, then, it is that I've had to actually *think* about these things and figure them out for myself. What I know, I've had to figure out slowly, over time, with the help of a lot of great books and many helpful fellow Flashers.

Stick around, and you'll reap the benefits of my long war with finicky Flash features such as shape tweening. Learn from my mistakes in virtually every part of Flash, and we'll have a little fun while we're at it.

By the end of the book, you'll be a Flash cartoonist, too.

CONTACT ME

Love me? Hate me? Want to make suggestions for my next book? You can contact me at www.markclarkson.com.

Mark Clarkson

KEY CONVENTIONS

I do all my work on a PC, and this book is written from the PC point of view. (Yes, another clear case of oppression by the majority.) Fortunately, the Flash interface is very similar on both the PC and the Mac. But there are some differences, arising from the differences between the mice and keyboards of the two machines.

For example, the Enter key on the PC is called the Return key on the Mac. Same key. Same functionality. Different name.

The Ctrl key on the PC is the equivalent of the Command key on the Mac. For example Ctrl+Z on the PC equals Command+Z on the Mac. Ctrl+clicking on the PC translates to Command+clicking on the Mac. Everywhere I say "Ctrl", Mac users should just pretend I said "Command," instead.

Where the PC has an Alt key, the Mac has an Option key. Alt+clicking on the PC is the same as Option+clicking on the Mac. When I say "Alt," Mac users should press the Option key instead.

Lastly, most Mac mice only have one button. When the text refers to right-clicking a screen item, Mac users should Control+click instead: hold down the Control key and click that item.

BOOKS FROM MY DESKTOP

These books never left my side while I wrote this book. I heartily endorse any and all of them:

- *The Elements of Style* by **William Strunk Jr. and E.B. White** (Needham, MA: Allyn & Bacon, 1995). Tiny, cheap, readable, under 100 pages long . . . the only grammar book you'll ever need.
- *The Illusion of Life: Disney Animation* by **Frank Thomas and Ollie Johnston** (New York: Hyperion, 1995). Legendary animators Frank Thomas and Ollie Johnston take you on a grand, coffee-table-book-sized tour of the glory years of Disney animation.
- *Cartoon Animation* by **Preston Blair** (Laguna Hills, CA: Walter Foster Publishing, 1995). No animator or animator wanna-be can afford to be without this book. Buy it now!
- *Bare Bones Camera Course for Film and Video* by **Tom Schroeppel** (Tampa, FL: Tom Schroeppel, 1982). A valuable resource on camera moves and scene layout.
- *The Cartoonist's Workbook* by **Robin Hall** (London: Sterling Publications, 1997). Although geared toward print cartooning — newspaper and magazine panels and strips — this book does a great job of introducing all the basics of cartooning, including faces, expressions, poses, and layouts.
- *The Animator's Workbook* by **Tony White** (New York: Watson-Guptill Publications, 1988). A comprehensive guide to the traditional animation process.
- *Everything You Ever Wanted to Know about Cartooning but Were Afraid to Draw* by **Christopher Hart** (New York: Watson-Guptill Publications, 1994). Mr. Hart has single-handedly written a small library of books on cartooning everything from mice to superheroes. All of his books are great, but this one is my favorite.
- *Chuck Amuck: The Life and Times of an Animated Cartoonist* by **Chuck Jones** (New York: Farrar Straus & Giroux, 1999). The most wonderfully delightful biography ever written by someone who wasn't Mark Twain. You'll laugh, you'll cry, you'll learn a lot about animation. (Well, okay, you won't cry so much . . .)
- *Cartooning the Head and Figure* by **Jack Hamm** (New York: Perigee, 1982) Some of the material is a bit dated — the section on caricature features Woodrow Wilson and Neville Chamberlain — but still a very useful book.
- *Digital Character Animation* by **George Maestri** (Indianapolis: New Riders Publishing, 1996). This book is really about 3D animation, but has a lot of good information about character movement and camera work.
- *Flash 4 Magic* by **David Emberton and J. Scott Hamlin** (Indianapolis: New Riders Publishing, 2000). Cool projects push Flash interactivity to the edge. A must if you want to build video games, jukeboxes, and other nifty toys in Flash.

- ***Flash 4 Bible* by Robert Reinhardt and Jon Warren Lentz** (New York: Hungry Minds, Inc., formerly IDG Books Worldwide, 2000). This was the definitive reference on Flash back in the early days when I first got the idea for the book you're holding.
- ***Producing Great Sound for Digital Video* by Jay Rose** (Gilroy, CA: CMP Books, 2000). DV columnist and audio expert Jay Rose tells you everything you need to know about recording and processing digital sound.
- ***How to Draw Comics the Marvel Way* by Stan Lee and John Buscema** (New York: Simon & Schuster, 1984). Great information on character design, poses, and layouts.

ACKNOWLEDGMENTS

I would like to thank the cartoonists and animators who have contributed tips, tricks, techniques, and art to this project; without them, this would have been a lesser book. A special big hug to fellow Flashers Vaughn Anderson, Brian Byers, Dean Dodrill, Janet Galore, Ibis Fernandez, Dave Jones, and Charles Kaufman, for their contributions above and beyond the call of duty. Thanks also to the guys and gals on the We're Here forums (www.werehere.com) for their help and input 24/7. Thanks to Beth for keeping me warm and fed while I slaved away in the basement. And of course, thanks to Hungry Minds, Inc., for giving me the wherewithal to create this book and get it out there for everyone to read.

Quotes from Jay Rose (www.dplay.com/book), courtesy of *Producing Great Sound for Digital Video*, by Jay Rose (Gilroy, CA: CMP Books, 2000).

Quotes from Ellen Finkelstein and Gurdy Leete courtesy of *Flash 5 for Dummies* by Ellen Finkelstein and Gurdy Leete, Hungry Minds, Inc., www.hungryminds.com.

CONTENTS AT A GLANCE

CONTENTS

CHAPTER 1
HOW TO WATCH CARTOONS   3

CHAPTER 2
LEARNING TO DRAW   11

CHAPTER 3

WRITING A CARTOON   41

CHAPTER 4

DÓNDE ESTÁ LA BIBLIOTECA?   53

CHAPTER 5
WHY DID YOGI BEAR
WEAR THAT NECKTIE? 69

CHAPTER 6
RECORDING DIALOGUE
AND OTHER SOUND 85

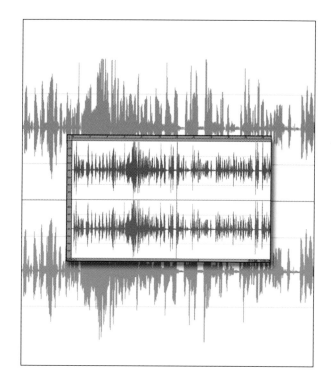

CHAPTER 7
KEYFRAMES, TWEENING, AND ANIMATICS   95

CHAPTER 8
TWEENING — MANUAL AND AUTOMATIC   113

CHAPTER 9
WALKING, RUNNING, AND CYCLING   133

CHAPTER 10
FACIAL ANIMATION   151

CHAPTER 11
LAYOUT, STYLE, AND
CAMERA MOVES   165

CHAPTER 12
INTERACTION, PART I   181

CHAPTER 13

INTERACTION, PART II 191

CHAPTER 14

MAKING A MOVIE 207

CHAPTER 1
HOW TO WATCH CARTOONS

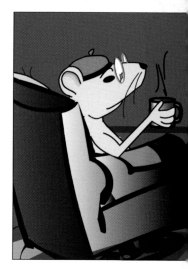

This chapter discusses cartooning on TV, in the movies, and on the Web, and highlights elements that are applicable to Flash. The chapter focuses on limited animation cartoons, from modern treasures such as *Dexter's Lab*, to classics such as *Rocky and Bullwinkle*.

Just what the hell has all this laughter got to do with the making of animated cartoons?

EDDIE SELZER, PRODUCER,
WARNER BROTHERS ANIMATION

REALLY WATCHING TV CARTOONS

I know, you've watched a lot of cartoons in your time, but did you really watch them? Did you pay attention to the way animators fake movement? To the way they create — or fail to create — the illusion of mass and weight in their characters? How characters are constructed to facilitate their animation? How characters' walks reveal something about who they are? The different line styles and thicknesses used to separate foreground characters from the background?

You did? Then you can skip ahead to the next chapter. See you there.

A MATTER OF STYLE

Super Important Rule #1: Pay attention to the style of animation effected by different cartoons.

As many styles of animation exist as do animators. You can make any style work for you. MTV's *Daria* (www.mtv.com/mtv/tubescan/animation/daria/), for example, is drawn in a relatively realistic style — the characters' heads are in proportion to their bodies; objects such as cars and houses closely resemble their real world counterparts.

© IBIS FERNANDEZ

3

Dexter's Lab (www.dexterslab.com) and *The Power Puff Girls* (www.powerpuffgirls.com), on the other hand, effect a very simple, stylized look. Dexter's head is a pentagon. The Power Puff Girls' arms and legs are just teardrops, and their mouths are simple curved lines. The colors on objects such as couches and paintings don't line up perfectly with the objects themselves.

None of this is by accident. These cartoons are supposed to look like that, and it's not because their creators can't draw. A lot of thought and planning has gone into those simple shapes, unrealistic hairdos, crooked lines, and misaligned colors. Don't make the mistake of assuming that this style is necessarily easier to effect; it's often harder to draw a recognizable phone with 12 lines and one flat color, than to draw a recognizable telephone with 50 lines and subtle shading.

CHUCK JONES AND WALT DISNEY

If you want to study the very best in animation, load up your VCR with some Warner Bros. cartoons such as *Bugs Bunny* and *Daffy Duck*, MGM cartoons such as *Tom & Jerry*, and, of course, almost any cartoon from Walt Disney studios — *Pinocchio* and *101 Dalmatians* to name but two. All these cartoons use *full animation*: Although they use a fair number of *held shots* — shots in which the character doesn't move — when a character does move, all of him or her moves. Every line of the body and face is drawn anew in every frame of the action, giving the animation the fluidity that is the trademark of full, frame-by-frame animation. Watch them next to *Scooby Doo* or the *Flintstones* and the difference is immediately obvious.

NOTE

Flash is easier to draw with than many of the current animation tools on the market. Many animators are doing their basic illustrations in Flash, and using high-end animation tools such as Retas! Pro, Crater Software's CTP, or AXA Studio to produce finished animation.

Thanks to Ibis Fernandez for this note.

Many of the full animation cartoons cited previously, such as *Tom & Jerry*, are essentially *pantomime* — they work just as well with the sound on your TV turned off. You do not need sound to enjoy the Coyote chasing the Road Runner, or Tom chasing Jerry. Even wordier offerings such as Yosemite Sam versus Bugs Bunny are easy to follow with the sound off.

This kind of full, frame-by-frame animation is rare in Flash cartooning mainly because an animation's playback speed in the Flash player cannot be guaranteed. Even if the cartoon plays back perfectly on your computer, it may lag or stutter on another computer, especially a slower one. The sound and the animation can fall *out of sync*, so that dialogue no longer matches the animation. Some cartoonists do use Flash for full animation, but they generally export the finished movie to another format — QuickTime or AVI (Audio Video Interleave), for example — or render it off to film or tape, to use outside of Flash.

HANNA-BARBERA AND LIMITED ANIMATION

Most Flash cartoons are *limited animation*. Limited animation, in contrast to full animation, is built around the idea of creating as few new drawings as possible and reusing the same drawings repeatedly.

Limited animation is associated with television, where the money and the production times are much smaller than in the motion picture world. The best known examples of limited animation cartoons are the works of Jay Ward (including *Rocky and Bullwinkle*, *Dudley Do-Right*) and William Hanna and Joseph Barbera (including *Yogi Bear*, *The Jetsons*, and *Scooby Doo*).

If you compare a Tom & Jerry cartoon directed by Hanna-Barbera , and a Yogi Bear cartoon also directed by Hanna-Barbera , you cannot mistake the difference in animation style. Full animation looks more fluid and believable . . . just plain better.

Consider this: the way characters move, even how they walk, reveals much about who they are. Take two characters walking down a path. If they're well animated, we can tell a lot about them — whether they're smart, dumb, young, old, strong, weak, happy, sad — just by the way they walk.

Limited animation, however, often takes a lot of this detail of movement away. Very little difference exists in the way Fred Flintstone and Barney Rubble walk, or for that matter, in the way each runs, laughs, or reaches for an object. In limited animation, characters and objects move from left to right, or right to left. Little to no movement occurs into and out of the scene. You rarely see Fred Flintstone or Scooby Doo moving toward or away from you at an angle, or even heading directly toward you or away from you. Instead, they usually walk across the scene from one end of the screen to the other, remaining at the same distance from the camera to get across. Limited animation typically relies much more heavily on dialogue, sound effects, and camera moves to convey the story.

HEY, DID THAT MOVE?

While you're watching cartoons, pay careful attention to what moves and what doesn't. Even full animation work, such as Bugs Bunny, uses plenty of held shots — shots with a strong pose but very little motion. Limited animation often freezes shots completely for several seconds.

Notice how cartoons distract you from the fact that so much of the screen is taken up a lot of the time by static images that aren't moving at all? Notice how they maintain a sense of life with a few eye blinks, a twitch of a hand, or a little movement of trees or clouds in the background?

When characters talk, what moves? Just their mouths? Their eyes? Who are they talking to? What are the characters doing? Are the actions happening at once or, more likely, is only one action occurring at a time: the mouth moves, the mouth moves some more, the eyes blink, the mouth moves again?

Stick a tape in your VCR and record an animation of your choice. Watch it again and again; play it back frame by frame if you can. Pay attention to how often the characters and objects are actually animated. Are the arms and legs moving? Is the face changing shape? Are the images just sliding across the screen? Is the camera simply zooming in and out?

NOTE

Many limited animation cartoons, however, do successfully convey characters' personalities. In *Dexter's Lab*, for example, Dexter's mother's personality can clearly be seen by the way she walks tippy-toeing on her tiny shoes, always a busy bee, baking, and cleaning up the house. Dee-dee is a free spirit; she skips around, almost dancing as she walks. Dexter is small; he has tiny feet, which he must move really fast to travel small distances.

Thanks to Ibis Fernandez for this note.

CAN YOU OUTLINE THAT FOR ME?

Super Important Rule #2: Pay attention to the thickness and color of outlines, and the differences in color between foreground and background in cartoons.

In almost all circumstances, you want your characters — and foreground objects — to stand out clearly from the background. If your cartoon bear takes a . . . well, let's say a walk in the woods, you want the bear to be clearly discernable from the woods. Pay attention to how the cartoons you watch distinguish foreground characters and objects from the background.

You can distinguish foreground characters and objects from the background with these three methods:

- Color
- Outline
- Motion

For example, this bear isn't very distinguishable from the woods he inhabits (1.1). To make him visible, I changed his color and his outline. Because the woods are dark, I made him light. Where before he was outlined with strokes about the same thickness as the background trees, now he is outlined in much thicker strokes. With these two easy changes, he becomes clearly visible against the background (1.2).

The third way to separate foreground from background is through motion. Usually, the foreground is in motion, but not always. In my cartoon, "Fishin'

1.1

1.2

1.3

NOTE

Backgrounds are sometimes blurred, softening both color and outline to contrast it from the foreground. Blurring the background simulates depth of field in a camera.

Ain't So Bad," the main character in the foreground is relatively colorless and motionless. The lake in the background, on the other hand, is very colorful and in a constant, wavelike motion.

The result is that the foreground character clearly pops out despite his lack of color and movement (1.3).

WATCHIN' WEBTOONS

Of course, if you want to make great Flash cartoons, check out the work of other Flash cartoonists. You can watch Flash cartoons at countless places on the Web, and the cartoons change daily. Here are a few of my favorites, to get you started.

The first great Flash cartoonist I came across was Nova Scotia-based animator Ed Beals (www. edbeals.com). Be sure to watch "Giant Cow!" You can see lots of Flash cartoons, including Ed Beals' Wenchell Boogem series, on the Hotwired Animation Express at www.hotwired.lycos. com/animation/. You can find another large collection of Flash cartoons, including some of mine, from AtomFilms at www.atomfilms.com (1.4).

For some terrific Flash animation with that classic twenties look, check out the adventures of Bulbo, at www.bulbo.com (1.5).

Also, check out the wonderful work of Dave Jones at www.transience.com.au (1.6). Mr. Jones proves that it's possible to pull off some wonderful, entertaining animation with surprisingly simple characters. Jones' Flash cartoon, "Teetering," is included on the CD.

The uncontested king of interactive, downloadable, e-mailable, pass-around Flash cartoons is Joe Cartoon (1.7). Joe is probably the most viewed, most popular, and most laughed at of all Flash cartoonists. Load up the Frog Bender 2000, included on the CD-ROM, or visit his site at `www.joecartoon.com`.

You'll probably notice that Flash cartoons suffer from a certain *sameness* of technique. This comes partly from a common toolset, and partly because Flash animators labor under two serious technical constraints: limited bandwidth and no guaranteed playback speed.

Simply put, *bandwidth* is a measure of how quickly data moves from one place to another . . . from your Web site to your viewer's PC, for instance. For a viewer watching a Flash cartoon on the Web, bandwidth is a measure of how quickly that cartoon can make it from the Web to his or her computer. For a Flash animation to play smoothly, every frame must be small enough to make its way to the viewer's computer before its turn comes to play, or the viewer must wait until all or part of the animation makes it down before playback starts. The bigger the animation, the longer this downloading takes, and the less likely that viewers will stick around long enough to watch.

Even if viewers are playing animations directly from their hard drives, you must be aware of Flash's second big constraint: no guaranteed playback speed. The slower the viewer's computer—the less powerful the CPU, the less RAM—the slower a Flash animation plays back. However, the simpler a Flash animation, the wider is the range of computers on which it plays smoothly.

These bandwidth and playback constraints give Flash animation a distinctive style. Flash animations

1.4

© 2000, AtomFilms

1.6

Copyright © 2000, Dave Jones, www.transience.com.au

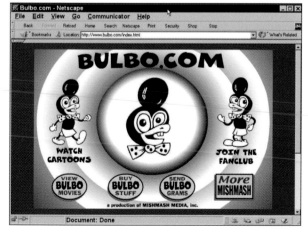

1.5

© 2000 Xeth Feinberg

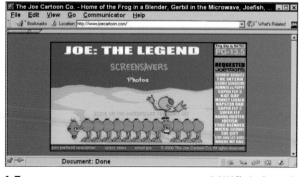

1.7

© 2000 The Joe Cartoon Co.

tend toward short run times, small file sizes, mediocre sound, low frame rates — the lower the frame rate, the less data that must be transferred every second — large areas of broad color, restricted color palettes, simple characters, and limited animation. Rather than animating smoothly, characters often flip between one of two or three poses. (Of course, if a character only has two poses, those poses had better be good.)

EVERYTHING I NEED TO KNOW I LEARNED FROM BULLWINKLE THE MOOSE

Super Important Rule #3: Story is everything.

Look at the animation classic *Rocky and Bullwinkle*. What is it about Rocky and Bullwinkle that makes them so endearing and enduring? It's certainly not the animation; *Rocky and Bullwinkle* is just about as bad as animation gets. These characters live on thanks to the writers who gave them funny lines to say, and to the actors who gave voice to those lines. In fact, as I write this, *Rocky and Bullwinkle* are back in theaters again.

At the opposite extreme from *Loony Tunes*, which you can enjoy with the sound off, *Rocky and Bullwinkle* are cartoons you can enjoy with your back turned. They are essentially illustrated radio plays, complete with the voice-over announcer to remind you of the plot twists that happened two minutes ago. Good writing can triumph over mediocre, or even bad, animation. (Witness *South Park*!) Technically great animation, conversely, does not triumph over mediocre writing.

CHAPTER 2
LEARNING TO DRAW

N o matter how easy Flash may be to use, drawing with a computer isn't like drawing with pencil and paper (or crayon and paper, for that matter). Computer hardware and software can add another layer of awkwardness, but the extra power and capability they bring to the process make it all worthwhile.

DRAWING IN FLASH

Before you can become a Flash cartoonist, you must come to terms with Flash's drawing tools, make friends with them, start calling them by little pet names . . . well, at least make friends with them.

Before we get started . . . a quick word about pressure-sensitive tablets. If you still don't own a graphics tablet, put down the book and go buy one. I'll wait. A graphics tablet consists of a pen-like stylus and a drawing tablet — basically a flat plastic hunk with some magic bits inside (2.1). The stylus replaces your mouse when you're drawing with the computer and does a much better job of emulating a pen or paint brush than do mice and trackballs. There are a number of choices on the market; I'm personally a big fan of Wacom tablets.

Better tablets are pressure and tilt sensitive. Flash responds to different pressure levels of a tablet — enabling you to vary the width of your strokes by varying the pressure on the stylus.

No other single change you make has as large an effect on how you draw in Flash, and other art programs, as does a graphics tablet. With a graphics tablet, tasks like sketching a tree or signing your name go from impossible to simple, instantly.

© 2000, Greg Kelly

Those things you don't see are very instrumental in how well your drawing is constructed, and how efficient it can eventually become.

PETER SYLWESTER

They'll get my Wacom tablet when they pry it out of my cold, dead lap.

MARK CLARKSON

2.1

PIXELS AND VECTORS

Two kinds of images are in the digital world: bitmaps and vectors.

Desktop wallpaper, or a scanned photograph on a Web site, are bitmaps, often called *raster graphics*. This scanned photograph of a baby is a bitmap (2.2), and so is this computer-generated car, rendered in the program LightWave 3D (2.3). Bitmaps are like incredibly intricate mosaics, made up from thousands of almost invisibly small tiles . . . tiny dots, called *pixels* ("picture elements").

Programs such as Painter, Paint Shop Pro, Photoshop, and Windows Paint work with bitmaps with individual pixels. Bitmap images are similar to photographs; if you zoom in too closely on them, or enlarge them too much, you can see the individual picture elements. The image becomes grainy—or *jaggy*—or pixilated (2.4).

2.2

2.3

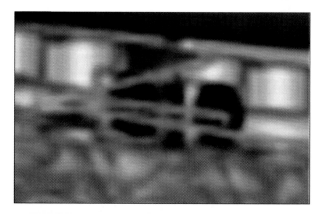

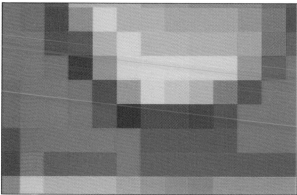

2.4

The file that holds a bitmap image must, in some fashion, remember every single pixel in the image. A typical piece of desktop wallpaper, an 800×600 image, contains 480,000 pixels of one, two, or three bytes each—between about a half a million bytes and one and a half million bytes.

Flash, on the other hand, works with curves. An object is defined by a set of curves. Zoom in as far as you like, and the image still looks smooth, because Flash redraws that same smooth curve at whatever resolution you like (2.5).

Graphics that are defined by their geometry—by the curves that make them up—are called *vector graphics*. (Vector is a math name for a type of line.) The file that holds a vector image, such as a Flash drawing, only remembers the definitions of that drawing's curves, not what they're going to look like when they're actually drawn. That is, it remembers that you drew a black circle of a certain size and color, but it doesn't remember whether the leftmost pixel, 312 down from the top, is black or white. Vector files are typically much smaller than bitmap files. Its vector graphic format is what makes Flash so well suited

2.5

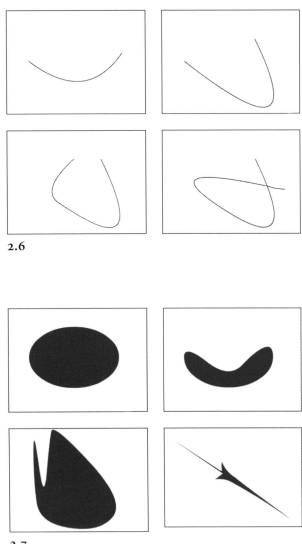

2.6

2.7

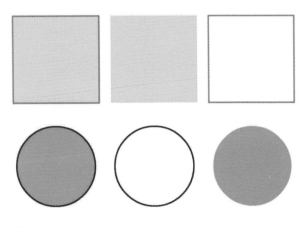

2.8

for the Internet: large Flash animations can reside in very small files; very small files download very quickly.

LINES AND FILLS

Images in Flash are made from lines and fills. Lines are like stretchy pieces of wire; they can be bent and twisted and stretched, but they don't get any thicker or thinner as you manipulate them; a 2-point line remains a 2-point line, no matter how much you stretch it. You can, as we see in a bit, change a 2-point line into a 4-point line, or .5-point, or whatever thickness you want. But just dragging a line around on the stage won't change its thickness (2.6).

Fills, on the other hand, are more like Silly Putty; they can be made thick or thin or round or square. They can be smaller than a line or bigger than the movie frame (2.7).

The Pencil tool and Line tool produce lines. The Brush and Paint Bucket tools produce fills. The Oval ⊙ and Rectangle ▢ tools produce either lines or fills or both, depending on how you set them up (2.8).

A fill can be any shape — just like a blob of paint — but a line is always a line.

SKETCHING, PAINTING, AND SCULPTING

That being said, these are the three approaches to creating images in Flash:

- Sketching
- Painting
- Sculpting

SKETCHING

You sketch in Flash with the Pencil tool ✏. You find the Pencil tool on the Flash Tool panel (2.9).

Open a new file. Grab the Pencil tool and sketch some lines (2.10). By clicking the Stroke Color button on the Tool panel ✏■, you can make lines in any color you want (2.11). If a line is selected when you choose a new line color, it instantly changes to the new color.

Open the Stroke panel (Window ➤ Panels ➤ Stroke). Here, you can change the thickness of the line, the point setting (2.12).

2.9

You can also change the Line Style, in case you want, say, a dotted line instead of a solid one (2.13). Notice that you can change your line color from the Stroke panel, as well.

Changing the Way Flash Interprets a Sketch

In a much more interesting approach, you can change the way Flash interprets your sketching. Open a new file. When you draw with the Pencil tool, you can choose from three different pencil modes—straighten, smooth, and ink (2.14). Depending on the mode you choose, Flash tries to straighten your lines, smooth them out, or leaves them just as you sketched them.

Select the different pencil modes and sketch some quick lines to get a feel for how they work. It's pretty straightforward. Notice that Flash isn't perfect in its interpretation of your movements, no matter which mode it's in; it doesn't always smooth or straighten your lines just the way you want.

Even the pencil's Ink setting, which tries to mimic your lines precisely, won't always catch every tiny nuance. In general, the slower you go, the more accurately Flash captures your strokes.

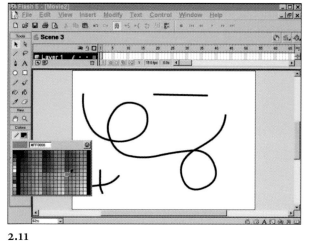

2.11

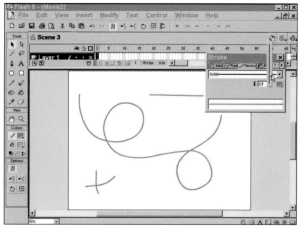

2.12

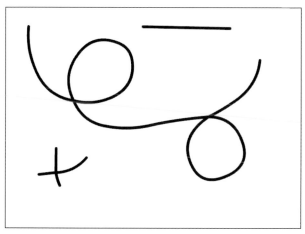

2.10

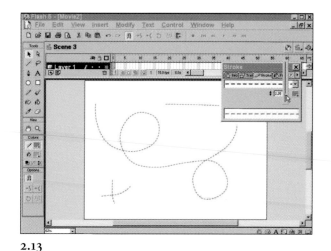

2.13

Flash also smoothes and straightens your lines after the fact, with the Smooth ⬚ and Straighten ⬚ tools. The Smooth and Straighten tools are on Flash's main toolbar (2.15). The Smooth and Straighten tools also enable you to be a little more selective. You can select parts of your lines and smooth or straighten them while leaving the rest alone, or even smooth part of the line and straighten another part (2.16).

It's usually a good idea to have Flash smooth or straighten your lines, as you draw them or after the fact, because it helps us—and memorize this, because it's to become our mantra—***Minimize Curves***. The fewer curves, the smaller the animation, and the happier everybody is. Trust me.

Let's say you want to draw a cartoon head, or perhaps copy one from a scanned image. Here is a sketch (2.17) of an old, cranky guy based on a cartoon head in Jack Hamm's *Cartooning the Head and Figure* (New York: Perigree, 1982).

Now, if you just try to trace this image in Flash, you're likely to wiggle a bit (especially if you're using a mouse!). Instead of, say, a single, smooth curve defining the top of the head, you're likely to get a dozen or more smaller curves (2.18).

Now, sometimes, wiggly is fine. In fact, sometimes that's just the effect you're looking for, to give your art a natural, sketched look. But make sure you're doing it because you choose to do it. Never use three curves where one will do. We want to *minimize* curves. With the Pencil in Smooth mode, the same motion results in fewer curves (2.19).

One last tool for smoothing and straightening your curves is Flash's Optimize tool (Modify ➤ Optimize) (2.20). Optimize looks for places with three lines where, in its opinion, two would suffice, and changes

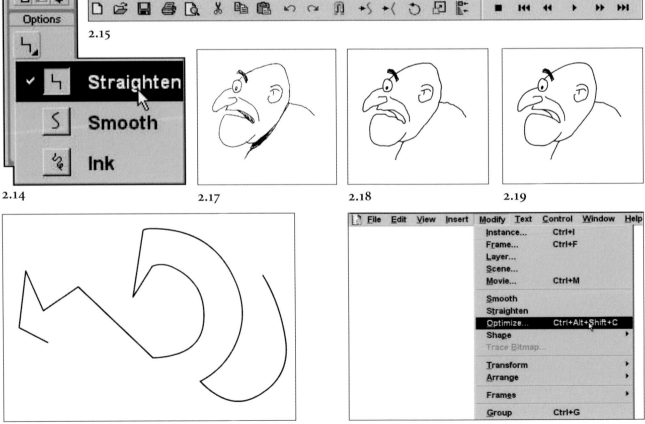

2.15

2.14

2.17

2.18

2.19

2.16

2.20

your drawings accordingly. You can tell Optimize how aggressive you want it to be in eliminating extraneous curves by dragging the slider to the right (2.21). It's a great tool, but Optimize often changes the shape of your drawings or even, depending on how it's set up, optimizes some curves right out of existence. Notice that Optimize has removed the inside of the old guy's ears, for example (2.22). If this goes too far, press undo and try again with smoothing set a little lower.

To give these techniques a try, open the Cranky Old Guy.FLA file and save it under a new name. Enjoy.

Shape Recognition

One very cool Pencil tool feature is shape recognition. You can set up Flash to recognize certain basic shapes when you sketch them and *clean* them up for you. Here's how to do this: select Edit ➢ Preferences and click the Editing tab (2.23). Here you can set up how Flash handles snapping to grid, snapping to lines, and so forth. Click the Recognize shapes drop-down box and choose Tolerant. Press OK to close Preferences. Now select the Pencil tool and set its mode to Straighten. Sketch a rough box on the stage (2.24). Flash recognizes the shape and turns it into a nice, smooth rectangle (2.25). Flash also recognizes ovals and triangles. I usually prefer to use Flash's Line, Rectangle, and Oval tools, but shape recognition gives you another option for sketching in Flash.

Go back to Preferences and set Recognize shapes to Off.

2.21

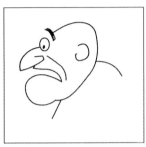

2.22

2.23

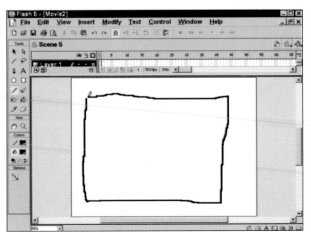

2.24

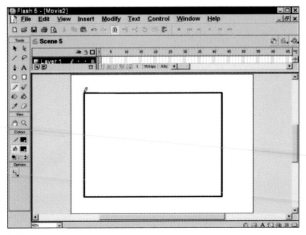

2.25

PAINTING

You can use Flash as a paint program by using the Paint Brush tool. You can paint in any color (2.26).

You can choose from an assortment of brush shapes (2.27). Different brush shapes give you different effects as you paint with them (2.28).

You can change the paintbrush size, to vary your stroke size (2.29).

If you have a pressure-sensitive tablet, select Use Pressure ✓ from the Tools window to have Flash interpret the pressure of your strokes as thickness (2.30).

Flash's Smooth, Straighten, and Optimize Curves tools all work with fills just as they do with lines. Shape Recognition only works with the Pencil tool.

Let's give it a try. Open a new file. Select the paint-brush ✓ and choose your color and brush size and shape. Paint a few strokes. Strokes left behind by the paintbrush are fills. You can grab them, move them, stretch them, and reshape them (2.31).

Here's how. Select the paintbrush and paint a rough circle (2.32).

Select the Arrow tool ▸. This is the black arrow at the upper-left corner of the Tools window, *not* the

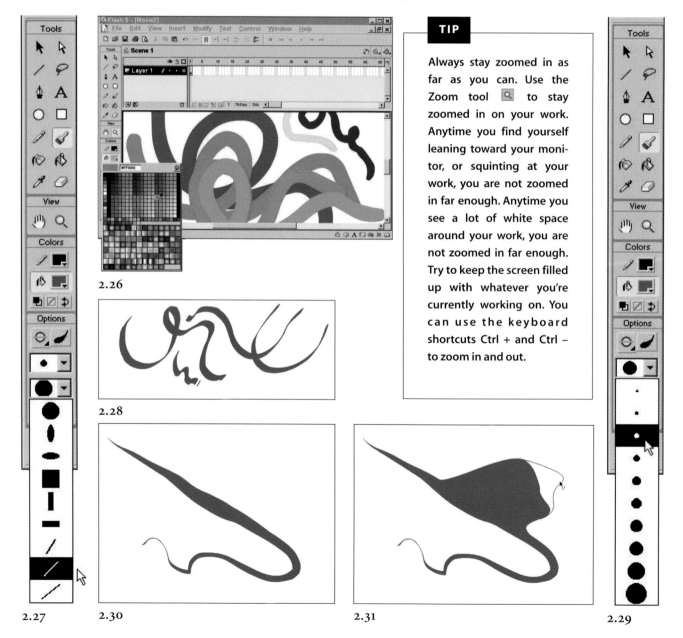

2.26

2.28

2.27

2.30

2.31

2.29

TIP

Always stay zoomed in as far as you can. Use the Zoom tool 🔍 to stay zoomed in on your work. Anytime you find yourself leaning toward your monitor, or squinting at your work, you are not zoomed in far enough. Anytime you see a lot of white space around your work, you are not zoomed in far enough. Try to keep the screen filled up with whatever you're currently working on. You can use the keyboard shortcuts Ctrl + and Ctrl – to zoom in and out.

white Subselect arrow beside it. With your circle unselected, move the Arrow tool around the circle's outside edge. The Arrow tool is really four different tools; as you move the tool, you see it change between four different icons to show you which is active at that moment.

The first ⌁ is the standard Arrow tool and consists of an arrow and a little rectangular marquee. In this mode, you can click your circle to select it, or click and drag to make a marquee selection. If you selected part of the circle, de-select it by clicking a blank part of the stage (or by pressing Ctrl+Shift+A).

The second Arrow tool ⌁ has a four-directional arrow below it. This is the move tool. If you click and drag while this tool is showing, you move the entire circle.

The third ⌁ has a dotted arc below it. This is the Adjust Curve tool, and it's considerably more inter-

TIP

To temporarily switch to the Arrow tool while you are using another tool, hold the Control (Windows) or Command (Mac) key while you select an object or objects.

This tip is from *Flash 5 for Dummies* (Hungry Minds, Inc., formerly IDG Books Worldwide, Inc., 2000) by Ellen Finkelstein and Gurdy Leete.

esting. You click and drag with this tool to change the curve's shape under it. Give it a try (2.33). Cool, huh? Notice that some curves are very small, while others are larger.

The fourth tool ⌁ has an angle below it. This is the End Adjust tool. You click and drag with this tool to move the endpoints of the curves that make up your shape.

If it's hard for you to see how the End Adjust tool is working, do this: select the Line tool ⌁. With the Line tool selected, click and drag from left to right across the stage to make a straight line. Now select the Arrow tool (V) again. Move the Arrow tool along the line. You see the Curve Adjust icon ⌁ appear when the tool is moving along the length of the line, and the End Adjust tool ⌁ appear when it passes the two endpoints. Play around a bit, moving the endpoints and adjusting the line's curve until it's clear to you how they both work.

Note that the line or shape must be unselected for you to modify its endpoints and curves; if it is selected, all you can do is move it.

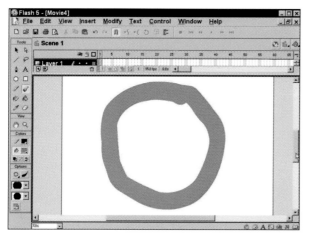

2.32

SCULPTING WITH LINES

This leads us to the third way of working in Flash: sculpting. Sculpting is my term for building images in Flash by using the Curve and Endpoint Adjust tools (and the Pen tool — more about this is discussed later) to bend lines and fills into your final shapes.

Sculpting gives much greater control over exactly how a character or object is constructed, exactly how many curves it has and how they are positioned.

Let's look again at our Grumpy Old Man (2.34). Notice that the top of the head is basically just a

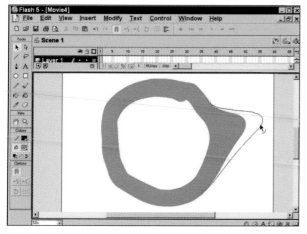

2.33

single curve running from the eyebrow to the back of the neck.

Open the Cranky Old Guy.FLA file and save it under a new name.

One of Flash's most fundamentally useful features is the layer. You can construct your Flash drawings and animations on many layers. Think of drawings made on overhead transparencies, or sheets of acetate, except that Flash's digital equivalent is perfectly transparent.

For example, this picture of Penguin (2.35) driving a car contains three layers: a background layer containing the sky, clouds, sun, and grass (2.36); a middle layer containing Penguin and his car (2.37); and a foreground layer with a little more grass (2.38).

2.34

To create a new layer, click the Insert Layer button at the bottom left of the timeline. Don't accept the default names; always give new layers descriptive names. You create, delete, and rearrange layers.

In Flash, the area where you've been doing your drawing is called the *stage*. Above the stage is the Timeline (2.39). Among other factors, the timeline shows you what layers are in the current scene, and on which one you're currently drawing.

At the left of the timeline, you see the layer names. The original sketch is in the layer named *Background*.

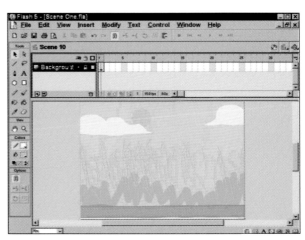

2.36

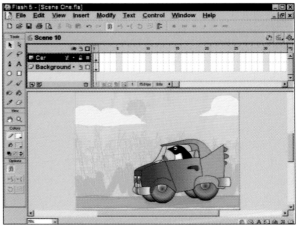

2.37

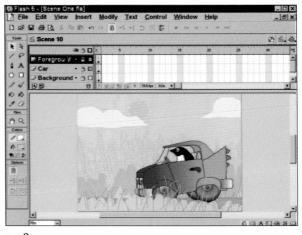

2.38

2.35

2.39

We'll leave it alone and trace a copy on a new layer, which is placed *above* it.

Click Layer 2 to select it. Notice that Layer 2 is, indeed, *above* the Background layer. Any items placed on this layer block out the corresponding area in any layers below it.

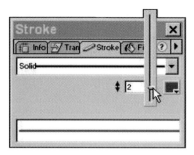

Select the Line tool (N). If the Stroke panel is not open, open it (Window ➤

2.40

Panels ➤ Stroke). Set it to a solid blue, 2-point line (2.40). When you're tracing over a reference image, as we are here, it's a good idea to use a line color that contrasts with the underlying image. If you used a black line, you wouldn't be able to see what we were doing, because the background drawing is also in black. If blue doesn't work for you, choose a color that does—be it red, green, or yellow. You can also make the line thinner or thicker, if that helps.

With the Line tool selected, click and drag from left to right across the stage to make a straight line running from the eyebrow to the back of the neck (2.41)—the beginning and end points of the curve define the top of the head. Select the Arrow tool and move it to the center of the new line, until you see the adjust curves icon ⬆. Click and drag the line upward to the top of the head. Use the Adjust Curve tool to drag the curve up and down, left and right, until it matches the original sketch as closely as possible (2.42).

Let's do the chin, next. The chin is actually a little harder, although it looks like a smoother curve. Draw a single line from the bottom of the mouth to the back of the chin (2.43). Now use the Arrow tools to adjust curves mode to pull the chin down, just as you pulled the head up. Try to adjust the curve until it matches the chin as closely as possible.

2.41

2.42

2.43

2.44

2.45

Can't do it, can you? No matter how you drag, the chin comes out too pointy; it won't match the original sketch (2.44).

Fear not, we can fix it. The problem is that the chin is really two curves; one line curves down from the bottom of the mouth to the bottom of the chin; the other curves up from the bottom of the chin to the back of the chin (2.45).

A single curve in Flash can only bend once, or not at all (2.46). To have a line that bends more than once, you have to make it from more than one curve. When you are sketching or painting, Flash takes care of this for you, but when you're sculpting, you need to learn to recognize situations where you need to add more lines to achieve the shape you want. Don't worry; it's pretty easy.

Erase the old chin line. Make sure snap is turned on. Now draw a new line from the bottom of the mouth to the bottom of the chin. Draw a second line

starting at the back of the chin and coming down to meet the first line at the bottom of the chin (2.47). With snap on, the two line ends should automatically snap together; when they get near enough, you see a thick circle at the line end under the arrow. Release the mouse button here, and the two lines snap together.

With the Arrow tool, click and drag the angle where

the two lines join, to make sure they are actually attached. If not, drag the endpoints together until they snap.

With the Arrow tool, click and drag on the first curve until it matches the sketch; turn snap off . Now adjust the second

2.47

TIP

You can zoom in until your work fills the screen, in a single step, by choosing View ➤ Magnification ➤ Show All (or Ctrl+3).

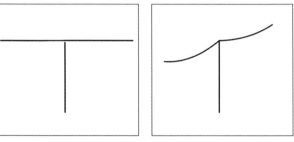

2.48

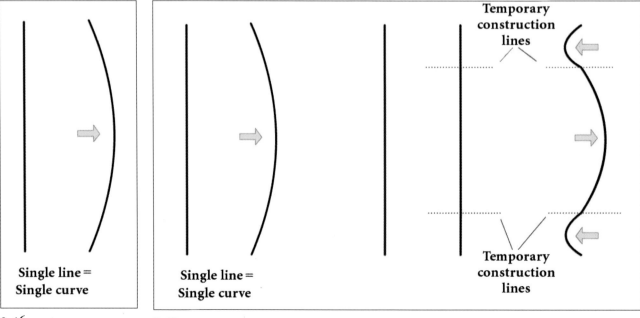

Single line = Single curve

Single line = Single curve

Temporary construction lines

Temporary construction lines

curve until it matches, too. *Viola!* (or vye-Oh-luh, as we say in Kansas).

When you find yourself fighting with a line that just won't bend the way you want it too, you probably need to add another curve.

Important note: Once you snap a line somewhere in the middle of a second line, that second line is broken, at the snap point, into two curves (2.48). This can provide a handy way of breaking a line in two when you're sculpting—simply draw a temporary *construction line* where you want a break, adjust your new curves, then delete the temporary line when you're through (2.49).

2.50

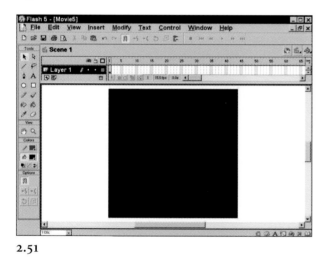

2.51

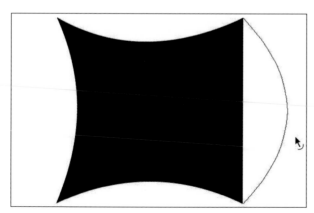

2.52

On the other hand, once you break a curve, it becomes very difficult to smoothly adjust the whole line as though it were one curve. Make sure you are done adjusting the overall curve of the line *before* you snap any other lines onto it.

Sculpting with Fills

The sculpting approach works just as well with fills (that is, shapes) as it does with lines. The process is similar. Select the Rectangle tool ▢. In Flash, rectangles—and ovals—have two parts: a solid fill and an outline, each with its own settings.

The outline is just a line, and has all the same settings as other lines: thickness, color, and style (dotted or solid). In this case we don't actually want an outline. Click the line color icon and select the crossed-out square outline in the upper right-hand corner of the color palette (2.50). This sets the line to *none* and tells Flash not to outline our object.

Next, choose a color for our new shape. The color really doesn't matter at this point; choose black. Now click and drag on the stage to make a rectangle (2.51). If you hold down the Shift key while you drag, Flash constrains the new shape to a square.

Select the Arrow tool and play around with bending the curves that make up the square (2.52).

You can use the temporary construction lines to break fills into additional curves, just as you did with lines. Play around a bit; see what you come up with. With a little imagination, you can push and pull even a simple square into almost any shape. I pulled these simple cartoon heads out of squares in less than a minute (2.53).

> **TIP**
>
> Wondering how I got those outlines around the cartoon heads once I'd worked out the shape? It's easy. To outline a shape, even a relatively complex one such as a head, select the Ink Bottle tool ⬢. Choose your line settings—I used 4-point solid outlines for my heads—and click your shape with the Ink Bottle. Flash automatically outlines your shape for you!
>
> Thanks to Phil "Uglydog" Tanner for this tip!

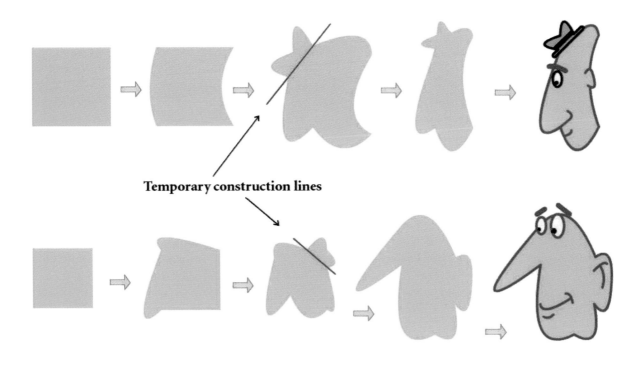

Temporary construction lines

2.53

The usual method of working in Flash is to outline the shape first with lines and then use the paint bucket to fill it in. Maybe I'm just contrary, but sometimes I like to do it this way, instead.

You don't have to design your characters this way, of course, but it's a fun way to work — a sort of *sketching*, if you will. To me, it feels a bit like working with clay. It leads you to designs you might not come up with in other ways. Once mastered, it also enables you to fine-tune shapes you've created in other ways, giving you more control over the final result.

Working with Fills

Flash enables you to do a lot of nice tricks with Fills. For starters, a fill doesn't have to be a solid color, it can be a gradient. A gradient is a range of colors fading from one to another. It might shade from black to white, or from red to blue (2.54). Gradients can fade between more than two colors, as well (2.55).

Flash comes with some gradients, and you can load more from Ibis Fernandez's collection on the CD-ROM (file). You can, of course, make or modify your own gradients. Let's do it.

Gradient fills are set up in the Fill panel. Open it now, with Window ➢ Panels ➢ Fill. In the drop-down box, select Linear Gradient. A lot of other options are here, but we can ignore most of them for now.

On the Fill panel, you now see a colored bar, probably fading from black to white (2.56). Below the bar are two little pointers, looking a little like houses, or fat pencils. These pointer pencils define your gradients. Click either pointer, and you see a gradient fill color

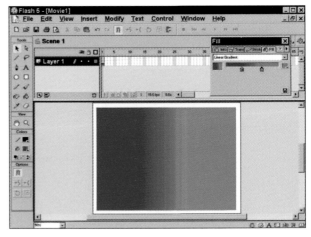

2.54

button ■ appear at the right side of the gradient. Click this button in turn, and you can select a color for the pointer (2.57). Do this now and select a deep color, such as red.

Click the other pointer and set its color to white. Select the Oval tool ⬭ from the toolbar. Click and drag on the stage to draw a gradient-filled oval (2.58). Holding down the Shift key constrains the shape to a circle.

You can have many colors in your gradients. Let's add another. Click just below the colored gradient bar, between the two pointers, and a third pointer appears. Click this new, middle pointer. This time,

select a light pink to get a nice, three-color gradient. You can repeat this step as many times as you want.

Drag the middle pointer to the left and right. Notice how this changes the way your gradient looks. You can drag the pencils at each end — the bright red and the white one — as well. Try this and watch the changes it makes to your gradients.

Make sure the Oval tool ⬭ is still selected, and click and drag across the stage to make a new oval. The oval is filled with your new gradient (2.59).

Select the drop-down box on the Fill panel again, and select Radial Gradient (2.60). A radial gradient shades from the inside, out, in concentric color rings.

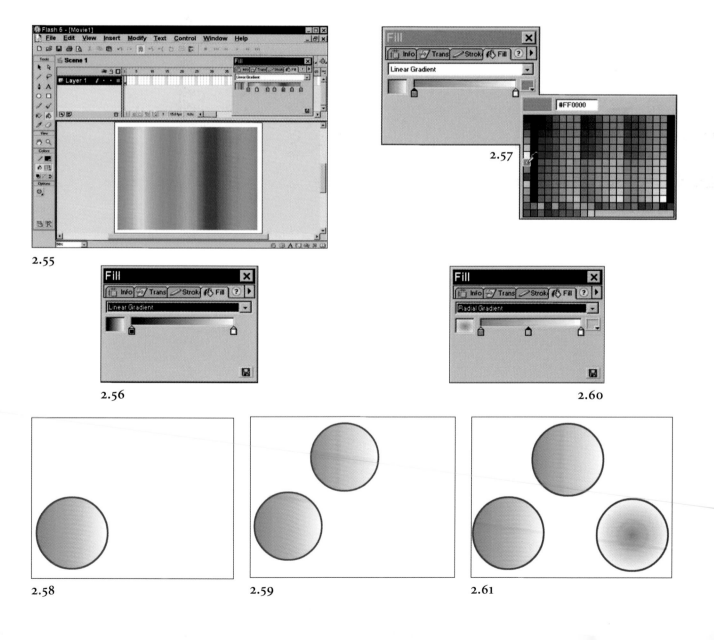

2.55

2.57

2.56

2.60

2.58

2.59

2.61

With the Oval tool selected, click and drag to make a third oval. This one is filled with the same gradient colors, but with a radial pattern (2.61). You can see that gradients, properly applied, can give a nice 3D effect to your objects.

By changing a color's Alpha setting in the Mixer panel (2.62), you can make that color partially or totally transparent. This is especially useful in gradient fills, where you can make a filled object fade off to invisibility (2.63).

The Paint Bucket and Gradients

To really work with fills, though, you need to understand some of the Paint Bucket features. The Paint Bucket fills empty areas inside of outlines and also replaces existing fills with new fills.

Fills Won't Fill

The Paint Bucket only fills enclosed areas. That is, you can't use it to turn the background a different

> **NOTE**
>
> Like the Ink Bottle, the Paint Bucket is an *attributer*. It assigns a color value to a shape without physically dumping any color pixels. And, just as easy as dumping the same fill into overlapping shapes, the Paint Bucket can combine shapes, too — a Unite filter in a bucket!
>
> Thanks to Peter Sylwester for this tip.

color, or to fill in the sky above a house. For the Paint Bucket to fill an area, that area must be completely enclosed on all sides by either lines or other fills.

It's a common problem for the Paint Bucket to refuse to fill an area that seems completely enclosed. When this happens, you can try two options. The Paint Bucket tool's Gap Size setting can tell Flash to ignore small gaps when filling an area (2.64). Try

2.62

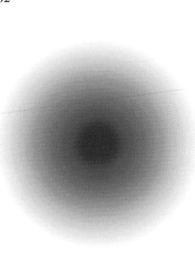

2.63

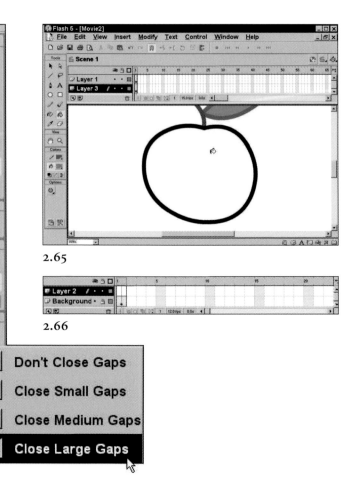

2.65

2.66

2.64

choosing a larger setting, such as Close Medium Gaps or Close Large Gaps, and then try to fill the area again.

If this doesn't work for you, then it means that some lines or fills that you think are joined really aren't. Some gaps are hiding in your picture.

There's a gap hiding in this picture of an apple (2.65), preventing the Paint Bucket from filling it, but you can't see the gap because the thickness of the lines hides it. To root it out, look above and to the left of the timelines. Just above the layer names are three icons: an eye ⬛, a lock ⬛, and a square outline ⬛ (2.66). Clicking the last of these, the square outline, changes your view to outline mode.

In outline mode, lines and fills are displayed as colored hairlines — in fact, usually a color that's impossible to see well. Select

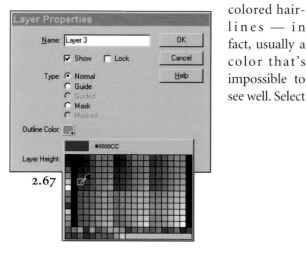

2.67

Modify ➤ Layer, then click the large color button at the bottom of the Layer Properties (2.67) to choose a new color for the outline, one that shows up well against your background color.

Use the Zoom tool ⬛ to zoom in and examine the joins in outline mode. It soon becomes apparent where the gap is (2.68). In normal viewing mode, the thickness of the lines hides this gap (2.69).

Outline mode is useful for times when you really need to see what's going on, in detail, in your Flash drawings.

Drag 'n fill

Open a new file and select the Rectangle tool ⬛. Make sure the Rectangle tool has some solid fill color selected; it doesn't matter what (2.70). Click and drag on the stage to make a rectangle.

Now select the Paint Bucket Tool ⬛. If it's not already open, open the Fill panel (Window ➤ Panel ➤ Fill). Choose Linear Gradient from the drop-down menu. Define a simple gradient.

With the Paint Bucket selected, click the filled part of the rectangle you just made. Flash fills the rectangle (2.71).

Sometimes, though, Flash doesn't place the gradient in the orientation you want; maybe the gradient goes from left to right, but you want it to go top to bottom. Easily fixed. With the Paint Bucket still selected, click and drag from left to right on the rectangle's fill. Flash fills from top to bottom (2.72). Click and drag from left to right, from right to left, or even at angles, and observe how Flash paints your fill differently every time. For some reason, Flash fills in at right angles to the direction you drag, making it a bit confusing, but you can always click and drag in different directions until you get objects where you want them.

Resizing and Reshaping a Gradient

There's another way to get your gradient fills to behave. Clear off the stage by selecting everything (Ctrl+A) and pressing Delete. Now select the Oval tool and draw a filled circle on the stage. Choose Radial Gradient from the Fill panel drop-down. Make a simple white-to-black gradient. Select the Paint Bucket tool and click in the center of the filled part of the circle you just drew to fill it with the new gradient (2.73).

2.68

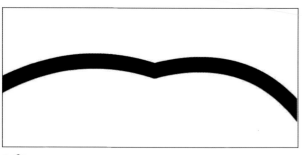

2.69

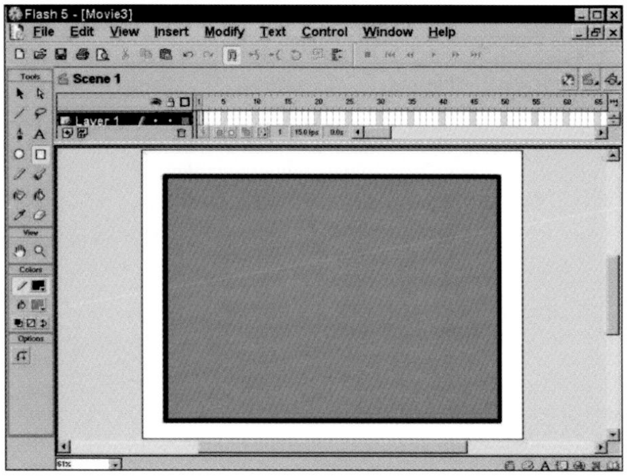

2.70

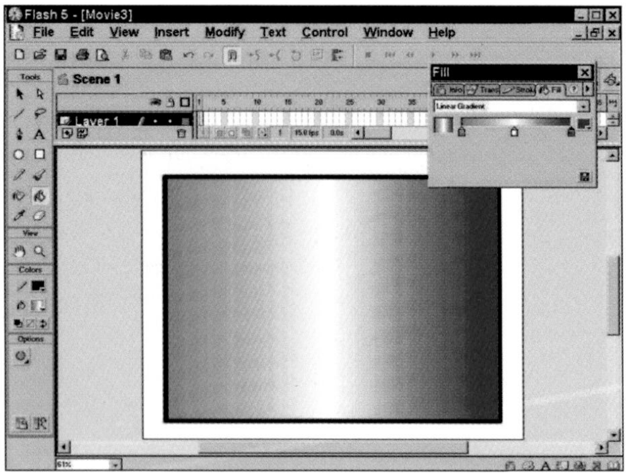

2.71

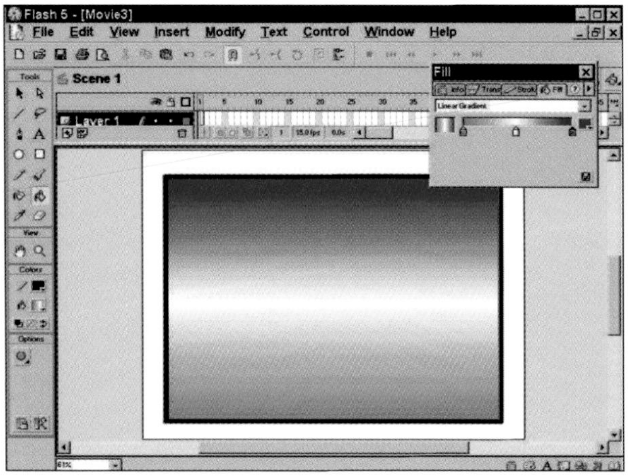

2.72

Among the Paint Bucket's settings is the Transform Fill button at the bottom of the Tool panel. Click this icon now. With Transform Fill selected, click anywhere on the gradient fill you just made. A *selection ring* appears around the fill (2.74). In Transform Fill mode, you can change the size, shape, and orientation of the gradient within the fill, without altering the filled shape at all.

The white circle in the center is the gradient's center. Click and drag this to move the center point of the gradient (2.75).

Click and drag the white square handle to the side of the gradient to squash or stretch the gradient from side to side or top to bottom (2.76).

Below the squash/stretch handle are two circular handles. The upper of these is the Size handle. Click and drag it to change the gradients overall size, making it bigger or smaller.

The lower square is the rotation handle; click and drag this handle to rotate the gradient colors around their center. This won't have a visible effect on a radial gradient unless you've squashed or stretched it (2.77).

The Transform fill works with linear gradients as well.

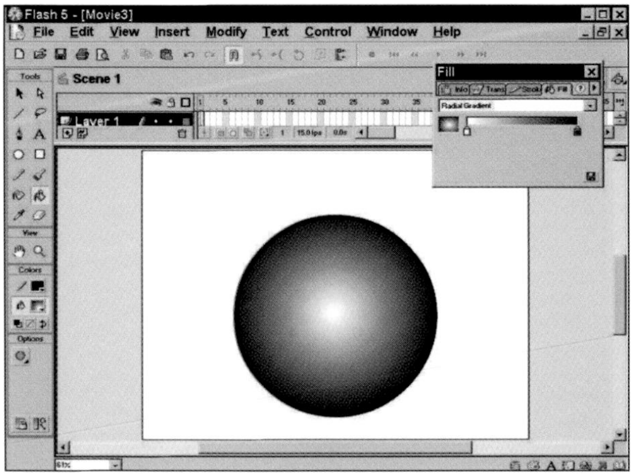

2.73

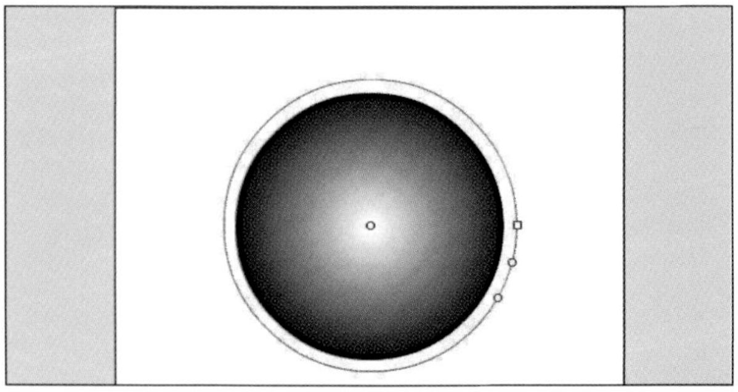

2.74

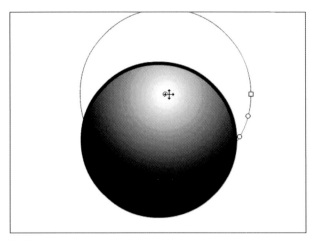

2.75

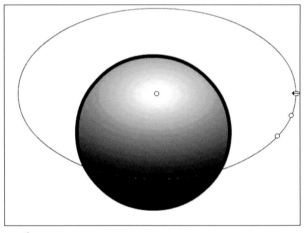

2.76

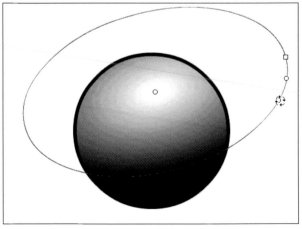

2.77

Lock Me Gradient Down, Sport

The last Paint Bucket control is Lock Fill. With Lock Fill selected, the center and orientation of your fills are locked into place. Normally, every time you make a fill it is centered wherever you click. Each fill has its own center and rotation. Once you select Lock Fill however, all subsequent fills have the same center and rotation. Let's look at how this works.

Select all the items on the stage and delete them. Select the Oval tool and make three small, filled circles in a line. If the black-and-white gradient is still selected, all of your ovals share the same gradient (2.78).

Select the Dropper tool (I) . The Dropper tool samples lines and fills so that you can copy them from one item to another. Click the filled area of your middle circle. Flash samples that fill and copies it to

---

TIP

If you like to create the soft look, you may want objects with softened edges. Flash provides three completely different ways to accomplish this. Use the one you like best. First create a shape with no outline and select the object. Choose Modify ➤ Shape ➤ Soften Fill Edges. Use the dialog box to define how soft you want to get. Next, create a radial gradient whose outside color matches the stage background. Finally, create a radial gradient whose outside color is semitransparent. You can use two or three levels of transparency of the same color.

This tip is from *Flash 5 for Dummies* by Ellen Finkelstein and Gurdy Leete.

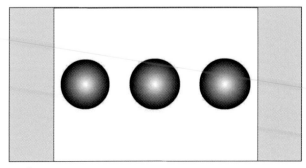

2.78

your Paint Bucket. Notice that Flash selects the Paint Bucket tool automatically. Notice also that Lock Fill is automatically turned on.

Click the center fill with the Paint Bucket. Nothing seems to happen, because we are filling the circle with the same gradient that's already there.

Now, click the fills in the left and right circles. Uh-oh. They both turn black (2.79). Don't panic; that's what we told them to do. The gradient shades from white to black in the center circle. At the outside of the center circle, the gradient is completely black. Because we have locked our gradients to that center gradient fill, and they are *outside* of the outermost part of that gradient, which is black, they are also black.

To better see how this works, select the Transform Fill button. Now click within the fill in any of your circles to edit the gradient. Grab the size handle and drag it outward until the fill covers at least part of all three circles (2.80). As the gradient expands, some gray tones make their way out to the outer circles. Click and drag the gradient's center handle to move the gradient center into one of the other circles (2.81).

This is a great tool for placing a single gradient — either radial or linear — across a range of items, or getting gradients to match across different areas of the same item. Penguin's car (2.82), for example, shades from dark blue to light blue, from front to back, but the car symbol is broken into different fills by the door and roof lines. Lock Fill ensures that the gradient matches across the entire car.

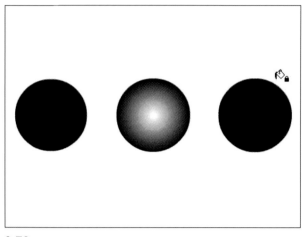

2.79

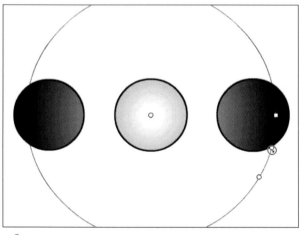

2.80

TIP

To precisely set the size of a bitmap image, or any object, in Flash, do this: Select the object. Open the Info Panel — Window ➢ Panels ➢ Info. Set the *x* and *y* values both to 0. Now set the width and height to whatever you want them to be. Note that the object inspector does *not* maintain proportions; you can significantly distort your object if you want to.

This is a good way to get a background to precisely fit the boundaries of your movie.

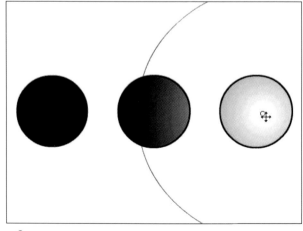

2.81

USING BITMAP IMAGES

You don't have to draw all your pictures from scratch in Flash. Flash also imports a variety of bitmap images, including JPG, GIF, and PNG. You can use bitmaps in your Flash cartoons in a number of ways.

The most common use for imported bitmaps is as background images, but bitmaps sometimes serve as items in your animation. You can also convert a bitmap into a Flash object, and even use it in place of a color or gradient when painting or filling.

IMPORTING A BITMAP

To bring a bitmap into Flash, choose File ➤ Import and select your picture. Flash brings the bitmap in as a single, solid object, such as a photograph or a post-card (2.83). You can stretch, resize, flip, rotate, and skew a bitmap, just like any other object.

CONVERTING BITMAPS TO FILLS

Beyond stretching and rotating, though, an imported bitmap cannot be edited to any great extent; you can't change its colors or erase parts of it or select bits and copy them elsewhere. If you need more control over your bitmap images, you have to convert them.

Flash turns your bitmap into a collection of fills with its Trace Bitmap command (Modify ➤ Trace Bitmap). Trace Bitmap examines the bitmap for areas that are all the same — or nearly the same — color, and turns those areas into a fill of the same size, shape, and color. You can specify just how similar colors must be to be considered the same color, how small an area should be before Flash ignores it, and how tightly Flash follows curves and corners (2.84).

Keep these points in mind as you work with bitmaps:

- The smaller the Color Threshold, the more different colors Flash sees and the more fills it generates. With a large color threshold, two similar shades of red, for example, are interpreted as a single block of red. With a small color threshold, they are interpreted as two differently colored fills.
- The larger the Minimum Area, the more little areas Flash ignores.
- The smoother the Curve Fit, the more Flash smoothes out jagged curves and outlines.
- The more corners selected under Corner Threshold, the less smoothing Flash performs around corners.

Countless combinations of the Trace Bitmap settings exist. (Well, OK, only nine million . . . but a lot!) Getting satisfactory results is usually a trial-and-error

2.82

2.83

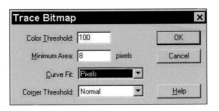

2.84

job; just keep using Undo and tweaking your settings until you get what you want.

This robot (2.85) was rendered in Lightwave 3D and imported into Flash as a BMP. He's been converted to fills under a range of settings. You can see how, as the minimum area and color threshold get higher and curve and corner following get looser, he looses more and more detail. You notice that he also gets smaller and smaller in terms of byte size, shrinking from 131K in the original bitmap to 7K in the last image.

Bitmap Fills

You can use imported bitmaps in another, really nifty way: as paint. Start with any old bitmap image such as, say, this one here (2.86). Import your image into

Flash. With the imported image selected, choose Modify/Break Apart (Ctrl+B). This tells Flash to pay attention to the individual pixels within the image.

Next, use the Eyedropper tool to sample the bitmap. When you select either the Paint Bucket or the Paint Brush, you see that the color button now displays a tiny thumbnail of your bitmap image (2.87). Now, when you fill or paint, instead of getting solid colors or gradients, you get a copy of your sampled bitmap (2.88).

Load the Tropico.FLA file, or import a bitmap of your own and try it out. As with gradient fills, you can use the Lock Fill and Transform Fill buttons to control where the filled image is centered and how it is scaled and rotated.

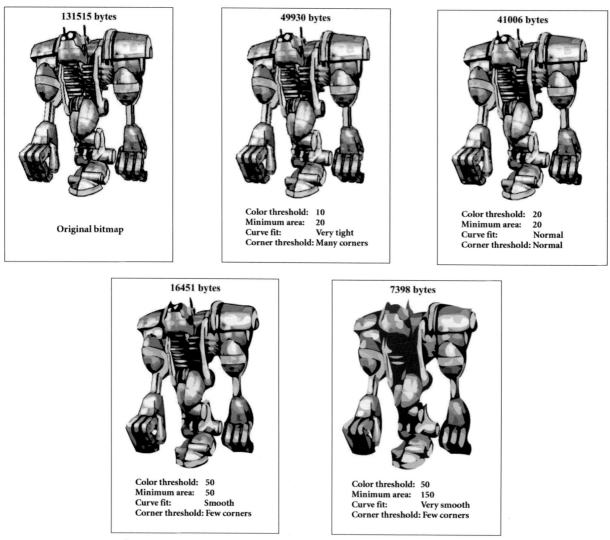

131515 bytes

Original bitmap

49930 bytes

Color threshold: 10
Minimum area: 20
Curve fit: Very tight
Corner threshold: Many corners

41006 bytes

Color threshold: 20
Minimum area: 20
Curve fit: Normal
Corner threshold: Normal

16451 bytes

Color threshold: 50
Minimum area: 50
Curve fit: Smooth
Corner threshold: Few corners

7398 bytes

Color threshold: 50
Minimum area: 150
Curve fit: Very smooth
Corner threshold: Few corners

2.85

> **TIP**
>
> You can use the Flash 5 Launcher Bar for quick one-click access to the Info, Mixer, Character, Instance, and Actions panels, as well as the Movie Explorer and the Library.

You can also use this method to erase part of a bitmap image. Perhaps you want to replace the sky in a photo landscape (2.89). (My vacation to the Virgin Islands . . . now deductible.) Make a rectangle (R) using that bitmap as the fill color, then erase that part of the filled rectangle (2.90). Finally, we can slip a rectangle with a new, gradient fill sky in behind (2.91).

USING THE TEXT TOOL

On its face, Flash's Text tool (T) is pretty straightforward and similar to text tools in any art or word pro-

cessing program. You can choose from any of your system's fonts. Text can be made bold or italic and any size from 8 to 72 points. Text can be any solid color but not a gradient or a bitmap (2.92).

But Flash text can be made to perform more tricks than that. Let's see some. Open a new file. Select the Type tool and click the left side of the stage. Type your name. Click the stage once to stop entering text.

Open the Character panel by choosing Window ➤ Panels ➤ Character, or by clicking the letter *A* on the Launcher Bar at the very bottom right of the screen (2.93).

Now select the Arrow tool and click once on your name to select the text object. The entire text is selected as one group. Select the Scale tool and scale your name up until it fills the stage (2.94).

Leaving your name as a single group, you can scale it, rotate it, flip it horizontally or vertically (Modify ➤ Transform) (2.95). If you double-click it, you can select the text and change its font, point size, or color using the Character panel settings.

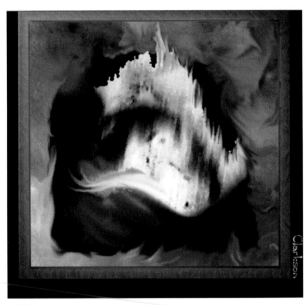

2.86

2.87

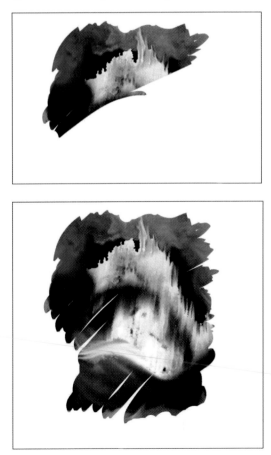

2.88

2.89

But to really make text dance, we have to break it apart. Select your name and choose Modify ➤ Break Apart. Flash breaks your name into a collection of curved fills (2.96).

After you break text apart, you can no longer use the Text Tool settings to change it. But now you *can* use all the tricks you've learned working with fills and gradients.

Click the stage away from your name to deselect it. With your name deselected, bring up the Fill panel (Window ➤ Panels ➤ Fill) and devise a colorful gradient by adding and moving gradient pointers of different colors.

Now, click the Paint Bucket 🪣. Make sure the Lock Fill button 🔒 is not selected. Select your entire name (Ctrl+A), and click it with the Paint Bucket. Flash

2.90

2.93

2.91

Now is the winter of our discontent made glorious summer by this son of York.

Now is the winter of our discontent made glorious summer by this son of York.

Now is the winter of our discontent made glorious summer by this son of York.

Now is the winter of our discontent made glorious summer by this son of York.

Now is the winter of our discontent made glorious summer by this son of York.

2.92

NOTE

If more than one fill is selected onscreen, Flash scales any gradient applied across all of them, at once.

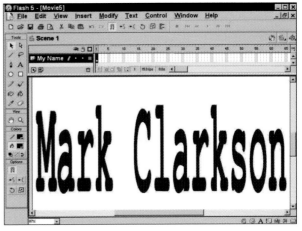

2.96

applies the gradient. Because all the fills were selected, the gradient is applied across them all (2.97).

Leave your name selected, and modify your gradient in the Fill panel; add or subtract some colors and move items around a bit. Notice that all the selected fills on the stage are automatically updated as you work. You don't need to use the Paint Bucket to apply the new gradient. This only applies to fills that are *selected* when you make a new gradient.

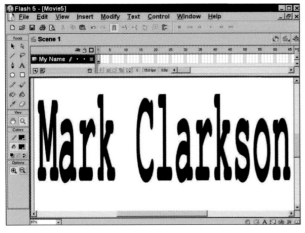

2.94

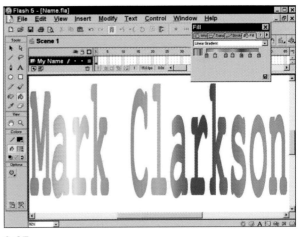

2.97

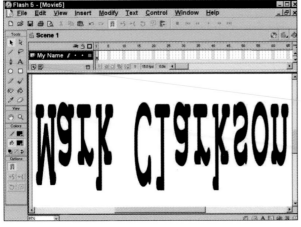

2.95

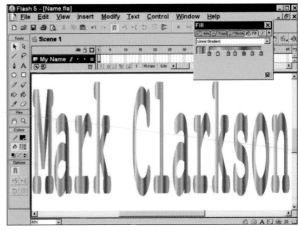

2.98

Click the stage away from your name to deselect it again. Click the Paint Bucket tool and click each letter in turn. This time, each letter is filled with the entire range of the gradient (2.98).

You can even fill the letters with a sampled bitmap image (2.99).

Because you broke up the text, each letter is now just a shape, or fill, and you can edit their shapes as you would with any fill. Deselect your name and click the Arrow tool (V). Click and drag on some of the lines and curves that make up your name to alter the text's look a bit.

To outline the letters, or any fill, open the Stroke panel. Choose a bright color which contrasts with your name's gradient fill. Set the line size to 4 points.

Click the Ink Bottle ⬚. With your name de-selected, click each of the letters with the Ink Bottle. All the letters are outlined (2.100). To change the size or color of the outline, change the Ink Bottle settings and click each fill again.

With the text broken apart, you can reposition individual letters, too (2.101).

USING THE PEN TOOL

With version 5, Flash adds a powerful new drawing tool to your arsenal of creation: the Bézier curve. (Named after French mathematician Pierre Bézier. Bézier is pronounced any number of ways; I prefer bez-ee-AY.) You create Bézier curves with the Pen tool ⬚.

2.99

2.100

2.101

TIP

The Pen tool can be hard to get used to. To make it easier, we suggest enabling the Pen Preview feature. Choose Edit ➤ Preferences. Click the Editing tab and check Show Pen Preview to display a preview of the line or curve as you draw. Click OK when you have finished setting your preferences. This helps you get a better idea of what the result will be as you work.

This tip is from *Flash 5 For Dummies* by Ellen Finkelstein and Gurdy Leete.

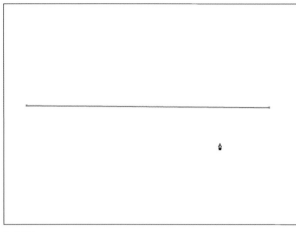

2.102

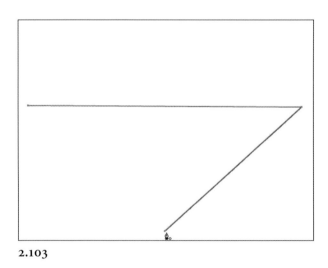

2.103

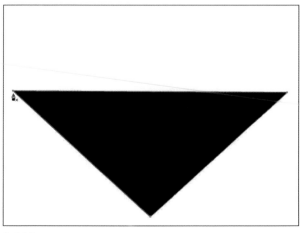

2.104

> **NOTE**
>
> **If pulling handles out of an anchor point results in a curve that loops across itself, drag in the opposite direction to reverse the positions of the handles.**

While you can sketch with the Pencil tool, drawing with the Pen tool more closely resembles the "sculpting" method described previously.

Curves built with the Pen differ from curves built with the Pencil in two basic ways:

- They are more complex; they can bend twice instead of once.
- You control them by pushing and pulling on "handles" instead of on the curves themselves.

Follow these steps to make some B-curves:

1. Open a new file.

2. Click the Pen tool on the Tools window.

3. Click once on the stage. The Pen tool leaves a tiny, colored, hollow dot on the screen. Click again with the Pen on another part of the stage, and Flash draws a line between the two points (2.102).

4. Click a third time on the stage, and Flash creates a second line at an angle to the first (2.103).

Now, move the Pen tool over the first point you created. The Pen cursor should change to a Pen tip with a little circle beside it ▨. This is the Close Path cursor; click now and Flash makes a last line, completing an enclosed triangle shape (2.104).

Another benefit of the Pen tool over the Pencil tool is that when you complete a shape with the Pen tool, it is automatically filled in with the current fill color, if any. But the operative word in Bézier curve is *curve*, and straight lines don't really show it off very well. Select everything on the stage (Ctrl+A) and delete it to give yourself a clean slate to work with.

With the Pen tool selected, click somewhere on the stage. Now, click and *drag* somewhere else on the stage. You get a pair of handles (2.105).

As long as you hold down the mouse button, you can drag these handles around, altering the curve's shape. Click and drag a few more times on different

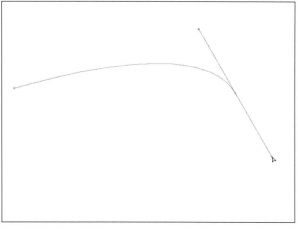

2.105

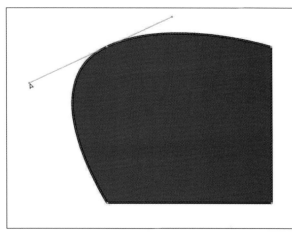

2.106

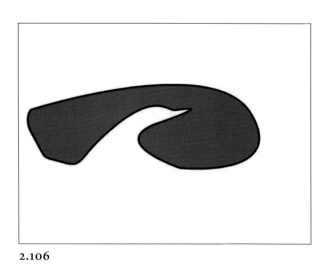

2.107

parts of the stage, to get a feel for how the Bézier control handles work. The farther the handle is from the anchor point, the more extreme the bend.

When you're done having fun, click the first point again to close, and fill, your new shape (2.106).

But the Pen is only half of the Flash Bézier story. The other half is the ill-named Subselect tool , the white arrow next to the regular Arrow tool on the Tools window. The Subselect tool is a Bézier curve editing tool; you use it to edit shapes that you've already built, as Bézier curves.

Click the Subselect tool and drag a selection marquee around the shape you just made. You should see little colored squares—*anchor points*—everywhere you clicked with the Pen when defining the shape. Click and drag any of these points to reshape the object.

If a node's handles are not visible, do this: click once on the anchor points, then Alt+click and drag (hold down the Alt key, and click and drag) the point to drag out its handles. You can use the Subselect tool to drag these handles around, refining your shape.

To add a new anchor point, select the Pen tool and click—or click and drag—on an existing curve. To delete an existing anchor, click it with the Pen tool.

Flash's Pen tool doesn't provide the intricate control of a program such as Adobe Illustrator; however, once you get the hang of them, Flash's Bézier curves enable you to define a curve very precisely . . . more precisely than you usually need for animation and cartooning. In fact, if the Pen tool has a problem, it's that it makes it easy to build shapes that are twice as complex as they need to be.

You don't have to create a shape with the Pen tool to edit it with Flash's Bézier tools. Click the Rectangle tool ▢ and click and drag on the stage to make a box.

Now, click the Subselect tool. Drag a selection marquee around the rectangle you just drew to reveal its anchor points. Alt+click and drag one of the anchor points to pull out its handles, and turn that corner into a smooth curve (2.107).

You don't have to keep Flash's two kinds of curves straight; you can build a shape with the Paint Brush and then edit it with the Subselect tool, or draw a curved line with the Pen tool and then edit it with the normal Arrow tool.

Load the movie Cranky Old Guy.FLA, and practice tracing him with the Pen and Subselect tools.

CHAPTER 3
WRITING A CARTOON

This chapter discusses various cartoon writing methods to prepare for animating in Flash. It also describes techniques you can use to plan and organize your animation project.

There was never a script at Warner Brothers.

CHUCK JONES, LEGENDARY ANIMATOR AND DIRECTOR

WHERE DO YOU GET YOUR IDEAS?

In all likelihood, if you're reading this book in the first place, you can skip right over this section. If you can't already think of funny ideas, nothing I say can change that. Concentrate on your technical skills and find yourself a funny partner who can't draw.

THE DRAWINGS THEMSELVES

Your own drawings are one of your most important sources of inspiration. As you sketch and doodle certain characters and postures, attitudes present themselves or emerge spontaneously.

The accidental curve of a character's back tells you that he is proud, or old, or a slouch. Go with that, and see where it takes you.

Does something about the gorilla's expression make him seem embarrassed? Why? Does he have a humiliating job? Does he hate being stared at in the zoo (3.1)?

Pay attention to which lines suggest these attitudes, to the postures they suggest to you, to the "happy accidents" that add character and expression to your drawings. If you can figure out how you achieved an effect by accident, then, with a little practice, you'll be able to do it again later, on purpose.

3.1

THE CHARACTERS

Your characters are a primary source of inspiration. The better you know them, the more easily they'll suggest situations and stories to you. Once you know who the Road Runner and the Coyote are, and what their relationship is, the situation establishes itself. You still have to write the *gags*, of course.

What do your characters love and hate? What do they *want* (3.2)?

EVERYDAY LIFE

An endless amount of material can be gleaned from the simple things that everyone does every day: waking up, going to work, going on a date, eating a meal, getting a speeding ticket, and playing with your dog; not to mention weddings, funerals, birthdays, graduations, elections, births, and deaths; as well as the things your kid did, the things your mother-in-law said, and the things your spouse keeps nagging you to do.

OBSERVATIONAL HUMOR

Observational humor is the great staple of stand-up comedians. Observational humor calls attention to something that everyone sees but most people don't notice . . . say, restaurant signs advertising menus in

Braille. One of my Flash cartoons, about a man fishing for deer, actually began as the observation that fishing is really hunting with hooks; people just aren't bothered because fish aren't cute and furry.

Pay attention. What do you notice that no one else seems to?

TRANSPOSITIONS

You can find unexpected humor in everyday situations by replacing one common element with a different, unexpected element. Many of Gary Larson's hilarious *Far Side* cartoons are based on this kind of simple substitution: what if a boy had a rhinoceros instead of a hamster for a pet? What happens when the phone rings . . . at a cow's house?

My own cartoons often start with a simple transposition: What if those psychic hotlines offered tech support instead of love advice? What if a guy went fishing . . . for deer? Many of you have read Kafka's hilarious romp, "The Metamorphosis" (`www.vr.net/~herzogbr/kafka/meta.htm`), which asks the comic question, "What if a guy turned into a cockroach?"

The immensely popular Joe Cartoon on the Web (`www.joecartoon.com`) is based on similarly simple ideas: What if a fly got drunk? What if you frappé a frog in a blender, and the frog talks back (3.3)?

Of course it still takes genuine wit and style to come up with an answer to that situation that's *funny* . . . or dramatic or tragic.

SATIRE AND PARODY

Feel like making fun of something? Then satire or parody may be your form.

The words satire, parody, and spoof are often used interchangeably to refer to movies that in some way make fun of other movies. (Well, not just movies. Satire and parody are exercised by columnists, cartoonists, musicians, playwrights, and more.)

Technically, they all have different meanings.

A satire has an axe to grind; a *message* to put across. Satires use humor and wit to expose stupidity, evil, social and political ills . . . whatever torques your jib. Satires are usually not derived from other stories.

3.2

A parody makes fun of a particular literary or visual style. Parodies are often intended to make fun of original story or the style in which it was told. A parody of the *Star Wars* movies, for example, would be making fun of the movies, themselves.

A spoof, on the other hand, isn't really making fun of anything but itself. Bugs Bunny and Elmer Fudd singing in Wagner's "Ring of the Nibelung" is a spoof. It's not poking fun at opera or Wagner, nor commenting on some social ill; it's having fun with the situation itself.

Whatever the definition, any and all of these are fertile ground for animation, especially comedy.

IF YOU THINK IT'S FUNNY, THEN IT'S FUNNY

Is there a particular subject that cracks you up? Politics? Rampant consumerism? Doodie? Run with it. Tim Winkler's Doodie.com (`www.doodie.com/`) is a successful cartoon Web site based on the simple premise of a new poop joke, every day.

The point is that great cartoon ideas are all around you. You want funny? Watch C-SPAN for an hour! You want tragic? Watch C-SPAN for an hour.

C'mon. You know you've got ideas to express, and if you think about it for a while, you'll realize what they are. To make a good cartoon, you've got to kick it up a notch (well, maybe not the poop jokes).

Okay, so you've got an idea. Now what?

A STORM IN YOUR BRAIN

The next step is the brainstorming session or, sometimes, the "story conference." Don't let the names scare you, though; this is probably the funniest part of the whole damned process. For the most part, it

Copyright © 1999, The Joe Cartoon Co.

consists of a few guys and gals tossing funny ideas around a room and laughing. Musicians call this "riffing" or "jamming." If you're lucky enough to be writing with a partner, this step is a whole lot easier.

To make brainstorming a success for you, keep in mind two simple rules.

Rule #1: First create, then criticize and edit. This is the single most important factor to keep in mind in almost any creative endeavor. Please take another look at it; I can't over emphasize its importance. Keep the creative process and the critical process well separated.

I am *not* suggesting that you not be critical of your own work. Far from it—you are your own first and best critic. I'm saying that you shouldn't try to be creative and critical *at the same time.* Don't think up a joke, then critique it, then think up another. Spend an hour writing and creating, wait a bit, and *then* go back and criticize the work.

Mixing the critical and creative processes sabotages your efforts on so many levels. The two activities rely on different modes of thinking—different parts of the brain, if you will. Thinking critically about your jokes diverts your mind away from the act of writing jokes. Just as bad, the more you criticize your teammates, the less they feel like contributing.

Chuck Jones called his story sessions, "Yes Sessions." The rule was, no one was allowed to say no. As Grandma used to say, if you can't say something nice, don't say anything at all. You can suggest new ideas, add to existing ideas, but under no circumstances attack existing ideas. Even the worst ideas can lead to something good. Sometimes you can't reach that good idea except by way of the bad ideas.

RIGHT: "Rat points at a clock."

RIGHT: "Rat gives Penguin his watch."

WRONG: "That won't work. Rat's watch wouldn't fit Penguin."

RIGHT: "Rat hands Penguin a tiny grandfather's clock."

RIGHT: "Rat says, 'Careful with this, it was my Grandfather's.' "

Rule #2: Write everything down. Rule #2 relates to Rule #1: even write down the bad ideas and jokes. You'll be amazed at the amount of perfectly good material you'll forget, otherwise.

SOME BASIC MOVIE-MAKING TERMINOLOGY

Odds are, thanks to your lifelong exposure to television and the movies, you're already familiar with all of these camera and editing techniques, and even with most of their names.

- **Shot:** A shot refers to an image or a piece of animation shown onscreen. You may have a shot of a tree, or a shot of an airliner plunging into a volcano. A shot can be of any duration, from a single frame to several minutes. (A shot that only lasts a few frames is called a "flash-frame.") Shots come in three basic types: *wide*, *medium*, and *close-up*, but these exist in infinite variety, they

ORGANIZE, ORGANIZE, ORGANIZE

I cannot stress the importance of organization in layers and timelines enough! The easiest way to begin is to always label your layers systematically, because there will be lots of them, no matter what you are doing. Personally, when I do an animation, I storyboard it first, and then I number each storyboard drawing. It is a nice way to stay organized.

I use letter paper divided into six sections. A typical two-minute short has around 30 storyboard drawings. If I work on storyboard drawing 15, which may be a three-second scene of meatball playing Parcheesi, I number all my layers, having to do with that scene, 15A, 15B, 15C . . . and so on. You get the idea. This way I can always quickly refer to my storyboard to find exactly what I am looking for within my animation.

The reason why I number the storyboard drawings instead of giving them descriptive name labels is a personal preference. I find it easier to visually stay organized looking at a layer menu filled with sequential numbers as opposed to names such as Left Arm, Right Arm, Tongue, or Hammer. But what works for me may not work for the next guy.

I do break my animations up into scenes, but I still seem to use a lot of layers, so numbers help me. My storyboards are like a card catalogue.

Thanks to Meredith Scardino.

3.4

are all relative, and no hard and fast lines exist between them. Extreme wide shots and medium close-ups are just a couple of possible variations.

- **Wide angle shot:** As the name implies, a wide angle shot takes in a lot of area. Characters seen in a wide angle shot are usually completely visible, from head to toe. Wide shots are often used as *establishing shots*.

- **Medium shot:** A medium shot moves a little closer to the action than the *wide shot*. Characters seen in a medium shot are probably visible from the waist up (or the waist down).

- **Close-up:** A close-up brings the camera in close to the action. In a close-up, you only see a character's face.

- **Extreme close-up:** A close-up to the *n*th degree. In an extreme close-up, a character's face — or even a part of the face — fills the screen. Watch any Sergio Leone western for lessons in extreme close-ups.

- **Cut:** In a cut, one shot is abruptly replaced with another. You may cut from an exterior shot of a house to an interior shot of the kitchen, or from one character's face to another. This animation (3.4) cuts from one character to another.

- **Establishing shot:** Usually a *wide shot*, the establishing shot establishes the scene. Are we outdoors in a park? In outer space? In a housing project? The establishing shot tells us.

- **Pan:** In a pan, the camera stays in place, but rotates from side to side. Like *dolly shots*, pans are simulated in cartoons by moving all the elements in the scene sideways.

- **Swish pan:** A very quick pan from one position to another, blurring the details between the two points.

- **Tilt shot** (or vertical pan): In a tilt shot, the camera stays in place but rotates up or down. Tilts are simulated in cartoons by moving all the elements in the scene up or down.

- **Zoom:** In a zoom, the camera remains stationary, and a special zoom lens is used to increase or decrease the magnification, changing the field of view. No change in perspective occurs in a zoom, as it does in a *dolly shot*. In Flash, you emulate a

3.5

zoom by scaling all elements in a scene up or down, simultaneously.

■ **Dolly shot:** In a dolly shot, the camera moves from side to side (dolly left and right) or front to back (dolly in and out). In animation, sideways dolly shots, like *pans,* are usually simulated by moving the entire scene from side to side. Movement into and out of a scene — dollying in and out — is simulated by zooming different elements of the scene up or down, at different speeds, to create the illusion of changing perspective.

■ **Tracking shot:** In a tracking shot, the camera moves along with the subject. In a motion picture, the camera is usually mounted on a dolly or crane, but in animation tracking shots generally have the characters walk in place while the background moves behind them.

■ **Reverse angle:** A shot pointing in the opposite direction of the preceding shot, for example, a shot of a man talking, followed by a shot of the woman he is talking to.

■ **Insert:** An insert is a shot of something other than the main action, but related to, and taking place simultaneously with, the main action. A shot of someone listening while another character talks is an insert. A close-up shot of a character's face while he works with his hands is an insert. A close-up shot of a character's hands while he talks is an insert.

■ **Jump-cut:** A jump-cut is a cut between two shots that appear unrelated. Jump-cuts are dramatic and disorienting; it takes the viewer a moment to re-establish his or her frame of reference. (Jump cuts are often accidental.)

■ **Cross-cutting:** Cutting back and forth between two related actions, usually to build tension. For example, a man swimming, then a shark fin cutting the water, then the man swimming, and so forth. Pull up the file, Cross-Cut Cars.FLA for an example of a cross cutting (3.5). After this build-up, any action less than a head-on collision is a major disappointment.

■ **Inter-cutting:** Cutting back and forth between two different locations that make up a single scene, for example, two people talking on the phone.

STORYBOARDS

Now it's time to actually write the cartoon down in some coherent form. From this point, different animators work in slightly different sequences, depending largely on what type of cartoon they're making. If your cartoon is mainly dialog driven, you may want to start there, with the dialog. My cartoon, "Fishin' Ain't So Bad," consists almost entirely of a fisherman, sitting still, rhapsodizing about hunting and fishing. For this cartoon I started by writing the dialogue.

But most cartoons, especially those with any kind of action, are laid out as storyboards — sketches remi-

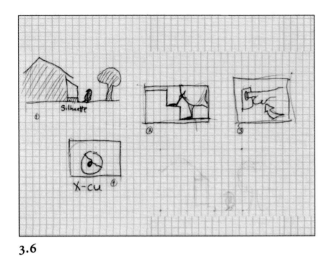

3.6

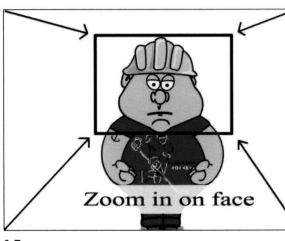

3.7

3.8

niscent of the Sunday funnies. The quality of the art in storyboards isn't very important, although good art never hurts. The purpose of the storyboard is to show every shot in the animation. Storyboards often include notations regarding corresponding audio, music, dialogue, and sound and video effects.

A storyboard can be anything from 3 × 5 index cards taped to the wall, to pages in a three-ring binder, to scenes drawn in Flash (3.6).

The storyboard is where you plan and stage the action: Where is everyone going to stand? What views of the kitchen do we need?

Here is where you begin to think about your "camera work." What different shots do you need? What close-ups? What establishing shots? Where will the camera pan? Where will it zoom? Will the action happen in one long shot? Or will it be broken into a number of shorter shots?

Because animation moves, but storyboard drawings are static, use arrows to indicate motion of the camera, or motion of the characters, within the scene (3.7).

Sometimes, a concept that seemed quite clear when you first thought of it can turn out to be a little more complicated to actually stage; you need to figure out how to get a character from the kitchen to the den, or how he can retrieve his toolbox from the truck without slowing down the action. You often find out you need more different shots than you originally thought you did. That's why you create a storyboard: to work out all the details before you commit to the animation. Sketches are cheap; animation is expensive.

Consider a short scene where Penguin walks up on a porch and rings the doorbell. This simple sequence can be handled in a myriad of different ways. He can walk up the stairs and ring the doorbell in a single, wide shot without any cuts (3.8).

NOTE

Some people prefer to start with a storyboard that is completely textual. They write descriptions of the action — Penguin hurts his back and falls down, moaning — and leave any actual drawings until later in the process. These text-only storyboards are sometimes called scripts.

Or you can break the action up into smaller segments, vary some details, and entirely change the feel of the scene (3.9). Here the action is shown in silhouette, giving the scene a little foreboding. The scene is broken into four shots, each closer than the last; the sequence moves from a wide establishing shot to an extreme close-up of one eye, further building the tension. We know something's going to happen when that door opens.

Either of these approaches is fine, depending on the effect you're after, but now's the time to decide, during the storyboard, and *before* you begin work on the cartoon itself.

Your storyboard tells you how you want your characters and other objects to be seen—do you need to animate him walking toward the camera? Or should he only ever walk left-to-right? Do we need a front view of the car? A view from the back of the house?

CASE STUDY: THE MAKING OF "THE LIZARD AND THE FLY"

It was Saturday afternoon and, as I started up Flash on my laptop computer, I wondered how fast I could make a short, presentable animation from start to finish, ready to go to my Web site for viewing. So with no ideas, I sat with a blank sketchbook, my laptop computer, and started. Four hours later "The Lizard and the Fly" was on my Web site.

I first started doodling in my sketchbook, doing some free-range brainstorming, trying to think up an idea. I drew the lizard and thought about how could I make that into a joke. Thoughts bounced around as I sketched the lizard: It's a rainforest. The lizard tries to catch a fly with his tongue. The lizard is on a branch in the jungle. He can't catch the fly that keeps circling. Keeps missing. Hmmm ... where's the joke? The end? The fly razzzes him. How else are flies killed? Fly swatter. Okay, after a few tries the lizard pulls out a fly swatter from nowhere and whacks the fly, which lands on the lizard's tongue.

From just looking at my sketch, I completed the drawing using Adobe Illustrator 8 (I now use version 9). First I drew the lizard, putting different parts of the lizard on different levels. Everything that moved had a separate level in Illustrator: eyes, legs, tongue, fly swatter, and other items. Then I drew the background as a separate illustration. And the branch the lizard is on is a separate illustration done in Adobe Illustrator. Then I exported all the Illustrator drawings with the .swf file type. In Flash, I imported all the Illustrator drawings into the library as symbols.

Everything that goes into a Flash animation is a separate symbol (even text) and put on its own layer in the animation.

In "The Lizard and the Fly" 3 separate scenes, total, exist. Scene 1 has 3 layers and 10 frames. Scene 2 has 24 layers and 180 frames. Scene 3 has 5 layers and 10 frames. Scene 2 is the cartoon. Scene 1 is just the first splash screen that is used while waiting for the rest of the animation to load. Scene 3 is the end splash screen with "See Again" button.

The key to this animation working is all in the timing (as it is with just about all animation). If the eyes did not move fast and jerky, or the tongue did not snap out and back quickly enough, or the fly swatter hit the fly just right, the animation would be less effective. So that is where I spent most of my time on this animation: tweaking the movements and coordinating it with the sounds.

One factor that I had not planned, but changed as I was making the animation, was the way the lizard walks backward after each strike with his tongue. The animation was done, but it seemed not to have enough action ... plus I was having space problems when the fly swatter hit ... so I redid the animation and drawings (I made movable legs for the lizard) and made it so the lizard walked backward. I originally only had one eye looking around. But after I was done I went back and made the back eye look around, too. That gave the lizard more realistic movements.

The sounds were mostly done with some freebie sounds I had laying around. I made the fly's "zzzzzz" sound by going "zzzzzz" into my computer's microphone and tweaking it in the program SoundEdit 16.

It only took four hours to get the entire thing done ... from start to finish! (3.10)

Thanks to Charles Kaufman (www.charleskaufman.com).

3.9

3.10

© 2000 Charles Kaufman

<u>SCENE ONE</u>

IRIS IN:

EXT. APARTMENT BUILDING -- MORNING

Falling snow partially obscures our view of an anonymous
apartment building. Assorted Christmas decorations are
displayed in some apartment windows. We hear an old-fashioned
ALARM CLOCK ringing.

                                                 FADE TO:

INT. BATHROOM -- MORNING

(Rat)

RAT is blearily BRUSHING TEETH. RAT sees a MAGAZINE AD taped
to mirror, advertising a sale on kittens.

RAT reacts.

                                                 CUT TO:

INT. KITCHEN -- MORNING

(Rat, Penguin)

RAT is seated at the table, reading the morning paper.
PENGUIN crosses behind him, dressed as a cook, mixing batter
in a bowl.

                         PENGUIN
                I circled a very interesting article
                in the paper for you.

RAT scans the paper. We see a circled article: "Pet a kitty
to lower your blood pressure, Docs say."

RAT reacts, scowling at penguin.

PENGUIN feigns innocence.

                         PENGUIN (CONT'D)
                I'm just worried about your blood
                pressure.

Will we see the porch steps in close-up, so they need to be drawn in detail? Or will they only appear in wide shots, so we can skip the detail? Let's say all the action takes place in silhouette; that affects the way you create your characters and other elements—a character seen only in silhouette doesn't need a face, but must have a recognizable profile.

The storyboard for a feature-length animation can consume the walls of a large room. The storyboard for some short gags may be only a couple of draw-

ings. It's most important that the storyboard cover every shot, and every gag, in your cartoon, to make sure you know what you're going to do before you begin animating the cartoon.

I admit it, you *can* get away with skipping the script and storyboard steps, *sometimes*, if your animation is very short. But if your cartoon runs any length, or has any complexity at all, you are saving yourself a lot of trouble in the future by storyboarding it in advance.

SCRIPTS AND DIALOGUE SHEETS

The script is an important part of almost every movie, long or short, but most animated cartoons, even big, feature length ones, don't have scripts, at least in the normal meaning of the word. Animated cartoons are almost always made from storyboards instead. If a script exists, it often comes late in the process, after the action has been worked out first in storyboard form.

Of course, even directors such as Walt Disney and Chuck Jones, who claim never to have made a cartoon from a script, had to write down the dialogue at some point. When Mel Blanc stepped into the recording booth, he needed to know what Bugs Bunny and Daffy Duck were supposed to say.

You can write the dialogue directly on your storyboard but, when the time comes to record the vocal tracks, you want to transfer it to a more manageable script, or dialogue sheets of some kind. The difference between a script and a dialogue sheet is that the script contains stage and (sometimes) camera directions (3.11). The dialogue sheet, on the other hand, only contains naked dialogue (3.12). Read by itself, it may make very little sense. Give the actors their own copy, and highlight their lines for them, to make their lines easier to find.

```
                PENGUIN
I circled a very interesting article
in the paper for you.


                PENGUIN (CONT'D)
I'm just worried about your blood
pressure.

                RAT
We are not getting a kitten.|

                PENGUIN
I didn't say anything!

                PENGUIN (CONT'D)
Gotta go - bye!

                PENGUIN (CONT'D)
Maybe Rat would like a kitten.

                PENGUIN (CONT'D)
Nah.

                PENGUIN (CONT'D)
Do you have this in a *much* smaller
size?

                RAT
No - no - no - no!

                RAT (CONT'D)
Hey.  Here's something!

                PENGUIN
Eureka!
```

3.12

CHAPTER 4
DÓNDE ESTÁ LA BIBLIOTECA?

Reusable library symbols are key to managing large projects and limiting the size and download time of your Flash animations.

BUILDING A LIBRARY OF REUSABLE PARTS

You'll save yourself a lot of work, and your viewers a lot of download time, once you learn how to make Flash's library work for you. Once created, a symbol can be used over and over as many times as you like, without your having to redraw objects, and without adding any size to your final animation.

THE IMPORTANCE OF SYMBOLS

The key importance of symbols in your Flash animation is to, say it with me now, *minimize curves*. Fewer curves mean smaller animations. The smaller the finished animation, the faster it downloads from the Internet. Thus, people spend less time waiting for it to load, and they are more likely to watch it and to recommend or send it to friends. Small is good. In fact, all other things being equal, smaller is always better.

Properly designed and organized, symbols make Flash animation easier and faster. Symbols also enable you to create cool special effects and interaction that you can't accomplish without them.

Flash keeps statistics on each symbol's size in bytes, and the number of times it is used. Those statistics are invaluable when you need to optimize your animation.

Importing the character pieces and building a library should be one of the first steps in creating a Flash movie. Naming conventions are important — the more organized you are at this point, the easier it will be to make changes later.

JANET GALORE, BITMAP ANIMATOR,
HONKWORM INTERNATIONAL, INC.

GRAPHICS, MOVIE CLIPS, AND BUTTONS

Anything you can do on the main stage in Flash can be done as a symbol. Symbols can contain sounds, multiple layers, and other symbols. In fact, I have at times made entire scenes, multiple layers and all, into symbols. Usually, though, a symbol is something less than an entire scene: a prop, a title, a character, or a part of a character. Flash symbols come in one of three flavors: graphic symbols, movie clips, and buttons.

Graphic Symbols

Graphic symbols are just pictures. They can be animated, or not. Graphic symbols, if they're animated, keep time with the scene in which they are placed. If you place a 20-frame animated graphic of a character walking into a scene that's 40 frames long, that animation repeats twice. Place it into a scene that's only 1 frame long, and you only see 1 frame of the animation.

Graphic symbols can move around within the scene independent of their animation. For example, you may want to create a graphic symbol that is an animation of a bird flapping its wings in place. Drop that symbol into your scene and have it move across the screen. The bird flaps its wings while it flies from one place to another. Place half a dozen copies of the bird symbol on the stage, and you have a whole flock of birds. In this image (4.1), the tent, boat, trees, ducks, and tufts of grass are all symbols. Each flying duck, each tuft of grass, and each distant tree is a copy of the same symbol.

Movie Clips

Movie clips are the same as graphic symbols with one big difference. They play back independent of the main timeline. If you place a 20-frame *movie clip* of a character walking into a scene that's only 1 frame long, you still see the entire 20-frame animation when you play the movie. Even if you stop the main movie, the movie clip symbol continues to run.

Buttons

Buttons are just what you think they are: special graphics that respond to the mouse (and the keyboard). You can program them to trigger different actions — play a sound, jump to a new scene, and so forth — when the user's mouse passes over them or clicks them, or when the user presses a key. Buttons can contain graphic symbols and movie clips. Each block of text on this screen (4.2) is a button. Clicking them restarts the animation, or fires off an e-mail to me, and so on.

Symbols as Mini-Libraries of Frames

A graphic symbol doesn't have to play straight through from frame one to the end and then stop, or loop. It can start and stop at any time. Your symbol may be a bird or butterfly that flaps its wings for a while, glides for some time, and then flaps again (4.3). It may be a counter that changes value slowly as the animation is loaded into memory, or played back (4.4). It may even be a series of images that can appear in any order, such as the expressions on a character's face (4.5).

4.1

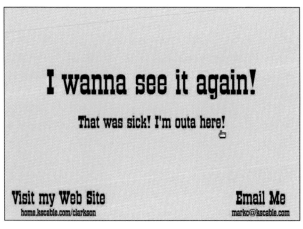

4.2

CONVERTING A MAIN STAGE ANIMATION INTO A SYMBOL

Y ou can turn any animation built on the main stage into an animated symbol, even if it has many layers and frames.

Click the first frame of the topmost layer. Now, hold down the Ctrl key and drag to the right-hand side of the bottommost layer, far enough to the right that every frame of every layer is selected. Right-click the selected frames and choose Copy Frames.

Choose Insert ➣ New Symbol. Give the symbol a good name (I like "Garnok," but you decide) and press OK to begin editing your new symbol.

Right-click the first frame in Layer 1 and choose Paste Frames. Every frame and layer from the main stage is copied to the new symbol, although the layer names are not preserved.

This process sometimes gives you extra frames on some layers. If Layer 1 is 10 frames long, for example, and Layer 2 is 15 frames long, Layer 1 will have 5 extra frames after the copy and paste. Every layer is padded to the same length. Select any extra frames and delete them (Shift+F5).

4.3

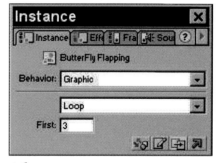

4.4

4.5

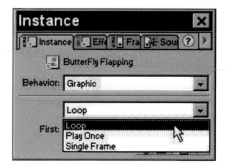

4.6

Load the file Butterfly.FLA and save it under a new name. Play the animation. The butterfly flaps across the stage.

Drag the playhead to frame 15. Press F6 to create a new keyframe (or choose Insert ➣ Keyframe). You can only change the properties of a symbol at a keyframe.

Right-click the butterfly symbol on the stage, and choose Panels ➣ Instance from the pop-up menu. The Instance panel tells you what's happening with this symbol at this particular frame.

In the lower part of the panel is the Play Mode option. You can see that the symbol animation is Looping, and that as of this keyframe, the animation is on frame 3 (4.6).

Click the Play Mode drop-down menu, which now says Loop, and choose Play Once. Play the animation.

4.7

The butterfly flaps its wings until frame 15, where it freezes and glides the rest of the way across the screen. Interesting, but not a very satisfying result. While a butterfly may glide, it would only be for a little bit. A few frames, let's say.

Move the playhead to frame 18, and press F6 again to create a new keyframe there. Click the butterfly once to select it. In the Instance panel, select Loop to start the butterfly flapping again (4.7). Change the first frame from 3 to 5. (This causes the butterfly to resume his flapping on the upstroke, which I, personally, like better. Play around and reach your own conclusions.) Now play the animation again. Much better, no?

You can stop and start an animated symbol at any time, and have it play from any frame, with a simple keyframe. Being able to play a symbol from any frame has some uses that aren't instantly apparent.

Load the file Face Expressions.FLA, and save it under a new name. This little guy is based on an exercise from Mark Heath's *Drawing Cartoons* (Cincinnati, OH: North Light Books, 1998) (4.8).

His eyes are an animated symbol with ten frames. However, the idea here is *not* to play the symbol as an animation, but rather to use it as sort of a mini-library of eyes. (Some Flashers refer to this as a *meta-library*.) If the Instance panel is not open, open it now by right-clicking the eyes and choosing Panels ➤ Instance. Notice that we're only playing a single frame. Change the first frame to a different number up to 10 and press Enter to change the eyes (4.9). Leave the Instance panel open.

The mouth is also a 10-frame animation. Click the mouth to select it, and change the first frame to any number from 2 to 10. Press Enter to change the mouths (4.10).

Admittedly, this is not the best organized method of keeping symbols — it can be hard to remember which mouth shape is at what frame — but sometimes it's the most convenient. It can help keep down the sheer number of symbols you accumulate in a large animation. It's also useful to think of your symbols as libraries of frames that you can access in any order (4.11).

You can use this method to leverage existing symbols and animations in other animations. For example, you may have built a facial animation of a character smiling, and then saying "Hello." You can

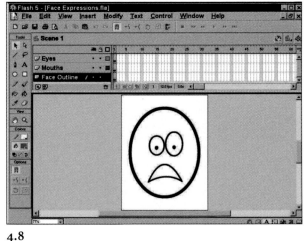

4.8

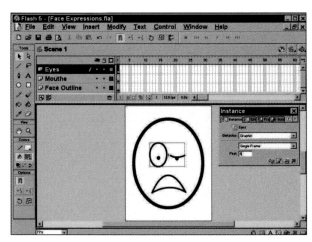

4.9

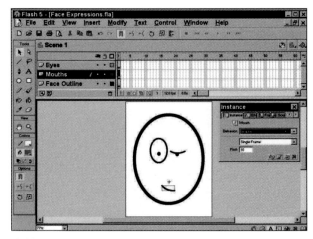

4.10

use this same animation, set to Single Frame mode, anywhere you need the character to just smile.

My animation "Fishin' Ain't So Bad" has several shots of the fisherman reeling in a line. I built a single animated symbol of his arm doing a circular, reeling motion, and then I stopped and started that animation as I needed. The fisherman reels, waits a while, reels a bit more, even backs up a little, all with a single animated symbol, stopped, started, and looped with simple keyframes (4.12).

Nested Symbols

Symbols can include other symbols. In my Penguin & Rat cartoons, I decided to animate Penguin's head separately from his body. When he needs to deliver a line, I make an animated symbol of his head speaking the lines (4.13).

I also have symbols that are Penguin's body walking, standing, turning, and so forth. If he needs to walk *and* deliver a line, I make a new symbol and drag both

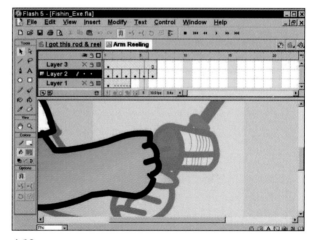

4.12

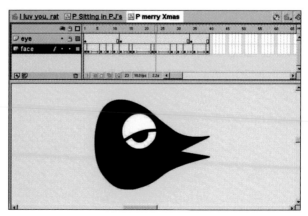

4.11

4.13

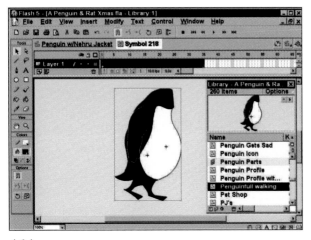

4.14

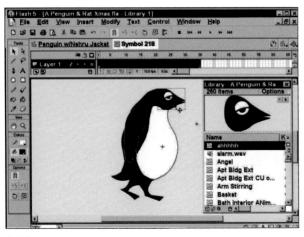

4.15

4.16

the body-walking symbol (4.14) and the head-talking symbol (4.15) both in there, creating a third walking-and-talking symbol, containing the other two. I drag the walking-and-talking symbol onto the stage and have it move across the screen while it plays: Penguin walks and talks (4.16).

To have Penguin run and talk, stand and talk, or deliver a different set of lines, I create new symbols made up of the appropriate head and body symbols.

Many opportunities exist to exploit nested symbols in your animation: an airplane may have two identical propellers, a firework may explode into many identical stars, or most characters have two identical eyes. Every time you use a second copy of a symbol instead of drawing a new one, your animation gets that much smaller.

Folders and the Library Window

Flash keeps all of your graphics, buttons, movie clips, and imported images and sounds in the movie's library. The command to open the library is found under the Window menu: Window ➤ Library (or Ctrl+L).

Open the file Bot Walk and Skip.FLA, and save it under a new name. If the library is not already open, open it (Window ➤ Library). Three objects are visible in the library window: two animated symbols and a folder called BOT parts. Double-click the folder to open it. True to its name, this folder contains all of the individual robot parts (4.17).

TRACKING SYMBOL USE

Flash keeps track of the number of times each symbol is used. Open the Library (Window ➤ Library). Select the Options drop-down menu and choose Keep Use Counts Updated.

If you can't see the Use Count column, click and drag the side of the library window until Use Count appears (4.19).

Use Count is a handy tool for tracking down any symbols and imported images and sounds that aren't used in your animation yet.

You can click and drag items to and from folders in the Library window.

> ### TIP
> You can move a number of library items en masse to a new folder: select the items via Shift+clicking or Ctrl+clicking, and then right-click the selected items and choose Move to New Folder.

Notice also that each of the parts is clearly labeled, and that their names follow the same format, for example, BOT_Rite Shoe. This much organization may be overkill for a simple animation like this one, but in a longer or more complex cartoon, it's a lifesaver.

Here is part of the library from my cartoon, "Fishin' Ain't So Bad" (4.18). "Fishin'" is a 2½-minute, 1700-frame animation. The library comprises some 90 objects, including 19 imported sound files (8 sound effects and 11 voice tracks), 14 imported bitmaps, 13 background objects, 18 props, 19 fishermen and parts thereof (including 7 mouths), and a handful of buttons and other miscellany. Giving every object the first name that occurs to you and then throwing it in one big pile is a recipe for confusion and lost time.

As you can see, folders can contain other folders— the Fisherman folder contains a Mouth folder, for example—to allow you to organize to your heart's content.

Movie Clips versus Graphics

Animated symbols come in two flavors: graphics and movie clips. The difference between animated graphics and movie clips is a little hard to grasp at first. Animated graphics are tied to the playback of the main timeline, whereas movie clips play back on their own time, regardless of what's happening on the main timeline.

The best way to understand that difference is by example, so let's look at one. Open the file Bot Skip. FLA, and save it under a new name.

This movie has a single frame (4.20) with Andy the robot poised for takeoff. Double-click Andy to open the symbol for editing. You see that the symbol itself has 20 frames, not 1. Click any area of the stage and press Enter to preview the symbol's animation: Andy skips across the screen (4.21). Click the Scene 1 tab above the timeline to return to the main timeline.

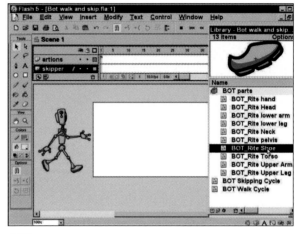

4.17

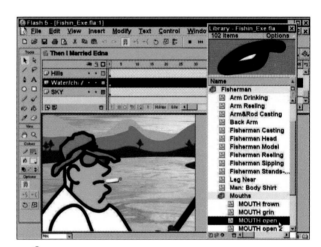

4.18

4.19

Test the movie by choosing Control ➤ Test Movie. Sure enough, because it's only a one-frame movie, it only plays the first frame of the animation. Close the Preview window.

Right-click the Andy symbol and choose Panels ➤ Instance from the pop-up menu. Notice that the behavior of this symbol is Graphic, meaning that it is an animated graphic. Graphic symbols are tied to the main timeline. Because the main timeline is only one frame long, the symbol only plays its first frame. Click the Behavior drop-down menu and change the symbol's behavior to Movie Clip (4.22).

Movie clips play back according to their own timelines, regardless of what's happening on the main timeline. Try it out. Choose Control ➤ Test Movie. Now Andy skips all the way across the screen, playing all 20 frames of his animation repeatedly, *despite the fact that the movie only has 1 frame.*

You can start and stop the main movie, and movie clips will keep running. You can also, as we will see in Chapter 13, tell movie clips to stop, start, rewind and jump ahead, independent of the main movie timeline.

Movie clips are great for animated background elements in your cartoons, and for making animated elements for menus on your Web site. You can build the menu itself with a single frame to hold the buttons and graphics, and then populate it with animated movie clips of whatever duration you want.

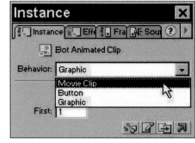

4.22

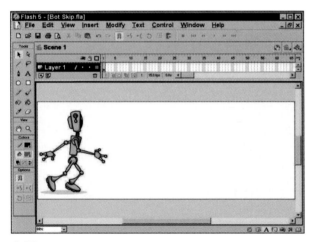

4.20

4.23

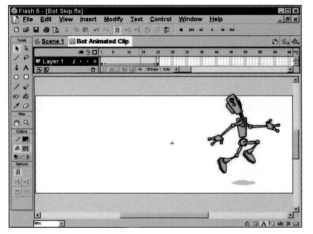

4.21

4.24

Instances

As I mentioned previously, your animation can hold any number of copies of the same symbol. You can build a forest out of dozens of copies of the same tree symbol, or a flock of geese from multiple copies of the same goose.

Each of these instances can be identical, or you can make each one subtly or grossly different. This forest background, for example, is built from only four symbols: two trees, one clump of grass, and one cloud, each copied, stretched, flipped, brightened, and darkened several times (4.23). The file size, and consequently, the download time, is essentially the same as a background with only two trees, one cloud, and one tiny clump of grass (4.24).

Multiple Graphics

You can animate different instances of the same symbol on different timings as well. Load the file 3 Butterflies.FLA, and save it under a new name (4.25). Press Enter to preview the animation. The butterflies all flap their way across the screen in sync . . . a highly unrealistic way for butterflies to fly, don't you think?

4.27

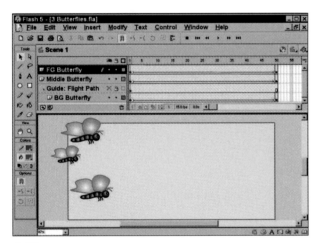

4.25

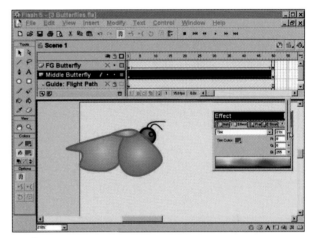

4.28

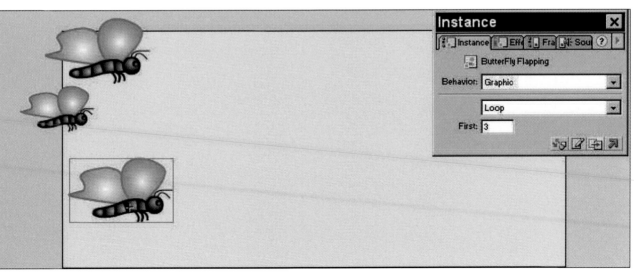

4.26

The butterflies' animation is six frames long. Currently, each copy of the symbol starts playing on frame one. Select one of the butterflies, right-click it, and choose Panels ➤ Instance. In the First frame field, type a number between two and six (4.26). Now this butterfly's wings will flap out of sync with the other two.

Select one of the two remaining butterflies and have it start on a different frame than the other two. Click the stage and press Enter to preview the animation. Sure enough, each butterfly now seems to be flapping to its own rhythm (4.27).

There are limits to what you can accomplish by using this method. You haven't changed the actual animation in any way, just juggled the order up a little bit. You probably noticed that I changed each instance's color a little bit (Window ➤ Panels ➤ Effects ➤ Tint) to further differentiate them (4.28).

Movie Clip Instances

So far, we've only looked at multiple instances of graphic symbols. You can have multiple instances of movie clips as well. Movie clips have an extra twist in that each instance can have its own unique name.

As I've alluded to once or twice, you can *talk to* movie clips, telling them to start, stop, back up, and so forth. By giving different instances of a movie clip different names, you can talk to each one individually

> **NOTE**
>
> A URL (Uniform Resource Locator) doesn't have to be the address of a Web site. A URL can refer to a file on your computer, on your local area network, or on the Internet.

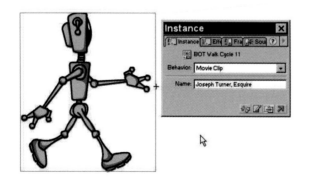

4.29

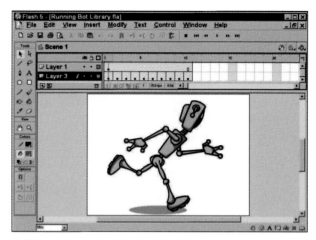

4.30

4.31

Wide state

Narrow state

4.32

(4.29). ("Bob, you back up. Gurdy, you stop playing. Ralph, jump ahead to frame 7.") We see how to actually use this cool feature later in the book. (Those of you who can't wait, skip ahead to Chapter 13.)

SHARED LIBRARIES

Flash 5 provides another great way to reduce the size of your movies, at least in some cases, and to make it easier for you to manage large cartoons and even whole series of cartoons. The *shared library* enables you to do this easily.

USING SHARED LIBRARIES OF SYMBOLS

The notion behind the shared library is pretty simple. As you've seen, every Flash movie has its own library of symbols. A shared library is a library of symbols that can be used by any number of different movies.

This is useful in several ways. Different animators working on the same project can all use symbols from a single library, ensuring that they are using the most current version of any given symbol. If that shared symbol gets changed — if you decide to make the red fish into a blue fish, or if you change the way your superhero dog's cape flaps when he flies — every movie that uses that symbol is instantly updated. You do not need to manually replace every instance of SuperDog throughout the entire 15-episode series.

Let's look at a quick example. Load the file Running Bot Library.FLA, and save it under a new name. It's just Andy (4.30).

We're not really interested in the movie here, though. As its name implies, this file serves predominantly as a library. In fact, no surprise, we're going to use it as a *shared library*.

Choose Window ➤ Library (or Ctrl+L) to open the movie's library (4.31). Click the Wide State button and drag the library's frame out far enough so that you see the column labeled Linkage.

SHARING SYMBOLS WITH OTHER MOVIES

If you intend to share these symbols with another movie, you have to tell Flash about it first. Symbols aren't shared with other movies by default.

Look at the library. Notice that the word Export appears in the Linkage column for every symbol except the symbol named, BOT Walk Cycle 11. Right-click any symbol *except* BOT Walk Cycle 11 — that is, any symbol that has the word Export in the Linkage column — and select Linkage from the pop-up menu (4.32).

This brings up the Symbol Linkage Properties panel (4.33). In this panel you tell Flash to make a symbol available to other movies, outside of the current one, by *exporting* it. Notice that "Export this symbol" is indeed checked.

Close the Symbol Linkage Properties panel.

Right-click the BOT Walk Cycle 11 symbol, and choose Linkage from the pop-up menu. As you probably suspected, I haven't yet told Flash to export this symbol; that's why the word Export does not appear

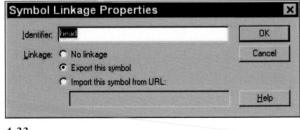

4·33

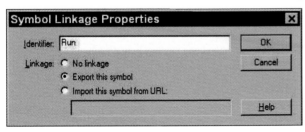

4·34

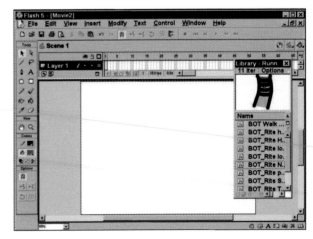

4·35

in this symbol's Linkage column. Go ahead and select the "Export this symbol" option.

Every exported symbol needs to have its own unique identifier, or name. The identifier can be the same as the symbol's name, or different. In the identifier field, type the word **Run** (4.34).

Close the Symbol Linkage Properties panel. You'll notice that the word Export now appears in the BOT Walk Cycle 11's Linkage column, showing

4.36

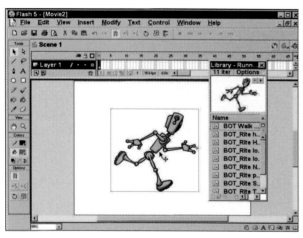

4.37

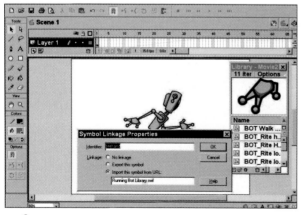

4.38

that you've told Flash to make it available to other movies.

Because the BOT Walk Cycle 11 symbol uses all of the other symbols in the library, you must mark each of them for export. As you can see from the Linkage column, I've already done that for all of the other symbols. (You're welcome, as always.) Every symbol in this library is now available to be *imported* into other movies. Save the file, but leave it open. Now, follow these steps to import some of those symbols into another movie, just to prove that it can be done:

1. Open a new file, and save it under an interesting name.

2. From the menu, choose File ➤ Open as Shared Library. Select the shared library file FLA file that you just saved (for example, My Running Bot Library.FLA). The shared library appears on the stage (4.35). The symbols in the library are grayed out (4.36) to remind you that you can't edit them here. You can only make changes to shared library symbols by opening the FLA file that holds the original library.

3. Select the symbol, BOT Walk Cycle 11, and drag it from the library onto the stage (4.37).

4. Move the playhead to frame 10 and press F5 (Insert Frame) to give Andy enough time to make a complete cycle. Click the stage and press Enter to preview the animation. Sure enough, it works.

5. Open the new movie's library (Ctrl+L).

6. Either close the shared library panel, or move it out of the way for a bit. Right-click any of the symbols in your new movie's library, and select Linkage from the pop-up menu (4.38). You'll see that, this time, the "Import this symbol from URL" option is selected, and the name of your shared library file — in this case, Running Bot Library.swf — is displayed at the bottom.

The identifier is the same one given that symbol in the original shared library.

If you select the Library's Wide State ▣ and drag the library frame out wide enough to see the Linkage column, you'll see that all of the imported symbols are labeled Import (4.39).

Notice also that you didn't have to manually select the Import option for every symbol, or specify the file

> **NOTE**
>
> A shared library must be published in SWF format before other movies can employ the shared symbols it holds.

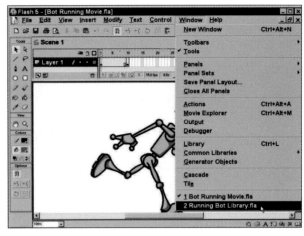

4.41

where that symbol is found. Flash did it for you. Test the movie by choosing Control ➢ Test Movie.

Whoops! It won't run (4.40). It's not your fault—I tricked you. But I did it to make two points:

- **Point #1:** There's nothing in this movie. The running robot and the parts that make him up all come from a shared library. They only exist within that shared library; Flash doesn't put them in your new movie at all. (I probably don't need to tell you that this reduces file size something considerable . . . .) If that shared library isn't there for some reason, your new movie can't run.

- **Point #2:** That shared library isn't there for some reason. That reason is that you didn't publish it in SWF form. (Of course, the reason for *that* is that *I* didn't *tell you* to do it.) If you remember, the

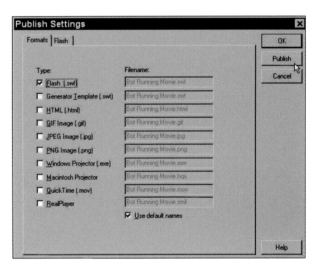

4.42

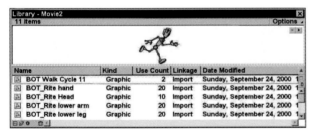

4.39

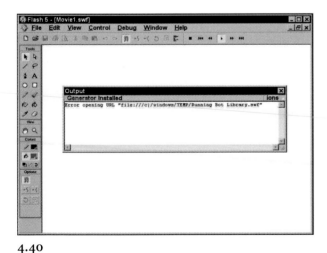

4.40

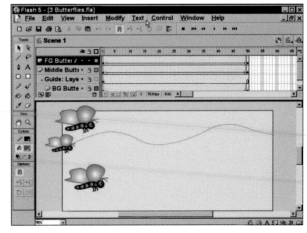

4.43

Linkage properties panel you looked at referred to the library it was importing from in its SWF form (4.38).

You can easily fix this error, though. Close the preview window, and from the Window menu select the movie containing the original shared library (4.41).

Choose File ➢ Publish Settings and select the Formats tab. Make sure that Flash (.swf) is selected, and that all other formats are unselected. Leave "Use default names" selected, and click the Publish button (4.42) to publish the shared library in SWF form.

Switch back to the movie that actually uses the shared library. Test the movie again (Window ➢ Test Movie). This time, because you just generated the SWF file it's looking for, the movie should play.

Now if you were to go back to the shared library file and make a change to any part of the robot, and then publish the shared library again, your new movie would automatically reflect the change. The next time you played the SWF file you would see the change. *You wouldn't have to edit the movie.*

> **NOTE**
>
> **Caveat: Unfortunately, you won't see changes in shared libraries reflected in the FLA files of movies which use them, only in published SWFs. Shared library symbols always appear in the FLA as they did when you first added them.**

WHERE'D I PUT THAT?: THE FLASH MOVIE EXPLORER

Flash 5 has added a nifty tool to let you keep track of large numbers of assets in your Flash movies: the Movie Explorer.

Close any open files. Open the file 3 Butterflies.FLA and save it under a new name. Open the Movie Explorer by clicking the Movie Explorer button 🔳 on the launch bar at the bottom of the screen (4.43), or by choosing Window ➢ Movie Explorer (4.44).

The Movie Explorer shows you every symbol, every imported bitmap or sound file, and every piece of

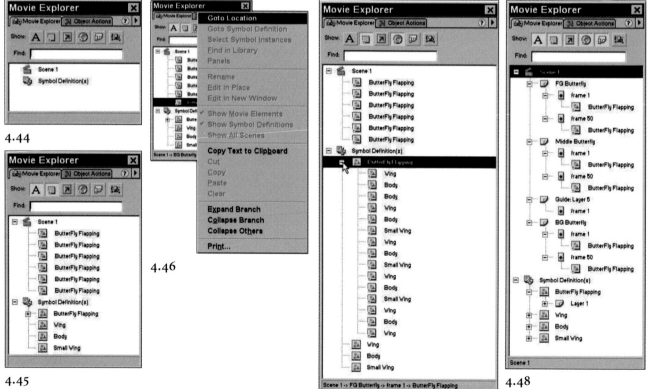

4.44

4.46

4.45

4.47

4.48

4.49

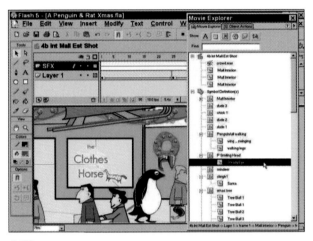

4.50

text in the current scene of your movie, as well as detailing which scenes, layers, and frames they appear in, and what actions, if any, they perform. You can browse for them, or search for a given bit by name.

Let's take a look. At the top of the Movie Explorer, beside the label Show, are six buttons. Click the first button **A**. This shows all the text in the movie. Because no text is in this movie, nothing appears. Click the second button ⬚. This shows all movie clips, buttons, and graphics in your movie (4.45).

Now we're getting somewhere. You can see six instances of Butterfly flapping under Scene 1, indicating that this symbol appears in six keyframes in that scene. Because three copies of this symbol exist, and each has a beginning and ending keyframe, this is certainly true. Right-click the last of these six and choose Goto Location from the pop-up menu (4.46). The Flash playhead moves to frame 50, the ending keyframe of the third copy of the symbol. Double-click any of the six instances of Butterfly Flapping in the Movie Explorer to edit the symbol itself.

Under Symbol Definition(s) in the Movie Explorer, you see all of the symbols that go into this simple movie. The plus (+) sign to the left of the Butterfly Flapping symbol indicates that it, in turn, is made up of other symbols. Click the plus sign to see them (4.47). When you expand the symbol, the plus sign becomes a minus sign, which you click to collapse the tree again. You'll see that the Butterfly Flapping symbol is made up of several copies of the symbols, Wing, Small Wing, and Body.

The third button ⬚ shows any action script in the movie. Because we haven't learned how to add actions yet, none exist. The fourth button ⬚ shows any imported bitmaps or sound files. Again, none exist in this movie. The fifth button ⬚ shows the actual layers and frames on which each item appears (4.48).

The sixth button ⬚ allows you to choose which assets (settings) the Movie Explorer shows and how it shows them (4.49).

All of the Movie Explorer's information can seem a little overwhelming at first, but it comes in handy when keeping track of elements in larger and more complex animations (4.50).

CHAPTER 5
WHY DID YOGI BEAR WEAR THAT NECKTIE?

Animated characters can look like anything, but not every character is easy to animate. This chapter examines the design of *animatable* cartoon characters and explores drawing and coloring them in Flash.

DESIGNING A CHARACTER FOR ANIMATION, OR, "WHY DID YOGI BEAR WEAR THAT NECKTIE?"

So why did Yogi Bear wear a necktie? He wore it to hide his broken neck. In fact, you've probably noticed over the years that *all* Hanna-Barbera's animal characters—Yogi, Boo Boo, Huckleberry Hound, Snagglepuss—inexplicably wear ties, even though none of them wears pants. And they all wear ties for the same reason: to hide the fact that their heads aren't connected to their bodies.

A staple of limited animation cartoons, such as those pioneered by Hanna-Barbera, is that characters are assembled from a collection of separate parts—heads, arms, legs, eyes, and so forth. The character's design must reflect this fact.

Consider Rat (5.1). If his head is not actually attached to his body then, as soon as I animate his head moving, cracks will show (5.2). Even if the body and head were extended to hide the most egregious fractures, getting the outlines of the neck to match up on both ends would be well nigh impossible (5.3). But a simple, Yogi-style necktie hides a variety of sins (5.4).

Learning to draw the characters may take anywhere from a few hours to several weeks. I spent a week just drawing the Fox's hands for my animation for Pinocchio. Unless the construction of the characters is well understood, there is the danger that the proportions will go astray during the heat of drawing the rough animation and all the animation will have to be redrawn. Why risk it?

ANIMATION LEGEND SHAMUS CULHANE

5.1

Of course, you aren't required to put a necktie on all of your characters, even if you make the heads a separate symbol (which I usually do). Most human characters already wear a shirt or dress ... even a tie ... an item you can use to slip the head behind without the seam showing (5.5). In fact, in the Penguin & Rat cartoons, Rat *doesn't* wear a necktie although he keeps the spiffy beret. (And yes, it is a pain to keep the drawing looking right when he moves his head.)

But you should definitely be aware of the problem. Almost every Flash cartoon character is made up of a number of independent symbols, assembled into a whole. Keep this in mind when you're designing characters. What parts will be attached (meaning that you must animate the whole, every time a part moves) and what parts will be separate (meaning that you can move one without worrying about the others)?

LOTSA LAYERS

When you are building your characters, use that Insert Layer button 🔳 early and often.

Don't just draw the nose on the face; draw the nose on a new layer *above* the face (5.6). This way, you avoid difficulties caused by lines snapping together, say, when the nose overlaps the cheek. More importantly, you gain flexibility on several fronts. Later, when you decide you need to slip a mustache under that nose, it's easily done (5.7). It's also easy to grab the nose and move it around the face, or rescale it, without altering the basic face shape (5.8).

By keeping everything on its own layer, you make it possible to animate each symbol separately. In fact, Flash can automatically animate symbols, moving and changing their shapes, by *tweening*. I talk more about tweening in Chapter 8, but the salient point here is that Flash only tweens a single object per layer. If you put more than one object on a layer, you loose the option of using tweening to animate those objects.

This nerd (5.9) is made up of many individual objects, most on their own layers (5.10).

NESTED SYMBOLS

As you saw in the last chapter, symbols can contain other symbols that can contain other symbols. If you have a complex character, it may be a little much to break every item up onto its own layer. It's also sometimes more trouble than it's worth to move, say, the head, if the head is spread over 15 layers.

The solution is to make a separate symbol for the head. Within that symbol, place the eyes, ears, nose

> **NOTE**
>
> If you need to fill an item, such as a sleeve, that isn't completely outlined, draw a temporary line to enclose the area to be filled with color. Once filled, select and delete the temporary line.

5.2   5.3   5.4

5.5

5.6

5.7

5.8

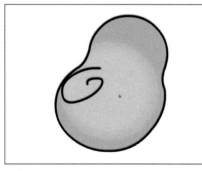

5.9

5.10

> **NOTE**
>
> Abe Lincoln said that a man's legs should be long
> enough to reach the ground. Make sure that your
> characters' arms and legs are long enough to do
> what they need to. Can she reach her own mouth?
> Can he walk with legs and feet of that length?
> Some characters that look cool just standing
> there simply can't be animated because their
> bodies and limbs are the wrong size or shape.

and so forth on separate layers (5.11), and then place the complete head on the Head layer of your cartoon in the main timeline (5.12). Now you can move the head as one object, but you can still easily adjust the positioning, rotation, and so forth of the individual parts of the head.

ONE BLOB OR TWO?

Speaking of heads, how do you draw them? You can draw two basic types of cartoon heads: the one-blob head and the two-blob head (5.13). Real people have one-blob heads, that blob being shaped more or less like an egg.

The rules of thumb for drawing a head are as follows:

1. The eyes are in the center of the head, vertically (5.14).
2. The head is about five eyes wide, with one eye's distance between the two eyes, and one eye's distance on either side.
3. The nose extends from between the eyes to a point roughly three-quarters of the way down the face — halfway between the eyes and the chin.
4. The mouth is on a line roughly one-third of the way down from the bottom of the nose to the chin. The mouth is about as wide as the distance from pupil to pupil (5.15).
5. The ears extend from about the top of the eyes to the top of the mouth (5.16).

How about from the side? Look at this nifty skull I dug up in my back yard last year while putting in a fish pond (5.17) and you'll notice that, seen from the side, a human head is roughly square.

These rules only apply to semi-realistic heads. Cartoon heads can have almost any proportions. Two blob shapes emphasize the cheek and jawline more. If you want a big, hairy ape with an overshot jaw, go with two blobs (5.18).

Virtually any blob can become a head (5.19, 5.20), as can virtually any combination of two blobs (5.21, 5.22).

5.11

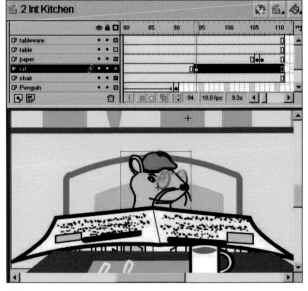

5.12

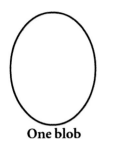

One blob   **Two blobs**

5.13

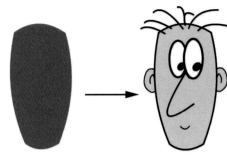

5.19

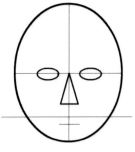

5.14   5.15

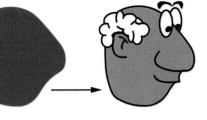

5.20

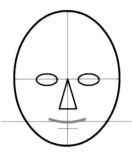
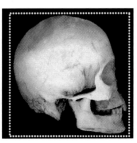

5.16   5.17

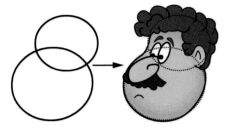

5.21

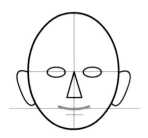

5.18

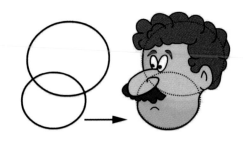

5.22

DRAWING HANDS

Hands are probably the single most intimidating features of a character to draw. Realistically drawn hands can be quite difficult to achieve — as can highly realistic drawings of any part of the body — but you can make quite serviceable cartoon hands simply out of a circle and four boxes (5.23).

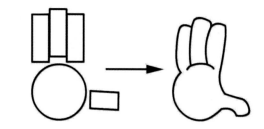

5.23

The hand is roughly twice as long as it is thick, and the fingers are about the same height as the palm — sometimes a little longer, and sometimes a little shorter, depending on the character and your style. On a real hand, the middle finger is the longest, but on cartoon hands, animators sometimes cheat and make the index finger the longest. The palm, or base, of the hand is usually drawn longer than the fingers themselves.

To position the fingers, orient each one on a line originating from the center of the palm (5.24).

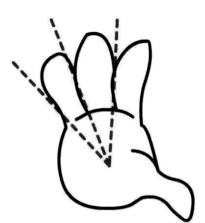

5.24

Notice that, while the fingers basically taper from the palm to the fingertip, the curve of the thumb is more complex. The inside of the thumb, nearest the palm, is concave; the back of the thumb, away from the palm, is convex.

Make sure all fingers *stack* in the same way — the index finger obscures part of the middle finger, the middle finger obscures part of the ring or pinky finger, and so forth (5.25). If not, the hand looks subtly wrong (5.26).

Notice that the side of the index finger curves down into the thumb, forming a concave bend. Remember that the wrist — the end of the arm — is narrower than the palm of the hand.

No matter what position the hand is in, remember to emphasize the ball of the thumb, the heel of the palm, and the backward curve of the thumb (5.27).

5.25

5.26

MOUTH CHOICES

If you pay attention, you'll notice that many, many cartoon characters are built so that their mouth never *breaks* the outline of their face. That is, even when the mouth is fully open, it never interrupts the line of the cheek.

When this guy's mouth opens wide, it breaks the outline of his face (5.28). This very similar guy's face is

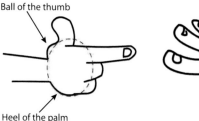

Ball of the thumb

Heel of the palm

Ball of the thumb

5.27

5.28

5.29

5.30

immune to such breaking (5.29). The advantage of the second design is that you can build a variety of mouths and drop them into the face without worrying about whether they break the cheek and the background shows through.

If you *must* have a character whose mouth breaks his face, you can still drop in different mouths from a library, by leaving a hole in the face, and building each mouth shape in such a way that it fills in that hole appropriately (5.30).

CHARACTER "CONSTRUCTION" COURTESY OF DEAN DODRILL

You can design and draw your characters in a thousand ways. To some people it comes easily; to the rest of us it's a struggle. This sections appears courtesy of the super-talented Dean Dodrill who knows it's easier to draw your characters in a variety of poses if you understand how they are constructed. It's adapted from one of his tutorials for traditional animation. Drop by www.noogy.com and read them all. You'll learn a lot.

BASIC CHARACTER CONSTRUCTION

Here is an image of my character, Bonnie (5.31), drawn using what I consider to be a general character design.

5.31   *© 2000, Dean Dodrill*

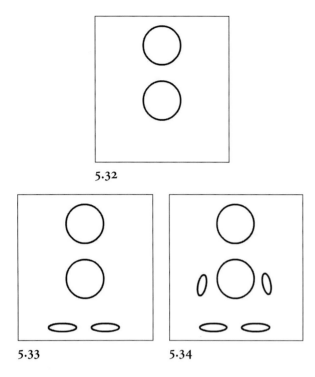

5.32

5.33   5.34

HOW TALL?

Just how tall should a character be? Animators measure characters in heads. The height of a character's head is one head. The rest of the body is measured in relationship to the head.

A normal human body stands about 6 to 6 ½ heads high. A superhero like Batman tends to stand 8 or 9 heads high, which gives the body bigger and more . . . well, superheroic proportions.

Less realistic characters can have any proportions at all, though they tend to the other extreme. Bennie (5.35) and Earl (5.36) from Wish Tank's Lovely Street cartoons are only a skosh over 3 and 2 heads tall, respectively. What's important is that characters remain consistent from shot to shot, pose to pose, and scene to scene.

You must be wondering how on earth I know where to place characteristics such as her legs and markings. It's easy when you use character construction.

Let's start constructing a character by opening a new file. Our generic character model is made out of these spheres, one above the other. The top sphere becomes the character's head. The bottom sphere becomes the character's waist and belly. I usually position the top sphere about half a sphere above the bottom one in a normal standing pose. Use the Oval tool to draw your spheres. Leave ample room below the characters where we will eventually add the legs (5.32).

Now, we place the feet. It's helpful to think of the location of the feet before you actually put your spheres down, but for our standard pose this is fine. Put little ovals where the feet will be. Place them below the waist sphere, about three-quarters to a whole sphere down. Mark a little horizon line below the feet if you want (5.33).

TIP

Hold down the Shift key to constrain the Oval tool to a circle, or the Rectangle tool to a square.

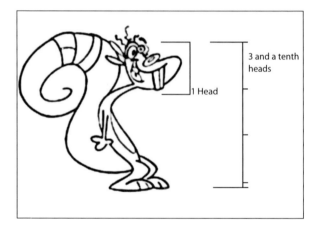

5.35   © 2000 Wish Tank Studios, LLC

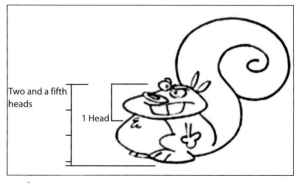

5.36   © 2000 Wish Tank Studios, LLC

Now do the same for the hands. I also use little ovals for the hands. Don't worry about details! Place the hands by the sides of the waist sphere, near the lowest part of the sphere. Hands normally hang down to about the groin level, but because our character is going to be so short you can make them just a tad longer (5.34). It's easy to place the arms and legs when you already know where the hands and feet will be.

The last step to constructing our character is adding his chest and shoulders. Use the Arrow tool to grab the top of the bottom sphere and pull it up where the bottom of his neck should be. The whole chest area looks like a fat teardrop from the front. Add a horizontal line at the top of the teardrop that goes across the whole character; this helps us locate the shoulders (5.37).

Our character needs arms and legs now. Start with straight lines that meet right in the middle of the character, at the lowest part of the lower sphere, and extend to the back of the feet. Draw another set of lines that extends from the top of the hip to the top of the foot, near the back (5.38).

Use the Arrow tool to bend the lines. The outer part of the leg should have a convex line, while the inner part of the leg should have a concave line. Note that the legs seem to get as fat as the sphere at top, but are very skinny when they finally reach the foot (5.39).

Now let's draw the arms. Use the horizontal *shoulder* line as a guide. Arms are generally fatter on the top end, and skinnier as they reach the hand. The arm meets the chest teardrop where the armpit should be. At the top the arm stops at the horizontal shoulder line and curves inward. Do this for both sides. Add a neck by curving up from the shoulder line into the head sphere.

The last step is to add a small grid on the face. You can use this later when you add the face. Simply draw a single horizontal and vertical line, crossing in the middle of the sphere. Presto, your character is drawn (5.40)!

CHARACTER PROFILES

Now we'll draw the character's *profile* (or side view), using the drawing we just made to help us.

Flash 5 adds a handy drawing tool called *guides*. Guides are reference lines that you can superimpose

5.37

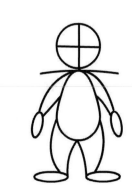

5.38

5.39

5.40

5.41

on the drawing stage to help keep objects in alignment. To make guides, turn on Flash's Rulers (View ➤ Rulers). Click one of the rulers and drag toward the stage and you'll pull out a guideline.

Pull out horizontal guidelines at the top and bottom of both spheres, the feet, the bottom of the hands, and the tips of the shoulders. If you want, you can add lines for the top of the legs, the middle of the head . . . anywhere you think they may help (5.41). These lines help you draw the profile. We'll draw him facing to the right.

In a normal standing pose a character's head is directly above his waist in a profile. Draw the two spheres again, using the guides you created. Alternatively, copy and paste the two circles you already made (5.42).

The chest teardrop shape is a bit different from the side. We'll make our character stick out his chest a bit, so make the front (right side) convex, and the back (left side) concave. Add a foot (you'll only draw one foot because we are viewing the character from the side) directly below the character on the ground. The heel, or back of the foot, should align with the left side of the spheres (5.43). Notice that the foot is longer from the side than it is wide from the front. Finally add a hand to the side of the waist. Make sure to use your guidelines!

Add the leg (again you only see one leg), making it concave in the back and convex in the front (5.44). Next, add the arm. The top of the arm is a bit harder to draw now because you can't really see the shoulder. The arm is a cylinder, and the shoulder is a sphere shape. Draw the necessary lines to show the shoulder. Finally, add the grid on the head again. You can't see the line going down the middle of the face because it is in profile, so just draw the horizontal line across the head. This line goes all the way around the sphere (5.45).

Now you have a basic character. Practice making a couple of characters, and memorize the location of their different curves.

TIP

To change the color of your guidelines, select View ➤ Guides ➤ Edit Guides.

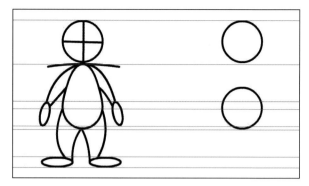

5.42

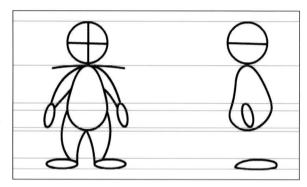

5.43

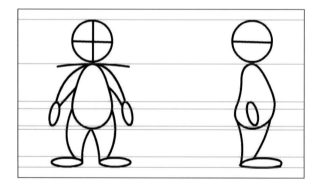

5.44

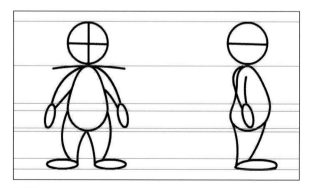

5.45

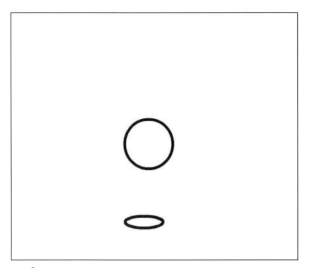

5.46

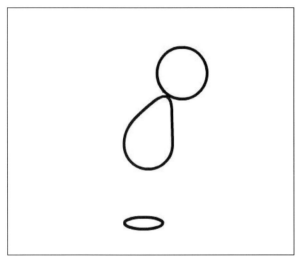

5.47

5.48

GESTURE, POSE, AND BALANCE

Using your new understanding of character construction, let's try a simple pose — let's have your character stand on one leg with his arms in the air. Because he is balancing his body on his foot, begin by drawing that foot, and then draw the bottom sphere directly above the foot, rather than off to the side (5.46). This way he isn't falling over.

Now draw the sphere for his head. Offset his head a bit to the right side, so his body seems to be bent. Add the lines for the chest. You'll notice that the orientation of the head, hands, and arms alters the shapes of the other parts of the body somewhat. The chest piece should bend slightly to accommodate the head (5.47).

Now draw the hands and the other foot. Place them wherever you like, as long as they are within a natural

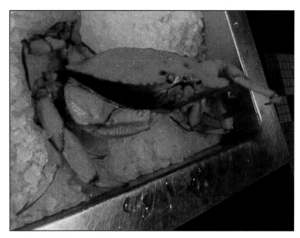

5.49   *©Honkworm International, Inc.*

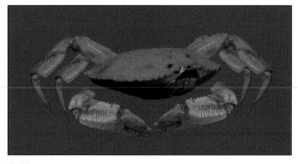

5.50   *©Honkworm International, Inc.*

NOTE

PNG and GIF are the only file formats that can be imported into Flash with a transparent background.

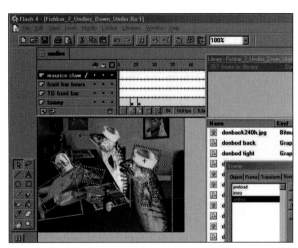

5.51   © Honkworm International, Inc.

distance from the body. Add the shoulder line, the arms and legs, and finally, the face grid (5.48). The legs should keep their mass, or total size, despite how they are bent or stretched. Just because an arm or leg is bent doesn't mean that it has gotten any smaller.

BUILDING BITMAP CHARACTERS IN FLASH

Can't draw at all, even with Dean's help? Well, there's more than one way to skin a cat, or to animate one. Case in point, Janet Galore. Janet makes hysterical Flash animations for Honkworm International, Inc. (www.honkworm.com). (My favorite? "Fish of War.") Unlike most Flash cartoons, which use Flash's vector graphics, Janet's cartoons are built from primarily scanned bitmap images and digital photographs of everyday objects (5.49), which are trimmed and prettied up in Photoshop, imported into Flash (5.50), assembled into characters (5.51), and animated.

How does she do it? Here's what Janet has to say:

"Characters in bitmap-based Flash movies are very much like puppets. To some extent the same is true with vector-based Flash animations, but it's very clear with bitmaps, because you create the characters outside Flash and bring them in piece by piece.

"Put each part of the character you want to be able to move (eyes, mouths, arms, hands, fingers, legs, bodies, and so on) in its own layer. Think about how you would make a marionette and you'll be on the right track. Build the character by working on each part separately and turning layers on and off to see how the elements fit together.

"Keep in mind how you will be animating the character—moving individual pieces such as an arm or hand; swapping out pieces to change the way it looks such as a blinking eye or different mouths to simulate talking; or squashing and stretching these elements. You also need layers for all the elements that make up other views of the character (that is, front, side, back, three-quarters view, and so on).

"To optimize the file size, it's important to crop each layer to the smallest size that will contain the image.

"You can import all the pieces of a character at the same time (File ➤ Import). Once the pieces are in, create a symbol for each bitmap you've imported. Naming conventions are important—the more organized you are at this point, the easier it will be to make changes later. It's useful to organize each character into its own folder. If you have imported portable network graphic (PNG) files, you won't have

5.52   © 2000 Wish Tank Studios, LLC

to cut out the pieces to remove the background. If you've used JPEG files, you have to break up each bitmap and erase the background by hand.

"The next step is to build a still image of the character, including all of its component parts — arms, legs, eyes, and so forth — as one symbol. To build the master character, in Symbol Edit mode, create a new symbol, and drag the elements (head, arms, legs, and so on) onto the stage and arrange the parts of the character as necessary to form the character in a normal pose. You will drop this master character symbol into the timeline, and use it as your base for creating animated symbols of the character, called behaviors.

"To animate the character, you can either drop the master character into the main timeline and break it up so that you can move the parts individually, keyframe by keyframe, or you can create animated symbols or movie clips in the library. Either way, you will have basic poses or movements that you can bring into the main timeline (the stage). You can tweak these poses at will, either by breaking the symbol apart, or by starting and stopping the animated symbol at strategic keyframes (for example, starting and stopping a walk, starting and stopping the mouth movement, or making the eyes blink)."

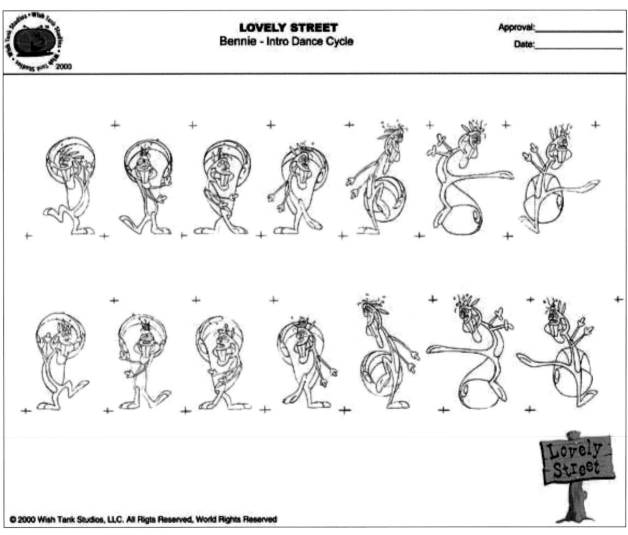

MODEL AND COLOR SHEETS

If you are planning a long cartoon, a series of cartoons, or, more importantly, if more than one person will be drawing characters for a cartoon, you need to work up a model sheet for each character. A *model sheet* is a collection of drawings of a character. It generally shows the character in a variety of poses, or seen from a number of directions, and points out that character's distinguishing characteristics. Here are some model sheets from Wish Tank's Lovely Street (5.52, 5.53).

Model sheets often include *callouts* pointing out special features ("Only one wrinkle on the forehead," or "Back of head alters as mouse changes expression.").

Animator Jim Zubkavich has a large collection of model sheets, and other animation resources, available for study on his Web site at http://www.crosswinds.net/~zubkavich/.

Model sheets can also include color information (5.54). If you make your model sheets in Flash, it's easy for animators to sample the colors.

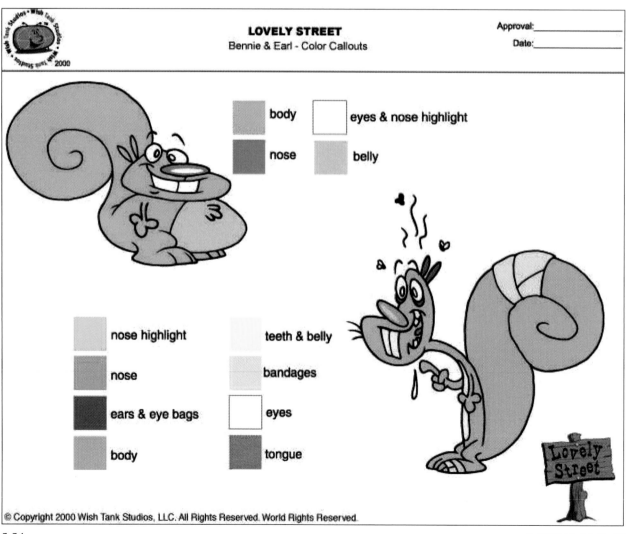

5.54

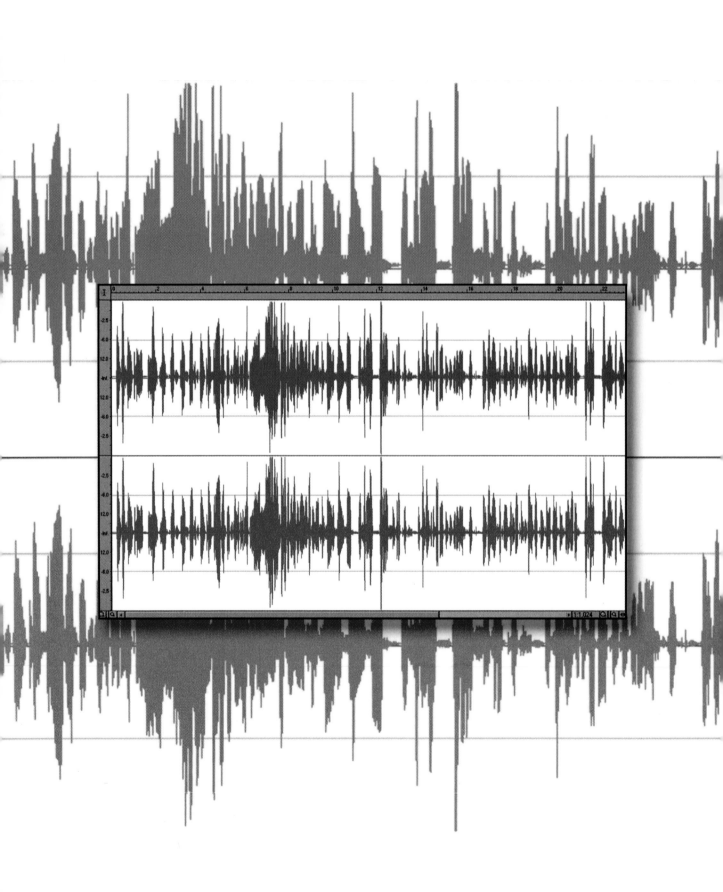

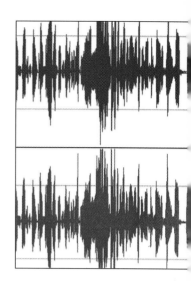

CHAPTER 6
RECORDING DIALOGUE AND OTHER SOUND

T his chapter covers the recording of sound-tracks for your Flash cartoons, from a lyrical depiction of the physical nature of sound and how it's stored in your computer, to practical tips for selecting a microphone, recording words and other noise, and tweaking your recordings with software in the computer.

You can fake almost anything else, and undo or change it if you're not happy with the result. But a bad dialog recording is forever.

JAY ROSE – *PRODUCING GREAT SOUND FOR DIGITAL VIDEO*
(GILROY, CA : CMP BOOKS, 2000)

WHAT IS SOUND?

Sound is the ear's way of interpreting vibrations in the air. (That's right: If a tree falls in the forest and nobody is around, it doesn't make any sound.)

Drop a rock into a pond and it sends ripples through the water in all directions. As the ripples pass under a floating leaf, that leaf bobs up and down in time with the ripples (6.1).

Drop a wrench on the driveway and the collision vibrates the air, sending ripples out in all directions. As the ripples smack into your eardrum, one after the other, your eardrum vibrates in time with them, and you "hear a sound."

The more widely spaced these ripples, or *waves*, the slower your eardrum moves, and the "lower" the pitch of the sound. The more closely spaced the ripples, the more quickly your eardrum moves, and the "higher" the pitch of the sound. Middle C on a piano, for example, produces 256 ripples — or *cycles* — per second. High C on a piano produces 4,096 cycles per second. (*Cycles per second* are usually called *hertz,* after the scientist who invented sound. No, really.)

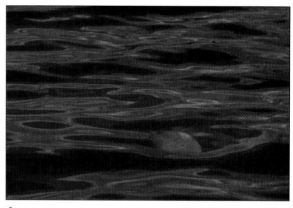

6.1

Your ear can't hear every vibration in the air. If the ripples are too widely spaced, your eardrum moves too slowly (or not at all) and you don't hear anything. These sounds are *subsonic*; they are pitched too low for you to hear. If the ripples are too closely spaced, your eardrum moves too quickly (or not at all) and you still don't hear anything. These sounds are *ultrasonic*; they are pitched too high for you to hear.

The human range of hearing runs from about 20 to 20,000 cycles per second, or hertz (Hz). Most human speech takes place at around 100 to 150 hertz, but speech also makes use of high-pitched "hisses." As you chop these off, speech becomes subtly less intelligible. "Tee" and "dee" sound almost identical over the telephone, for example, because phones don't transmit the higher pitched sounds that distinguish between them.

TURN IT UP

The loudness of sound is measured in *decibels (dB).* (As you might guess, a decibel is one-tenth of a bel; but no one ever uses bels so you can forget about them now.)

Decibels are measured on a logarithmic scale. Two decibels is not twice as loud as one decibel; two decibels is *ten times* louder than one decibel. Ten decibels is *a hundred million* times louder than one decibel (6.2).

In rough terms, the quietest audible sound is 0 dB. A whisper is about 30 dB, a thousand times louder. Conversation is about 60 dB, a thousand times louder again. A blood-curdling scream is a thousand times louder yet, a million times louder than a whisper, at about 90 dB.

SAMPLING

Here is a hypothetical perfect sine wave (6.3), which you would hear as a simple tone. It is continuous and unbroken. No matter where you examine it, or how closely you examine it, it remains continuous and unbroken. It is made up of an *infinite* number of points. (In fact, every tiny segment of it is made up of an infinite number of points.)

A computer doesn't have an infinite amount of memory so it can't record an infinite number of points. A computer handles this problem by

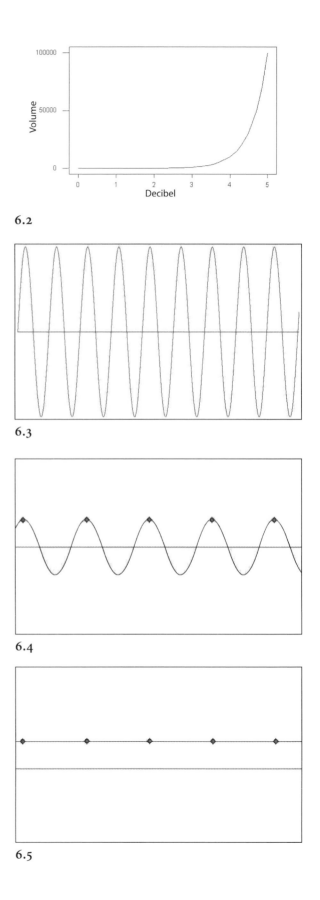

6.2

6.3

6.4

6.5

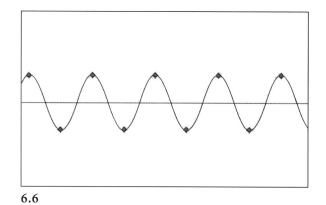

6.6

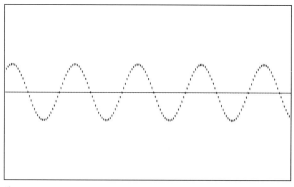

6.7

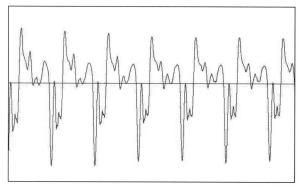

6.8

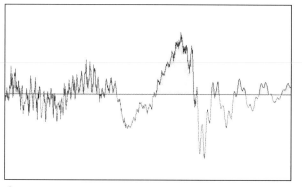

6.9

> **NOTE**
>
> **Odd as it may seem, boosting a sound by six decibels always doubles its volume. That's just the way logarithms are.**

sampling. It can't record the entire sound, but it can take a sample of it; reading the level of the sound (say, 2.0231 dB) at a particular instant in time (say 1.00021 seconds), and recording it as a number.

In fact, it can do this over and over, very, very quickly, tens of thousands of times per second, and record each of those samples, in sequence. And it turns out that if you take enough samples, frequently enough, you can do a pretty good job of reconstructing the original sound wave.

Say that your hypothetical sine wave has a pitch of 1,000 cycles per second, or 1,000 Hz.

If you sample at that same frequency — that is, if you take 1,000 samples every second (6.4) — you don't actually record any sound at all. The sample comes from the same place on the wave each time, resulting in a straight line (6.5).

To derive the rudest approximation of the original waveform, you need to sample at least twice the frequency of the sound you're trying to capture (6.6).

If you sample at 40,000 samples per second, 40 times the frequency of the sine wave, (and roughly the sample rate of an audio CD), you get a pretty accurate picture of the original sine wave (6.7). The faster your sample rate — the more frequently you sample your sound — the more accurate the digital recording will be. Of course, the more frequently you sample, the more samples you accumulate, and the bigger the resulting recording will be.

Real-world sounds are significantly more complex than a simple sine wave — the waveform of a saxophone (playing a G, if you want to know) is more complex than the sine wave (6.8), human speech is even more so (6.9) — but the same basic rules apply.

In theory, a high-fidelity sound system accurately produces sounds up to 20,000 Hz, the upper limits of human hearing. Audio CDs are recorded at roughly twice that, 44,100 samples per second. FM radio is broadcast at 15,000 Hz (15 kHz), although FM talk radio sometimes broadcasts at half that — 7.5 kHz. Telephones only go up to 3.5 kHz. The odds that the person watching your animation is listening on a system that can reproduce sounds accurately at above 15 kHz are remote.

HOW DEEP IS THAT NOTE?

In addition to deciding how often — at what *frequency* — you should sample a sound, you must also decide on the sample *depth*.

Sample depth refers to the resolution of the sample; that is, when the computer records a level, how precisely does it record that level? Consider the difference between giving your height to the nearest foot and giving your height to the nearest inch; that's a difference in precision.

> **NOTE**
>
> To retain any semblance of its original form, a sound must be sampled at at least twice the original pitch.

When working with Flash and most consumer-level sound-editing software, you're restricted to either 8-bit or 16-bit sample depths. With 8 bits, you can record 256 levels of sound — everything from 0 to 255. With 16 bits, you can record 65,536 levels of sound — everything from 0 to 65,535. At 16-bit resolution, there are 256 levels for every one level at 8-bit resolution, but the resulting file is twice as big. As a rule of thumb, 8-bit samples sound like crap. Only use 8-bit sampling if you don't mind your cartoon sounding like crap.

So what sample rate and resolution should you record at? A good starting place is 22,050 Hz, 16-bit, mono.

RECORDING

Now that you know what sound is, it's time to go get some. First you'll need a few pieces of hardware and software.

FINDING THE RIGHT MIC

Virtually all microphones have the equivalent of your eardrum — something that vibrates when it's bumped by pressure waves in the air (that is, sounds). Dynamic mics have a polyester eardrum (called the *diaphragm*) that moves a coil of wire in and out of a magnet as it vibrates. Condenser mics have a thin, metal, electrically charged eardrum. Both transform sound vibrations in the air into electrical voltages.

Condenser mics "hear" a wider spectrum of sounds than do dynamic mics — both lower and higher — but they are a bit more fragile and often require a separate power supply.

More important than the particulars of a given mic's internal workings is its *sensitivity pattern* (sometimes called the *polar pattern*).

Generally speaking, microphones are either omnidirectional (they hear in all directions), bidirectional (they hear in two directions) or unidirectional (they hear in only one direction). Unidirectional mics are called *cardioids* (yes, it's a conspiracy). Extremely unidirectional mics, such as shotgun mics, are called *hypercardioids*.

For recording voices and most sound effects, you want a cardioid mic. Few of us can afford to build a perfectly quiet, echo-free recording studio. Cardioid mics record what you point them at — say, your mouth — and do a fair job of ignoring the myriad of other sounds coming from everywhere else. Prices for decent dynamic cardioids start at around $150.

> **NOTE**
>
> Condenser microphones are also called capacitor mics and electret mics.

SOUND SOFTWARE INVESTMENTS

Buy yourself some sound-editing software. I know, your computer came with some free stuff but, in most cases, that free software is worth the price. You don't have to spend a fortune. I do all my sound work in Sonic Foundry's SoundForge XP — the "lite" version — which I bought for under $50. There's a demo version on the bonus CD-ROM that's included with this book (6.10). Fellow Flash cartoonist Ibis Fernandez favors Digidesign's Pro Tools, which are available for download, absolutely free, at `www.digidesign.com`. Pro Tools is the exception to the rule above: free software that's well worth owning.

Even "basic" sound software allows you to control volume, equalize sound, convert mono to stereo and vice versa, and cut and paste bits of sound from here to there. SoundForge XP even lets you speed sounds up and slow them down, change pitch, and add a handful of effects such as reverb. Make sure the software at least displays the actual waveform.

SOUND EFFECTS

You can get your sound effects one of two ways: either buy them from one of the many companies that offer professional sound effect libraries, or you can record your own. My recommendation is that, wherever possible, you make your own.

Of course some sounds, such as cannon fire or automobile accidents, are a little hard to come by, but you may be surprised what you can come up with if you try, especially if you throw in some effects — reverb, pitch bend, and so on — in software.

Beware: Most cheaper sound effects collections — the kind you find down at the record store — specifically prohibit the use of their sounds in your productions. Professional sound effects libraries, which you *may* use in your work, run about $50 to $100 per CD.

> **TIP**
>
> **For voice recording, use a cardioid dynamic microphone. Some good choices are the Audio Technica AT804, the Electro-Voice N/D767, the Sennheiser MD431-II, and the Shure 12A. Be ready to spend $150 to $400 or more, or to look around for a used one. Studio quality microphones can cost as much as $10,000. The little one that came with your cassette deck or your computer is useless (unless you're specifically going for a "cheap" or "tinny" effect).**
>
> © 2000 Steve Young, Webwelders, Inc.

ROLL YOUR OWN

Foley effects are sound effects produced using practical props. Foley is named for sound legend Jack Foley.

The salient feature of a Foley stage is the floor, which is tiled with an array of hatches. Each lifts out to reveal a small pit with a different kind of surface: ceramic tile, linoleum, dirt . . . you name it. Foley artists walk, jump, and slide around in the pits to create a wide variety of footstep sounds. Odds are your wife, landlord, or significant other isn't likely to let you tear up the floor and build a Foley stage, but you can make a Foley pit or two. Build yourself a sturdy wooden box, about 3 feet on a side and 1 foot deep. Line it with plastic and you can pour a variety of stuff in there, from gravel to broken glass.

Foley effects aren't limited to footsteps; they also include swooshing swords, tinkling ice cubes, jingling change, scraping silverware, and so on — any sound effect created with a real-world prop. Foley props are literally all around you. Cabbage, lettuce, and phone books are popular for simulating various body blows and falls, and I'm told a watermelon dropped from a step ladder makes a wonderfully realistic busting-head splat. Jars with screw-on lids make great grinding and scraping noises. You've probably got a coat with zippers and pockets great for all manner of clothing noises.

Blow up a balloon. Squeeze it, rub it, twist it. In his autobiography, *Chuck Amuck*, Chuck Jones says of

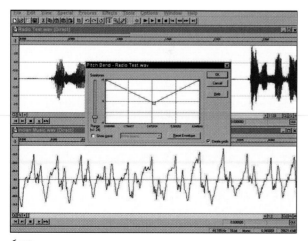

6.10

SETTING UP AND RECORDING

Record in as small a room as possible with sound-damping material on the walls. You don't need to buy professional "egg-crate" recording booth material (it's very expensive). You can use draped blankets, foam mattress pads, carpet samples — anything that will absorb and not reflect sound.

Use a gooseneck floor stand. Don't handhold your microphone or use a desk stand. The microphone will pick up vibrations from computer fan motors, shuffling papers, cycling hard drives, and so on. Isolate the microphone from these possible sources of unwanted sound.

Brush your teeth and tongue thoroughly.

Avoid milk products before recording.

Loosen up your neck, jaw, and face with a few stretching exercises. Make faces.

Hyperventilate — but carefully. I've seen people pass out. Just breathe rapidly until you feel slightly light-headed. Avoiding "oxygen debt" makes your recording sound more relaxed and natural.

Fit the physical mold. If you want a "happy" sound, you have to smile. Angry? Frown. You get the idea.

Work 3 to 6 inches away from the mic and across it at about a 45-degree angle. Don't speak directly into it or away from it. Experiment until you get a natural sound without breathing noises.

Your best speaking voice originates from the back of your throat and is shaped by your mouth, tongue, and lips. Practice using your diaphragm and chest as the "origin" of your voice, rather than forming the sound in your mouth. This takes patience and time and is possibly the biggest difference between professional announcers and wanna-bes. As time goes by and you keep practicing while adhering to the basic rules, you'll get better and you'll sound better than you ever thought possible.

Be sure to pause. A common mistake is to rush through copy. A good pause is a very effective way to naturalize your delivery.

If you edit your sound files, leave space where the breath occurred.

© 2000 Steve Young, Webwelders, Inc.

---

sound effects genius Treg Brown, "He could contrive more sound effects with an inflated balloon (earthquakes, wrestling grunts and groans, branches breaking, bullfrogs croaking, etc., etc.) than most editors could with all the sound devices at their command."

Paper, properly crinkled, is a favorite for creating all kinds of fire effects. Pour rice into a bucket or large bowl for the sounds of rain. If you've got a kid or, like me, you *are* a kid, then you've got tons of sound effects material strewn across the living room right now. Look around you: That clicking sound of a school bus wheel can become a fishing reel.

POST-PROCESSING

Recording the sound is only the first step. All of your recorded sound is going to be processed further at some point before the viewer hears it. Even if you do nothing, Flash kneads the sound a bit when it publishes.

Before you start processing, however, remember to always retain your original recordings! Only work with copies. Make sure that, no matter what you do and what mistakes you make, you always have the option of going back to the beginning and starting over.

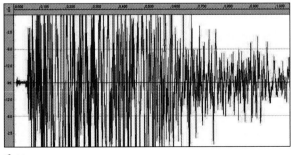

6.11

TIP

The only important characteristic of a sound effect is how it makes the viewer feel. It doesn't matter where you get it, what the label said, or what frames it's applied to. If an effect feels right, it *is* right. If not, change it.

Thanks to Jay Rose, *Producing Great Sound for Digital Video* (Gilroy, CA: CMP Books, 2000).

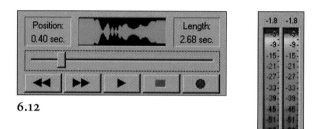

6.12

6.13

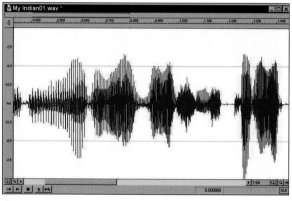

6.14

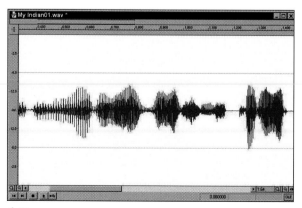

6.15

CLIPPING

Clipping is the most common sound mistake I see . . . I mean, hear. Clipping happens when a sound is too loud for some part of your recording or playback system to handle. The extremes of the waveform — the loudest bits — get "clipped off" and the bits near them get distorted. This is a clipped sound waveform viewed in sound editing software (6.11). This is a clipped sound waveform viewed in the Windows sound recorder (6.12). In both cases, the waveform is clipped off at the top and bottom; it's too loud.

Clipping is bad. Avoid it. Clipping is characterized by loud, blurry, crackly noise. The details of the sound are lost, and the extremes are distorted.

When you're recording, especially when you're recording voice, your input meters, whatever form they take, shouldn't be pegging all the way to the top. Try to arrange yourself and your microphone so that the peak recording levels are *almost* all the way to the top (6.13).

IS THAT A NORMAL VOLUME?

There are two ways to adjust the volume (or "gain") of your sound. You can either adjust the volume control until you get what you want or, if your sound software offers the option, you can *normalize* the clip.

Normalize is really just an automatic volume control. If you normalize a clip to 100 percent, it is adjusted so that the very loudest peak is at exactly 100 percent volume (6.14). If you normalize to 50 percent, the clip is adjusted so the loudest peak is at exactly 50 percent volume (6.15). The rule of thumb

COMMONLY MISPRONOUNCED WORDS: THE FIVE DEADLY SINS

It's *for*, not fir; *get*, not git; *your* not yore (that's *you* with an *r* at the end); *hundred*, not hunnerd; *nuclear*, not nucular. Sample sentence, "He decided to get you a hundred nuclear weapons for your arsenal." You don't need to sound like an elocution instructor, but you don't want to sound like a clueless amateur, either.

© 2000 Steve Young, Webwelders, Inc.

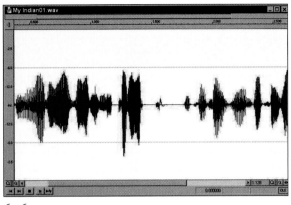

6.16

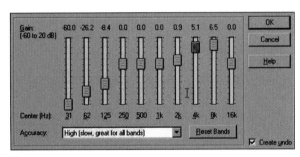

6.17

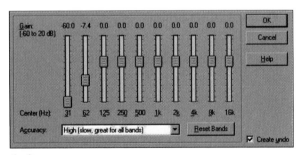

6.18

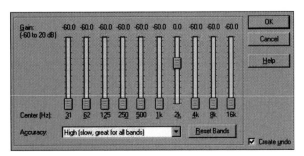

6.19

TIP

Some sounds, especially very loud sounds such as explosions, actually sound better — *bigger* — if they are turned up until they clip. But if you do need clipping, try to record the sound clean. Add clipping by cranking up the volume or normalizing in post-processing. Lastly, always use Normalize or Volume to turn the sound back down to 95 percent or so. The sound retains its characteristics but doesn't clip further on playback.

NOTE

Boosting or suppressing *all* bands equally simply turns the volume up or down.

is to normalize to about 95 percent but, in my experience, this makes most sounds, such as voice, too loud.

For normal, spoken dialogue, I like to keep the peaks at around –5 or –6 dB — about 50 percent of the maximum volume (6.16).

ALL THINGS BEING EQUALIZER . . .

To further tweak a clip, you may want to equalize it. An equalizer is basically a whole array of volume controls, each of which operates on a range of tones — bass, midtones, and so forth. The simplest equalizer is a tone knob, which turns from bass (emphasizing low tones and suppressing high tones) to treble (emphasizing high tones and suppressing low tones).

This is SoundForge XP's graphic equalizer (6.17), which allows you to adjust each of 10 *bands* (ranges of tones) individually.

A graphic equalizer allows you to emphasize some tones and eliminate others. You can suppress just the bass, for example, by turning those sliders down (6.18). Or you can recreate the "tinny" sound of a phone conversation by cutting off the low and high tones, leaving only those around 2,000 Hz — the middle of a telephone's frequency range (6.19).

Once you've got your sounds recorded, you're ready to build a cartoon for them to go in.

CHAPTER 7
KEYFRAMES, TWEENING, AND ANIMATICS

K eyframes and *tweening* are two essential concepts to grasp before you can get on with the task of making an animated cartoon. This chapter explains the basics of keyframing and motion tweening and explores how to use them to build an animatic for your cartoon.

Inbetweening — producing drawings in between key drawings — is of fundamental importance to the success or failure of animation technique.

TONY WHITE, *THE ANIMATOR'S WORKBOOK*
(NEW YORK: WATSON-GUPTILL PUBLICATIONS, 1994)

WHAT IS A KEYFRAME?

The term *keyframe* comes down to us from the dark prehistory of animation, when cartoons were actually drawn and painted *by hand*.

Now think: Old *Looney Tunes* cartoons ran six minutes, or 360 seconds. At 12 drawings per second (and sometimes, even worse, 24 drawings per second) that works out to about 4,000 drawings per cartoon (or 8,000, at 24 frames per second). That's 125–150 drawings a day for six weeks (which is how long Chuck Jones had to crank out his immortal *Looney Tunes*). That's a whole boatload of drawing, but the reality is far worse. If your cartoon has several characters, and it probably does, then that means several thousand drawings for each character, not to mention incidentals such as bouncing balls, cars, trees, ray gun blasts, and what have you.

That's way too many drawings for anyone to do in a reasonable time. To paraphrase those great philosophers of our time, Beavis and Butthead, in animation, you've got to draw thousands of coyotes falling off a cliff to get one coyote falling off a cliff.

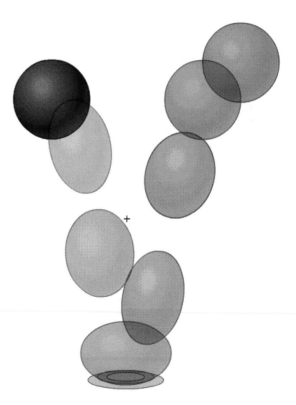

The upshot of all this is that the best animators would only draw a few of those 12 frames per second, those frames where the character is in the most important poses — the *key* poses.

As an example, take a look at the figure (7.1). Stickman is on the mound, throwing his famous spitball. Although this action spans a full 13 frames, there are only four images here, showing the four key poses in the pitch. Note that these keyframes move Stickman from one extreme to another.

A frame with the character in a key pose was called, you guessed it, a *keyframe.* Junior animators, whose time and talent were considered less valuable, got the work of drawing in all the frames in between the keyframes — a processed called *in-betweening*, or *tweening.*

THE FLASH TIMELINE

So, what does this all have to do with Flash? Flash uses keyframes, too. If you want to animate a plane flying through the sky, a safe plummeting earthward, a kangaroo boxing, or a robot dancing, you'll do it with keyframes.

Nowadays, the computer does a reasonable amount of the grunt work involved in simple tweening. Flash does simple tweening automatically; it can move an object across the screen, or have an object follow a path, but it isn't really equipped to perform tweening on complex character animation. If you need more frames to fill in Stickman's pitch, you have to draw them yourself.

READY, SET, GO!

Ready? Let's make some keyframed animation. Do this: Fire up Flash and open a new file (7.2).

> **NOTE**
>
> If you are doing a motion tween and the object refuses to move smoothly between keyframes — instead "popping" suddenly from one position to another — your problem is usually that there is more than one object on the layer.

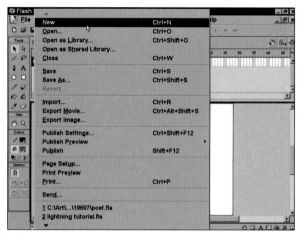

7.1

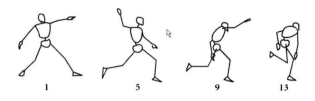

7.2

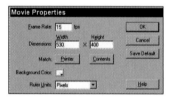

7.3

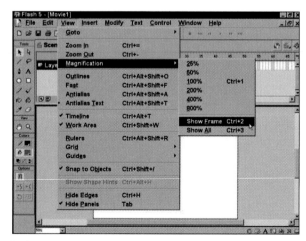

7.4

Choose Modify ➤ Movie to bring up the movie's properties (7.3). Set the Frame Rate to 15 and the background color to white. Set the dimensions to 530 width by 400 height. Press OK.

Select View ➤ Magnification ➤ Show Frame (or Ctrl+2) to make sure you can see the entire drawing area onscreen (7.4).

Ready to draw? Select the Circle tool and make a filled circle somewhere on the left side of the

TIP

If the timeline's dots and boxes are too small for you to see without leaning forward in your seat and squinting, click the Frame View button 🔳 at the top of the timeline on the far right side (7.12), adjacent to the frame numbers. The pop-up menu allows you to increase or decrease the size of the frame boxes in the timeline. Selecting Short squashes the frame boxes to half their normal height, letting you see more layers at once.

screen (7.5). Done? Great. From now on, pretend it's a rubber ball.

Look at the Flash timeline, above the stage (7.6). You'll see a series of alternating light and shaded rectangles. These are the frames of your animation. The red box above the timeline is the playhead; it shows what frame you're currently viewing.

At the moment, there's only one frame — frame 1 — with anything in it. That frame 1 has a solid black dot in it, indicating that there is something on that layer at that frame.

Click the Arrow tool ▶ (or press V) and select your ball object by dragging a marquee around it. Make certain that you select the entire thing, including the outline. Choose Group from the Modify menu or press Ctrl+G (7.7). Your ball is now a group. This step is important and here's why: Only one object can be tweened per layer. Your ball object, as drawn, was actually two objects: the solid fill and the outline. If you'd left it like that, motion tweening wouldn't have worked. By grouping those two elements, you create a single object that can be tweened.

Click the timeline at frame 10. From the menu, choose Insert ➤ Keyframe (F6). A black dot appears in the timeline on frame 10, indicating a new keyframe there (7.8), and the area between frames 1 and 10 is filled in, showing that there is something on that layer on all 10 frames. The white rectangle at frame 9 marks the end of the keyframe starting on frame 1; from frame 1 to frame 9, nothing changes.

Make sure frame 10 is still selected. Now click your ball object and drag it to the right side of the screen. Press Enter (or choose Control ➤ Play from the

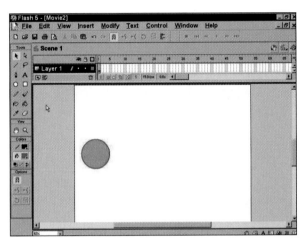

7.5

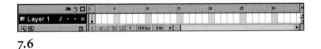

7.6

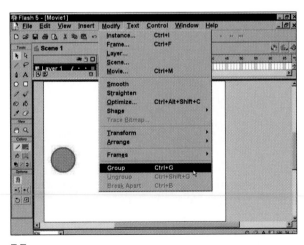

7.7

7.8

menu) to play the animation. The ball jumps from one side to the other (7.9), but this isn't what you want. You want the ball to move smoothly from side to side, so there's one more step: You need to tell Flash to fill in all the in-between frames for you.

Right-click the keyframe at frame 1, and choose Panels ➢ Frame from the pop-up list to bring up the Frame panel (7.10). Click the Frame tab and select Motion from the Tweening drop-down box.

Notice that an arrow appears between the two keyframes on the timeline (7.11) telling you that there's some tweening going on. The tweened frames are now blue instead of gray.

> **TIP**
>
> If your playback doesn't loop, select Loop Playback from the Control menu.

Press Enter to watch your animation play. Now the ball moves smoothly, more or less, from left to right. Flash has filled in eight in-between frames for you.

It took a lot of words to describe the process of setting up a motion tween, but don't despair; it's really not that hard to do. And now that it's set up, it's fairly easy to make changes. If you've closed the Frame panel, right-click frame 10, the second keyframe, and choose Panels ➢ Frame to open it again. Set the second keyframe's tweening to Motion.

Click once on the second keyframe in the timeline to select that frame. Now click and drag that frame to the right, and drop it at frame 30. Press Enter (or Control ➢ Play) to watch the new animation. The ball now takes around two seconds to make its way across the screen, and Flash has filled in all the new in-between frames for you.

Try one more. Click and hold the first keyframe in the timeline. The cursor should change to a closed fist. Now, hold down the Alt key on your keyboard. Your cursor becomes a fist with a little plus sign 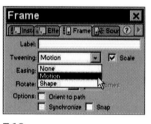 to show that you're getting ready to duplicate a keyframe. Now hold down the Ctrl key and drag the first frame out past the last keyframe, to

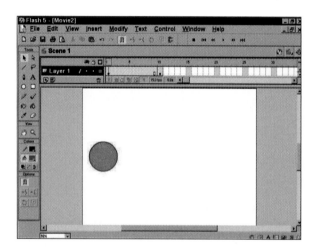

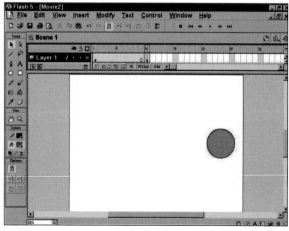

7.9

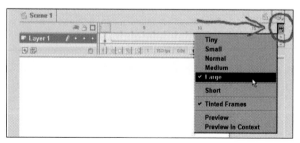

7.10

7.11

7.12

7.13

TIP

Select Window ➤ Toolbars ➤ Controller (or Window ➤ Controller on the Mac) to bring up a standard, VCR-style controller for your animation (7.13).

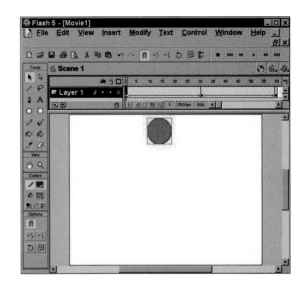

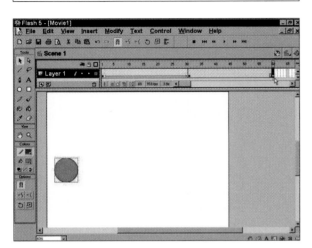

7.14

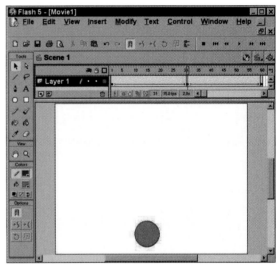

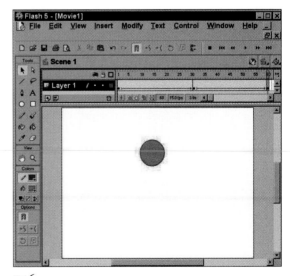

frame 50 or 60 (7.14). You should now have three keyframes. The last keyframe is a copy of the first; the ball now returns to its starting place at the end of the animation; the animation loops.

7.15

But wait! Before you press play . . . notice that there's no arrow between the middle keyframe and the end keyframe. In fact, Flash has inserted a blank keyframe on the newly created frame 11. Notice that everything between frame 10 and frame 30 is blank. Move the playhead to frame 11 and choose Insert ➤ Clear Keyframe.

The arrow and color change in the timeline show you that Flash tweens between the second and third keyframes. Play your animation. *Voila*—a looping motion.

Now, stop the animation before it hypnotizes you, 'cuz there's more. You're going to make your ball bounce. Go to the Control menu (7.15) and make sure Loop Playback is unselected.

7.16

Select the first keyframe in the timeline. Grab the ball and move it up to the top of the frame, near the middle. Select the second keyframe, and drag the ball to the bottom near the middle. Select the third keyframe, and drag the ball to about three-quarters of the way up, again near the middle (7.16).

Play the animation. ("Wow, Mark, that's the lamest bouncing ball animation I've ever seen!" I know. Bear with me; it's going to get better in a minute.)

EASE IN, EASE OUT

It's time to see if we can fix this animation up a bit. The primary problem is that the ball falls at a constant speed, then bounces instantly back up at a constant speed. In the real world, the ball should pick up speed as it falls, and then lose speed as it bounces back upwards. It's time to make that happen.

Right-click the first keyframe in the timeline and choose Panels ➤ Frames to bring up the Frame Properties panel. Under the Tweening tab are several controls I've ignored until now.

Notice the box marked Easing. It currently reads 0. Click the arrow to its right to bring up the slider control. By default, it's right in the middle (the number to the right reads 0) meaning that there is no easing in our motion.

What's *easing* you ask? Simple: If you ease into a motion, you start slow and pick up speed toward the

TIP

To snip off extra frames at the end of an animation, select the range of frames by clicking the first unwanted frame and then Ctrl+dragging to the right, to the last unwanted frame. Right-click the selected frames and choose Remove Frames from the pop-up menu, or press Shift+F5 to delete the frames.

NOTE

You should always build your animatic at the same frame rate you intend to use for your final animation. That way, any work you do in the animatic can be readily transferred to the final cartoon, or you can slowly transform the animatic into the final animation.

end. If you ease out, you start fast and gradually slow to a stop. A car pulling away from a red light is easing into its motion. A car stopping at a red light is easing out of its motion.

Of course, not all motion calls for any ease at all. Birds flying across the sky or spaceships darting through space may neither speed up nor slow down. Our ball, though, needs to pick up speed as it falls. Grab the slider and pull it all the way to the bottom, until the number reads −100 (7.17). The ball now eases into motion.

Play the animation. The ball now starts out falling slowly and picks up speed until it hits the bottom of the screen. The second half of the animation still doesn't work, however. It's time to fix that.

Click the second keyframe. If you closed the Frame panel, open it again (right-click, and then choose Panels ➤ Frame). Under Tweening, set Easing all the way to the top, until it reads 100 (7.18).

7.17

7.18

7.19

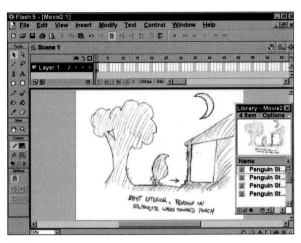

7.20

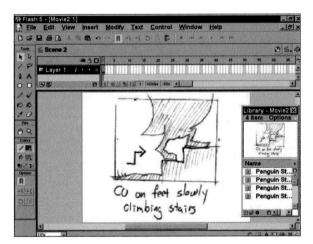

7.21

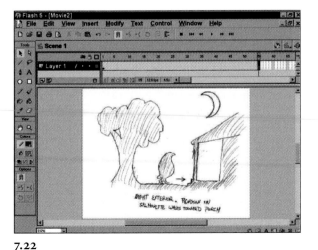

7.22

Play the animation. Now the ball starts out fast after the bounce and loses speed as it rises back up into the air. Better, huh?

BUILDING AN ANIMATIC

With some basic motion tweening under your belt, you're ready to build an animatic for your cartoon. "Oh, no!" you cry. "Not another step!" Not to worry; the animatic isn't really an extra step in building your Flash cartoon; all the work that goes into making your animatic goes directly toward your finished cartoon.

An animatic is basically an animated storyboard with sound. It's a planning tool, used to "tighten up" your cartoon, to be certain that the timing and pacing are going to work before going through the process of actually animating an entire cartoon.

The animatic has the same length and timing as the planned final cartoon. Traditionally, an animatic is a movie of the storyboard — a series of stills with dialogue. Each cell of the storyboard is onscreen the same length of time as the scene it represents will be onscreen in the final animation. Sometimes an animatic includes some music and sound effects.

Watching the animatic shows you where you need to expand and trim scenes, and maybe add or remove scenes. You may decide that you need additional dialogue, or can eliminate dialogue, or that some takes need to be re-recorded.

Some simple animations don't really warrant this step (a one-second animation of a character waving to welcome visitors to your Web site, for example).

7.23

But anything bigger than that—especially any cartoon with a *story*—really benefits from an animatic.

SCAN IT

One way to make your animatic is to start by scanning in your storyboard. Each cell in your storyboard becomes one scene in your movie.

Open a new file. Select Modify ➤ Movie (Ctrl+M) and set the movie's frame rate to 10. Ten frames per second is the bare minimum needed for convincing animation. Set the width to 400 and the height to 300.

Use File ➤ Import to import the four image files: Penguin Storyboard porch nite 1.gif, Penguin Storyboard porch nite 2.gif, Penguin Storyboard porch nite 3.gif, and Penguin Storyboard porch nite 4.gif. Flash puts all of the images on your stage. Select them and delete them from the stage; they're still in the library.

If the Library window isn't already open, open it (Ctrl+L). The four images you imported are displayed (7.19). Grab the first storyboard cell (Penguin Storyboard porch nite 1), and drag it to the center of the stage (7.20).

From the main menu, choose Insert ➤ Scene to create a new blank scene. Grab the second storyboard cell from the library (Penguin Storyboard porch nite 2), and drag it to the center of the stage (7.21).

Create a third new scene and place the third cell (Penguin Storyboard porch nite 3) there. Create a last scene and place the fourth cell (Penguin Storyboard porch nite 4) in it.

Jump to Scene 1 (7.22). In this scene, Penguin walks to the porch. How long should it take him? Two seconds? Five? You decide. Move the playhead to that position on the timeline (for example, 2 seconds equals 20 frames.).

> ### TIP
>
> To easily center an object on the stage, cut it (Ctrl+X) and then paste it again (Ctrl+V). By default, Flash automatically centers all objects when it pastes them. To paste an object in the same position you cut it from, use Edit ➤ Paste in Place (Ctrl+Shift+V).

Insert a new frame there with Insert ➤ Frame (or F5). Press Enter to play. Not much happens, huh?

Jump to Scene 2 (7.23), the close-up on Penguin's feet climbing the stairs. How long should this take? Decide and put a new frame there.

Decide how long Scene 3 and Scene 4 should last and give them the extra frames they need (7.24).

Open the Control menu. Make sure that Loop Playback is unselected. Select Play All Scenes (7.25). Jump back to Scene 1 and press Enter to play your animatic. Are you still happy with the timing? If not, go back and add frames (F5) or subtract frames (Shift+F5) until you're satisfied. That's why you build an animatic in the first place.

When you're done, save your file and close it.

SIMPLE MOTION

Open the file Animatic Penguin Storyboard with Motion.FLA. This is a slightly more sophisticated ver-

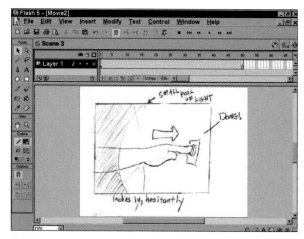

7.24

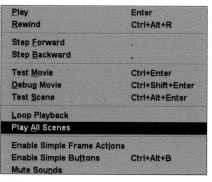

7.25

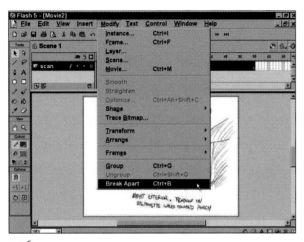

7.26

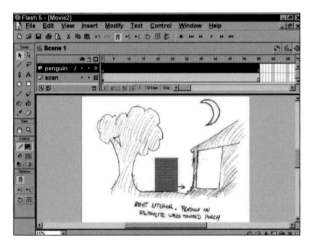

7.27

7.28

sion of the animatic you just created, incorporating a couple of tricks. Go to Scene 1, make sure that Control ➤ Play All Scenes is selected, and press Enter to play the animatic.

This animatic has some simple motion: I used cutouts of Penguin and his parts to rough in the motion for the finished cartoon. To create the cutouts, I employed the Bitmap Fill trick you learned in Chapter 2.

First, I broke the scanned bitmap image apart, by choosing Modify ➤ Break Apart (7.26). I sampled it with the Eye Dropper tool [icon]. Next, on a new layer above the scanned image, I created a simple shape, just large enough to hide Penguin (7.27). I used the Paint Bucket to fill this shape with the scanned image (7.28). I grouped the shape (Modify ➤ Group) because only groups and symbols can be animated with motion tweening (7.29).

Lastly, I copied this shape and pasted it into the layer holding the scanned image. I double-clicked the shape to open it, and then filled it with white. This effectively "erases" Penguin's image from the scan (7.30).

On the new layer, above the scan, I created my beginning and ending keyframes and applied motion tweening to make my Penguin cutout move across the screen (7.31).

I used this method on the first three scenes. For the fourth scene, I added a zoom in on Penguin's eye by scaling the scanned image up between two keyframes.

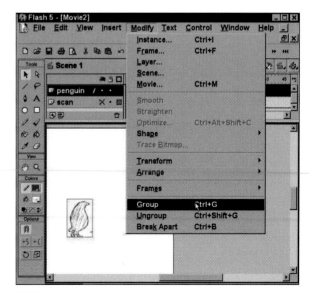

7.29

MAKING A BLACK MATTE

Another trick employed here is a black matte, which blocks out the part of the objects that extend outside of the frame (7.32). If you just see the scanned image getting bigger or moving from side to side, but you can't tell where the frame is, it can be hard to judge the effect. This matte trick also works to hide extra offstage bits in your completed animations. If the person viewing the cartoon resizes the frame, he or she can inadvertently expose parts you've left hanging over the edge (7.33).

To create a matte that exactly matches your movie's frame size, do the following: Select the Rectangle tool. Set the Line Color to none and the Fill Color to black (or whatever other color you want your matte to be). Create a new layer above the other elements of your animation, and create a black rectangle large enough to cover the entire frame and any objects that may lie outside of it (7.34). Hide this matte layer from view .

Create another new layer, above the black matte. Select the Rectangle tool and set the fill color to red. Click and drag to create a red rectangle on the stage. We're going to use this new rectangle to cut out the area in the matte that the movie shows through, so we need it to be exactly the same size as the movie frame. Select the rectangle, and then choose Window ➤ Panels ➤ Info. Under Dimensions, set the *x* and *y* values to 0. Set width (w:) to the width of your movie. Set height (h:) to the height of your movie. The red rectangle's size and dimensions exactly match those of the movie.

Select and copy the red rectangle. Hide the red rectangle layer and unhide the matte layer. Paste the red rectangle in place (Edit ➤ Paste in Place) on top of the black rectangle (7.35). Deselect everything (Edit ➤ Deselect All). Now click the red rectangle to select it, and press delete to delete it. Finally, delete the layer that displays the red rectangle.

TIP

To temporarily hide a layer from view, click that layer's eyeball icon . Hidden layers can't be edited, but they still render in your final animation.

7.30

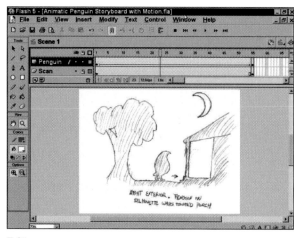

7.31

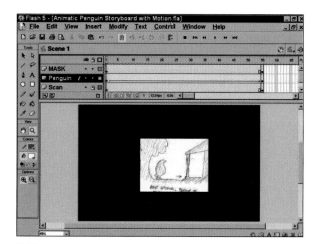

7.32

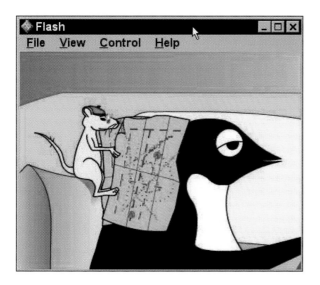

TIP

To use scanned artwork or other images as reference drawings for your Flash cartoons, place them on a layer of their own, at the bottom of the stack. Give the layer a name such as "reference" or "scanned storyboard," and lock it. Set the layers type to Guide (Modify ➤ Layers). Guide layers show up when you are editing your work, but they do not render in the final animation.

You're left with a large black rectangle—the matte—with a perfectly sized hole cut out of the middle, where the red rectangle used to be. If you're going to use the same matte in more than one scene, you should make it a symbol.

BUILDING AN ANIMATIC FROM SCRATCH

Of course, you don't have to start by scanning in your storyboard. If you've already created some of your characters, backgrounds, and props, you may want to start building your animatic by using them instead. Or you may choose to use a combination of scanned images and Flash objects (7.36).

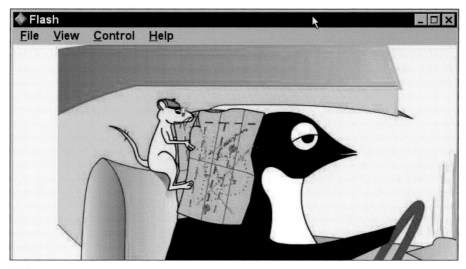

7.33

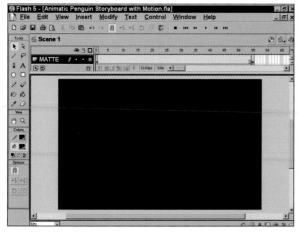

7.34

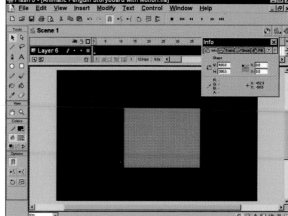

7.35

7.36

7.37

However you build it, the idea behind the animatic is the same. You are creating a rough draft of your cartoon to practice the timing and the layout of your shots *before* you actually begin animating.

I prefer to work in a large number of relatively small scenes. I feel that it makes it easier for me to organize my work and to make changes later. Other animators prefer to work with a few longer scenes; some build entire multi-minute cartoons in a single scene, although I don't recommend it.

There should be a rough correspondence between your storyboard and your animatic. If a bit was distinct and important enough to warrant its own drawing in the storyboard, then it probably warrants its own scene in your animation.

If you feel that this gives you too many scenes, then devote one scene to each location, as you would in a movie or a stage play. For example, you may have one scene for the exterior of a house. Then you may have a scene for all the action that takes place in the living room. Then you may have another scene for all the action that takes place in the dining room, and still another scene for action that takes place outside again.

> **TIP**
>
> You easily can turn any symbol into a silhouette. Right-click the symbol and choose Panels ➤ Effect to bring up the Effect Properties panel. Choose Brightness from the drop-down box, and set the brightness all the way to 0. Instant silhouette!

7.38

7.39

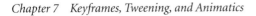

7.40

7.41

7.42

TIP

An entire scene can reside in a symbol. When I used the kitchen scene (7.51) in "A Very Penguin Christmas," I actually built the whole thing as one animated symbol, and then placed that symbol in my scene. To zoom in and out and follow Penguin as he crosses the room, I simply resized and repositioned the symbol with a few keyframes.

Remember: You can always break long scenes up into shorter ones later on. You can combine shorter scenes into longer ones, too, but it's a little trickier.

Flash's default scene names, Scene 1, Scene 2, and so forth, aren't very descriptive. Don't accept these defaults when you create a new scene; always name your scenes. Choose Windows ➤ Panels ➤ Scene to open the Scene Inspector. Double-click a scene's name to rename it (7.37).

These images show a scene I sketched using the scanned storyboard cell as a template. I added and sized a symbol of Penguin, which I made when I designed the character (7.38). I turned the symbol brightness all the way down to produce a silhouette. Then I used the paintbrush to sketch in the ground (7.39), the house, and the tree (7.40). I placed a simple, gradient rectangle on a lower layer for the nighttime background (7.41). Finally, I dropped in a crescent moon and a porch light (7.42).

ITERATIONS SAVE YOU WORK

As you work on your cartoon, make everything into symbols, even if you are just throwing in rough sketches, or scans, of your characters and objects, and plan to create better, finished artwork later. Rather than creating the final version as a separate symbol, edit your rough symbol through as many iterations as necessary. That way, when you arrive at a finished symbol that suits you, it's already in place in all of your scenes, properly sized and positioned.

Here, for example, is Penguin cooking (7.43). He begins as a scanned pencil sketch and becomes a rough Flash symbol, a finished Flash symbol, and,

7·43

finally, gets all of his cooking accoutrements (accoutrements, Fr., *noun*: stuff).

Because I made a symbol from the first scanned pencil sketch and kept editing that symbol instead of replacing it with new ones, Penguin stays sized and positioned, just like I want him, throughout the process. I never have to repeat the process of placing him in the scene.

ADDING SOME DIALOGUE

One of the most important jobs of the animatic is to preview your dialogue, *in situ*, as it were. In fact, the dialogue is often the primary consideration in deciding how to *cut* your movie—that is, where to break the shots: switching from one character to another, or from a wide shot to a close-up. This is where you can fine-tune the overall length of your scenes, as well.

You don't want your scene to be shorter than the characters' dialogue.

Open the file Penguin & Rat Kitchen Animatic (7.44). This is a single scene from an animatic of "A Very Penguin Christmas," a Flash cartoon starring Penguin and Rat. (The cartoon is included on the CD-ROM that accompanies this book.) It's breakfast time, and Penguin has been hinting about getting a kitten for Christmas.

There are three lines of dialogue in the scene:

> PENGUIN: I made your favorite breakfast—pancakes, bacon, and eggs!
> RAT: We are not getting a kitten!
> PENGUIN: I didn't say anything.

You bring a sound file into your animatic with File ➤ Import. But the three bits of dialogue for this

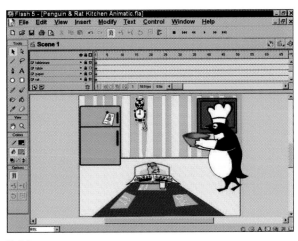

7.44

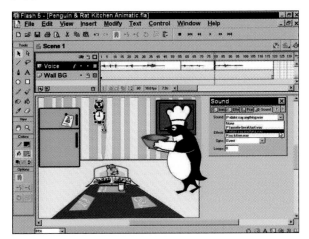

7.45

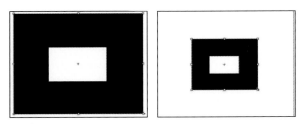

7.46

7.47

scene are already in your library. (You're welcome.) Now it's time to add them.

Create a new layer, and name it Voice. Right-click the first frame in the Voice layer and choose Panels ➤ Sound to bring up the Sound Properties panel. From the Sound drop-down list, choose "P Favorite Breakfast.wav." You can see the .wav file in the timeline; it lasts about 45 frames.

With the Voice layer selected, move the playhead to a frame after the end of the first piece of dialogue. Create a new keyframe here (Insert ➤ Keyframe, or F6). If you closed the Sound panel, reopen it (Window ➤

7.48

7.49

7.50

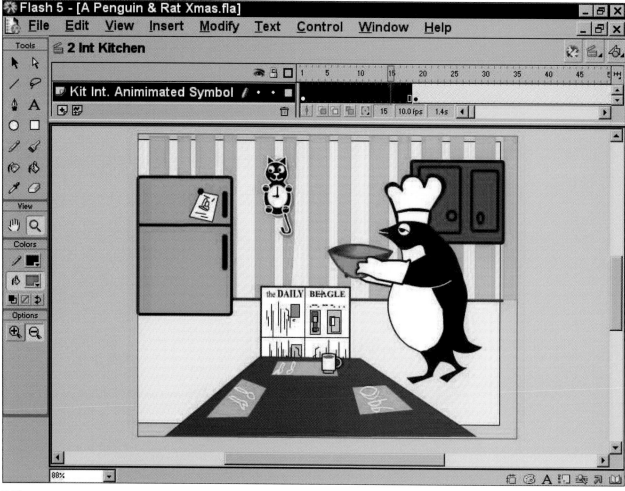

7.51

Panels ➤ Sound). This time, choose the "R No Kitten. wav" sound clip from the drop-down list.

Select a third frame in the Voice layer, somewhere beyond the end of the first two pieces of dialogue, and create a new keyframe. Assign it the "P I Didnt Say Anything.wav" sound clip (7.45).

Press Enter to preview the movie. Chances are you're not happy with the timing of this first effort. Adjust the timing by clicking and dragging the keyframes on the Voice layer to new positions. If you feel the scene needs to be longer, add more frames at the end of each layer (Insert ➤ Frame, or F5). If you feel it needs to be shorter, delete the extra frames from the end of each layer (Insert ➤ Delete Frame, or Shift+F5).

QUICK FRAMES, ZOOMS, AND PANS

You can quickly test different framings, pans, zooms, and so forth by using the matte, itself, to frame different shots. Sometimes, it's a lot easier to shrink the matte than to stretch every object in the scene. If you always resize the matte (or any object) using the corner handles, it retains its aspect ratio so that the hole is always in proper proportion to your movie size (7.46).

Load the file Penguin & Rat Kitchen Animatic FINISHED.fla, to see an example of using a matte to rough out camera shots. The scene begins with a wide establishing shot (7.47), cuts to a close-up of Penguin (7.48), cuts to a close-up of Rat (7.49), and then cuts back to a close-up of Penguin (7.50).

CHAPTER 8
TWEENING —
MANUAL AND AUTOMATIC

Just moving an object from place to place isn't always adequate to your animation needs. Sometimes you need more complex motion, such as motion along a curve. Sometimes you need to animate a person walking or throwing a ball, and Flash's simple motion tweening isn't quite up to the task. Here are some tricks and techniques to create more believable motion.

A LITTLE SQUASH AND STRETCH

In their book, *The Illusion of Life: Disney Animation*, longtime Disney animators Frank Thomas and Ollie Johnston describe *squash* and *stretch* as "by far the most important discovery" of the early days of animation way back in the twenties. Squash and stretch are just what they sound like. The simplest example is a soft rubber ball, bouncing on the ground. As the ball hits the ground, it deforms, flattening out — it squashes.

Only the most rigid of objects — a kitchen chair or a vintage Buick convertible — remain stiff and unchanging while moving or being moved. People and animals — especially cartoon people and animals — deform, flex, and warp as they move.

Disney animators used the example of a half-filled flour sack. Drop the flour sack on the floor and it squashes flat. Grab it and pick it up and it stretches out. To be realistic, the object should maintain its volume. The flour sack, for example, maintains its volume, no matter how you lift it, drop it, or fling it about (unless you split a seam . . .). Its *shape,* on the other hand, changes considerably.

©1999, 2000 oprosti.com

Everything that moves in life, moves in curves.

TONY WHITE, *THE ANIMATOR'S WORKBOOK*
(NEW YORK: WATSON-GUPTILL PUBLICATIONS, 1988)

The animators continued to search for better methods of relating drawings to each other and had found a few ways that seemed to produce a predictable result. . . . By far the most important discovery was what we call Squash and Stretch.

LEGENDARY ANIMATORS FRANK THOMAS AND OLLIE
JOHNSTON, *THE ILLUSION OF LIFE: DISNEY ANIMATION*
(NEW YORK: HYPERION, 1995)

©1999, 2000 oprosti.com

You see squash and stretch in cartoons as characters gather themselves up, and then spring into action, and even in facial animation as a character smiles, laughs, and chews. Notice how this little guy squashes down in anticipation before he stretches out, leaping off the screen (8.1).

As this sheep nods his head (8.2), his snout stretches unrealistically out of shape but, ironically, the resulting animation is made that much more believable.

Cartoons can, of course, feature wildly exaggerated squash and stretch, but even a little bit can really help sell an animation by bringing it to life.

RED RUBBER BALL

Load the file BouncingBall.FLA. It's the bouncing ball animation from the last chapter. It's pretty good, but what it needs in order to be even better is a little squash and stretch; it should deform a bit when it hits the ground, just as a real ball would. We'll add one frame each of squash and stretch. It's not much, but it really helps sell the motion.

The squash frame comes immediately after the middle keyframe and takes place in the same location on the screen. The ball has just hit the ground and is flattening out somewhat.

Because the ball is in the same place as on the middle keyframe, you can duplicate that keyframe. Click once on the middle keyframe to select it. Now, Alt+click and drag the middle keyframe one frame to the right, duplicating it. Flash actually generates two new keyframes so you should have three keyframes right next to each other (8.3).

We need one last keyframe. Again, move the playhead to the right of the three middle keyframes—frame 33—and press F6 to make it a keyframe. You should now have four keyframes all in a row in the middle of the timeline (8.4).

Here's why we need them: The first keyframe is the end of the fall; the ball has almost reached the ground but hasn't squashed yet. The second keyframe is the squash keyframe. The ball stretches on the third keyframe as it bounces back off the ground. The forth keyframe is the beginning of the ball's flight back into the air.

© 2000, Dave Jones, www.transience.com.au

8.1

© 2000, Alen Puaca, www.oprosti.com

8.2

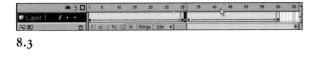

8.3

8.4

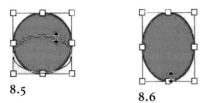

8.5   8.6

ANIMATING FROM THE ENDING POINT

Sometimes, you can more easily set up an animation from the end first. Say you want a whole bunch of bubbles to merge into one bubble. It's hard to tween each one so that it ends up in the exact right place. But you can easily create the end keyframe — lots of bubbles on top of each other. Just create them on different layers and cut and paste each one so it's in the center of the stage. Then you can move them all to a new location if you wish.

To animate from the ending point, create the object you want to animate in an empty keyframe where you want the animation to start, and convert it to a symbol. Create a keyframe where you want the animation to end. Now click the first frame again — this is the added step for animation from the end. Move the symbol to where you want it to start. Make any other changes you want to make (rotation, size, color). Open the Frame panel and select Motion from the Tweening drop-down list. Make any other adjustments you want to the settings in the Frame panel. Now the animation goes in the direction you want — for example, from the edges of the stage to the center — in the bubble example.

This sidebar is from *Flash 5 For Dummies* by Ellen Finkelstein and Gurdy Leete, Hungry Minds Inc., formerly IDG Books Worldwide Inc., 2000.

NOTE

Setting new keyframes in the middle of a tween can confuse Flash. It's always best to check your settings, just in case.

Now it's time to add squash. Select the second of the four middle keyframes. This is our first squash frame. Now select your ball and click the Scale tool ▣. Grab the *top* of the ball and pull it down until the ball is a little more than half its previous height (8.5). By scaling from the top, you leave the bottom of the ball in place.

As the ball bounces back off the ground, it should return to its previous, round, shape, but not instantly. We want the ball to deform a bit in the other direction, to stretch, as it comes off the ground.

Select the third of the four middle keyframes. This is our stretch frame. The ball is already back up in the air on this frame, because it was on its way back up when Flash created this keyframe. Select the ball, and then click the scale tool. Grab the top of the ball, and this time pull it *up*, stretching the ball until it is half-again as tall as before (8.6).

The last of the four keyframes have no squash or stretch to it. Leave the ball just as it is. Why do you need this keyframe at all? Without it, Flash would be tweening between a frame with squash and a frame without squash, and it would tween the squash as well as the motion. The ball wouldn't return to round until the very top of the bounce, which wouldn't look right at all, unless you're animating something very jiggly, like a water balloon. When you set this last keyframe, Flash is tweening between two frames with no squash and it won't try to stretch the ball as it flies up.

One last step. Because you've been shuffling things around quite a bit, Flash has probably lost track of the Easing. Right-click the last of the four middle keyframes and choose Panels ➤ Frame. Under Tweening, make sure that Easing is set all the way to the top, toward Out.

Press Play. Not too bad, huh? Feel free to drag the keyframes around if you're not happy with the timing. You can also adjust the height of the ball in the first and last keyframes until things look right to you.

GUIDE LAYERS AND YOU

This approach is all well and good, provided that your objects always move along straight lines. Few things *do* move in straight lines, however. In fact, most motion happens along arcs. Luckily, it's *almost* as easy to tween along a curve as it is to tween along a straight line. Here's how:

1. Open a new file in Flash (File ➤ New). Under Modify ➤ Movie, set the frame rate to 12 frames per second. Press OK.

2. Double-click Layer 1's name, and change it to Guide. Because this is a two-second animation, select frame 24 (2 frames at 12 frames per second equals 24 frames) and create a new frame there (Insert ➤ Frame, or F5). Flash fills in the intervening 22 frames automatically (8.7).

3. Bring up the Stroke panel (Window ➤ Panels ➤ Stroke) and choose a solid, black, one-point line. Select the Line tool (N) and click and drag to draw a line across the stage from side to side, near the middle (8.8). With the line unselected, use the Arrow tool ![arrow tool icon] to bend the line up in the middle, to form an arc about half as high as it is wide (8.9).

4. Bring up the layer's properties (Modify ➤ Layer) (8.10). Notice that the layer can be one of five types: Normal, Guide, Guided, Mask, or Masked.

5. Set the layer's type to Guide, and press OK.

As you may remember, a Guide layer does not show up in the final animation. Sometimes, you'll use a Guide layer as a place to put reference images so that you can "trace" over them. But Guide layers can serve another function as well, one more suited to their name. A line on a Guide layer can act as a path that tweened objects follow as they move across the screen.

6. Create a new layer, and name it Ball.

7. With the Oval tool (O), click and drag to draw a colored ball on the new layer. Select the entire ball and group it (Modify ➤ Group, or Ctrl+G).

8. Select the Ball layer. Click *only once* on the layer's name, and drag the Ball layer beneath the Guide layer. You should wind up with the Ball layer underneath the Guide layer in the timeline (8.11). Notice that the Guide layer's icon has

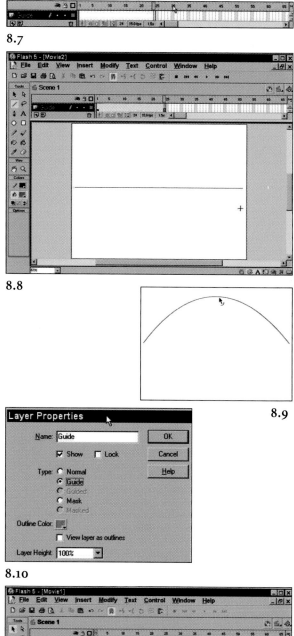

8.7

8.8

8.9

8.10

8.11

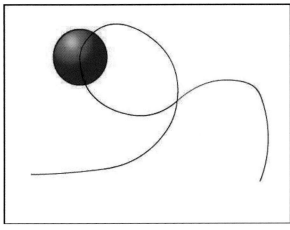

8.12

8.13

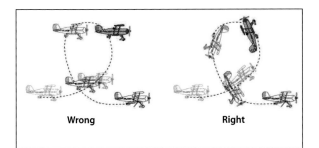

Wrong   Right

8.14

8.15

changed to . . . can it be? Yes! A ball moving along an arc. Why, this is perfect for us!

Notice also that the Ball layer's icon is now indented to show that it is under the influence of the Guide layer. Sometimes, you can wind up with a layer that is under a Guide layer, but not properly indented. If your icon is *not* indented, click and drag the Ball layer above the Guide layer, and then back into place beneath it again.

9. Right-click frame 1 in the Ball layer, and select Panels ➤ Frame. Set tweening to Motion. In the options that appear at the bottom of the Frame panel, select Snap (8.12). Snap assures you that the ball always stays in contact with the guide path. Leave the Frame panel open.

10. Click and drag your ball to the left-hand end of the arc. Because you turned on Snap, your ball automatically snaps to the arc in the Guide layer if you get anywhere close.

11. Create a new keyframe on the Ball layer at frame 24. Either turn on Snap, or bring up the Frame Properties panel (Modify ➤ Frame) and select Snap to Guide. With frame 24 selected, click and drag the ball so that its center snaps to the right-hand end of the arc. Make sure Snap is selected in the Frame panel.

12. Press Enter to preview the animation. The ball should smoothly follow the arc, from one end to the other. If it doesn't, then you don't have the ball's center snapped to the end of the guide arc at one of the two ends; snap the ball in place and try again.

A guide line doesn't have to be a simple line or single curve. It can be quite complex; it can even loop. Select the Guide layer, and delete your curve. Select the Pencil tool (Y), and draw a more complex path on the Guide layer (8.13).

Don't get too carried away; Flash can get confused if your guide lines loop or cross themselves too often. If you need a complex path that Flash can't seem to follow, you may have to break the animation up into two or more pieces.

A PROPER ORIENTATION

When a ball follows a path, it doesn't usually matter which way it's pointing. Some objects look silly if they point in one direction while following a curve in another. An airplane, for example, should always be pointing in the direction it's moving (8.14).

Flash keeps your symbols oriented as they follow a path. Open the file Guide Layer with Plane.FLA. This is exactly the same exercise as the ball you just animated, with a few minor adjustments (8.15). I've substituted an airplane from the Flash library (Window ➢ Common Libraries ➢ Movie Clips) for the ball, so you can tell if the symbol stays oriented to the path. Preview the animation and you'll see that it does.

Right-click the first frame in the Plane layer and select Panels ➢ Frame. Notice that the checkbox near the bottom, labeled "Orient to path," is selected (8.16). This tells Flash to point your symbol in the direction it's moving; as the path twists to point this way and that, so does the object. If you use "Orient to path," make sure that your object is properly oriented at both ends of the guide path or it may spin around more than you intended.

Go ahead and close the Frame panel.

TWEENING ROTATIONS AND SUCH

Despite its name, Flash's motion tweening isn't strictly limited to motion; you can tween between different rotations, sizes, and even colors and transparencies. You can use motion tweening to animate objects growing, or shrinking, or, to a limited extent, changing their shape.

Higher! Higher!

Load the file Ball Bouncing Really High.FLA (8.17). Press Enter to preview the animation. Yes, it's yet another bouncing ball animation. This time, however, the ball is bouncing high enough to bump its head on a Comsat.

The ball itself is a four-frame animated symbol of a red, spinning ball, which I've stolen from fellow Flasher Vaughn Anderson (*Thanks!*). The ball moves along a path in the Guide layer. Unhide the Guide layer by clicking the red *X* in the Show Layer column to see the path.

The ball has three keyframes: a beginning, a middle, and an end. The keyframes are at the beginning, middle, and end of the guide path, respectively. As you can see from this example, keyframes don't have to be at the beginning and ends of a guide path; they can occur anywhere along it. I used motion tweening between both sets of keyframes to move the ball along the path.

I needed a third keyframe, in the middle, because I wanted the ball to slow down (or ease out) as it approached the peak of its bounce, and then pick up speed (or ease in) as it plummeted earthward again. That means it needed to ease out along the first half of the path, and then ease in along the second half. Because a single keyframe can't both ease in and ease out at the same time, I needed two pairs of

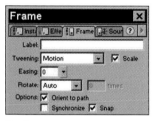

8.16

8.17

8.18

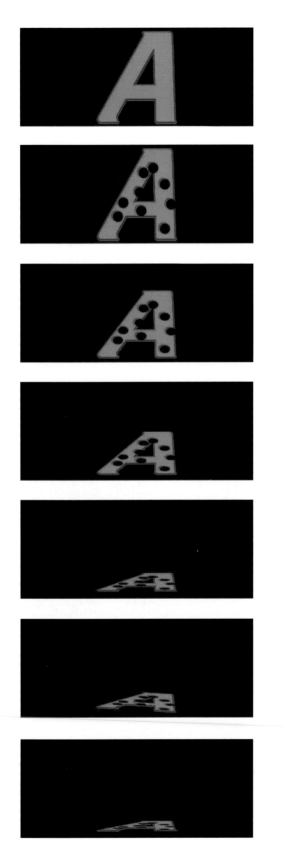

keyframes. The ball eases out between frames 1 and 20, and then eases in between frames 20 and 40.

Of course, the ball doesn't just move along the path; it also grows and shrinks to convey the illusion that the bottom of its bounce is a long, long way beneath.

At the beginning and end keyframes, I've sized the ball down to about 1 percent of its original size. At the middle keyframe, I've sized the ball up to about 120 percent of its original size. Flash motion tweening automatically tweens the size transformation, as well as the motion along the path.

A Is for Assassinate

In an especially cheesy animated logo for a friend's Web site (8.18), I wanted some of the letters to react as you passed the mouse over them. The letter *A*, for example, is assassinated, and falls over backward (8.19).

Because Flash doesn't actually do 3D motion, I couldn't really make the letter *A* fall backward; I had to fake it. To achieve the effect, I scaled the *A* down

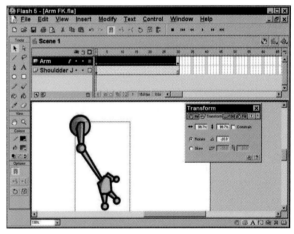

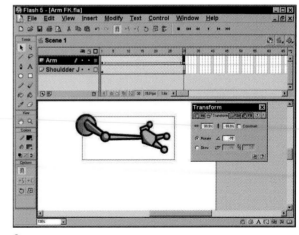

8.19

8.20

from the top, making it shorter but no narrower. I used motion tweening to go from the full-sized letter to the squashed one.

Lastly, I added a few frames of the squashed letter rocking back and forth to suggest it rattling a bit as it hits the ground.

When played back, the effect is surprisingly effective; the letter seems to fall over backward. Load the file Jump Arena.FLA. Test the movie (Control ➤ Test Movie) and pass your mouse cursor over the *A* to see for yourself. This simple approach may not always work for you. The shape of the letter helped me out here; the pointed top of the *A* gives the impression of diminishing into the distance.

Skewing for Fun and Profit

Flash's motion tweening also interpolates rotation to raise and lower drawbridges or animate clock hands between keyframes. This robot arm rotates smoothly from –20 degrees at frame 1 to –75 degrees at frame 30 (8.20).

To animate an object such as a propeller or a bicycle wheel, which rotates all the way around, you use a different method. Follow these steps:

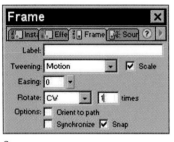

8.21

1. Open a new file. With the Rectangle tool (R), click and drag on the stage to make a box that is much wider than it is tall. With the Arrow tool (V), drag a marquee selection around the entire rectangle and group it (Ctrl+G).
2. Create a new keyframe at frame 30.
3. Right-click the first keyframe, at frame 1, and select Panels ➤ Frame. Set Tweening to Motion.

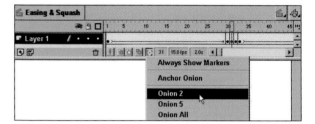

8.23

8.24

8.25

8.22

4. Click the Rotate drop-down box. Select either CW (clockwise) or CCW (counterclockwise) from the list and type 1 in the "times" field (8.21). You've told Flash to rotate your box ".1 times" in whatever direction you chose, which, grammar aside, is pretty easy to interpret. Preview the animation and sure enough, that's what it does. Try rotating the box different numbers of times.

MANUAL TWEENING

"But Mark," you say, "enough with the bouncing balls and such. I want to do sophisticated character animation! Can Flash tweening help me there?"

No. Not really. Sophisticated character animation is beyond Flash's limited tweening capabilities. But there are some tricks that make tweening easier than it may seem, and Flash provides the tools to help you tween. Read on.

ONION SKIN

Foremost among these tools is Onion Skin. Traditional animators labored over a light table or light box — a box or table, illuminated from the inside to facilitate tracing. When they wanted to make slight changes from one drawing to the next, they traced over the first drawing using a light box.

Flash emulates a light box with Onion Skin. In Flash, onion skinning allows you to see several frames at the same time, as though you were looking at a series of animations drawn on a stack of onion-skin paper. (Onion skin is a type of very thin paper, used for tracing.) Click the Onion Skin button below the timeline (8.23), and then click the Modify Onion Markers button to the right of the Onion Skin button. From the pop-up menu, choose Onion 2 (8.24).

> **TIP**
>
> To rotate an object, such as the propeller on a plane, that is seen at an angle, create the rotating object as a separate symbol; then place that symbol in your scene and scale and skew it to obtain the proper perspective (8.22).

If you look above the timeline, you see that brackets have appeared on either side of the playhead (8.25). If you're currently on the first or last frame, you only see one bracket. Drag the frame marker to the middle of the animation to see both brackets. The space between the brackets is shaded.

These brackets mark the extent of your onion skinning. Because you chose Onion 2, Flash onion skins two frames in front of and behind the current frame.

Grab the playhead and drag it back and forth (this is called *scrubbing*) to see how onion skin works. You can clearly see the effects of easing in and out: At the beginning and end of the animation, consecutive images of the ball are much closer to each other; in the middle of the animation, they are farther apart. Onion skin is an invaluable tool when you are doing the in-between frames yourself.

BREAKING AN ANIMATION INTO FRAMES

It's time to do a couple of animations where you are responsible for all of the tweening yourself. Don't

> **TIP**
>
> Flash motion tweening also tweens between colors and even transparencies, but only on library symbols, not on simple groups. Set the first keyframe to motion tweening, and then right-click your symbol and choose Panels ➤ Effects. To vary transparency, choose Alpha from the drop-down list. Select the next keyframe and vary transparency, Tint, or Brightness. Flash tweens between the two keyframes. (Use the Advanced setting to vary color, brightness, and transparency all at once.)

1   5

8.26

worry, though, because there's a secret that makes tweening a whole lot easier than you may think: *You tween from the middle out.* That way, the motion in every tweened frame is exactly halfway between that in the two keyframes. How far does the head move? Exactly halfway from the first keyframe to the next. How far does the arm swing? Exactly halfway. How far does the ball fall? Exactly halfway.

"Aha!" you say. "What about all that ease in, ease out business?" Aha! I say right back. Even with ease in or ease out — or both! — you only have to tween halfway.

Here's how it works. Here's Stickman again (8.26). To tween the three frames between keyframes 1 and 5, we don't draw them in order. Rather, the first tween goes on frame 3, halfway between the keyframes. (The first tween between two keyframes is called the *breakdown drawing*.) The next tween goes on frame 2, halfway between 1 and the new frame at 3. The last tween goes at frame 4, halfway between 3 and 5.

Here is a breakdown diagram of the Stickman tween (8.27). The keyframes are circled in green. The breakdown drawing is in the broken blue circle. The last two tweened frames are below the line.

Easing In, Easing Out

"Ahem!" you ahem. I know, I know: What about easing in and out? It's better if I draw you a diagram. Here's another breakdown drawing (8.28).

Notice that this breakdown drawing has all the tweens on the left side and that as the frames progress, the distance between them gets longer and longer. That is, the object being animated picks up speed.

This breakdown drawing is for this animation of a hammer falling (8.29). Onion skin is on, showing all five frames. Just like our ball, the hammer picks up speed as it falls, easing in.

Notice in the breakdown diagram that all the tweens still take place exactly between two other frames. They are just done in a different order. The breakdown frame, the one exactly halfway between

TIP

You can manually drag the onion skin markers to select the number of frames for Flash to onion skin, before and after the current frame.

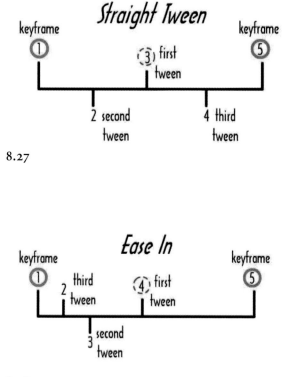

8.27

8.28

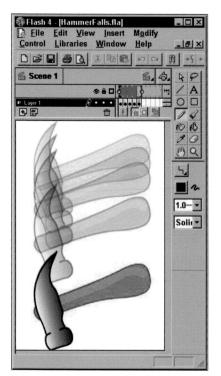

8.29

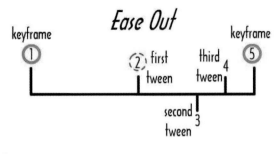

8.30

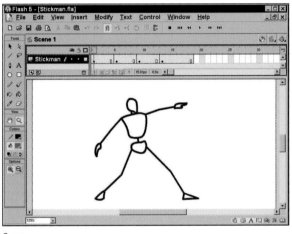

8.31

TIP

If you have a hard time positioning lines because they keep snapping into place in the wrong position, click the Snap to [] to turn snapping off.

the two keyframes, is now frame 4. The next tween is frame 3, halfway between frame 1 and frame 4. The third and final tween is frame 2, halfway between 1 and 3. With each passing frame, the hammer moves twice as far.

To ease out, we reverse the process (8.30) so that, with each passing frame, the hammer only moves half as far. (Those of you with a college philosophy course under your belt will recognize this as Aristotle's brilliant proof that a dropped hammer never reaches the ground.)

Moving in Arcs

"So, enough with these cheesy bouncing balls and falling hammers," you say. "How can tweening help me with a *real* animation?" Well, I'll show you. Load the file Stickman.FLA and follow along (8.31).

Start the second set of keyframes, at frames 5 and 9. This is a straight tween — no easing in or out — so the breakdown drawing (the first tween) goes right between the two keyframes, on frame 7.

Select frame 7 in the timeline, and turn on onion skinning. Click the Modify Onion Markers button and choose Onion 2. The entire range of your tween is now onion skinned.

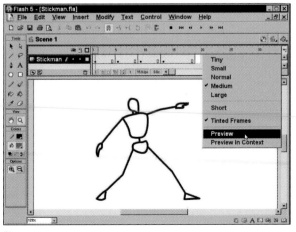

8.32

8.33

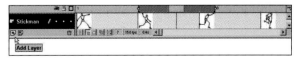

8.34

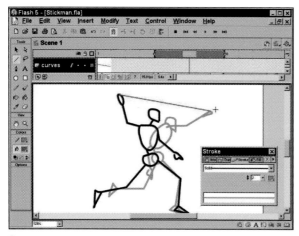

8.35

8.36

8.37

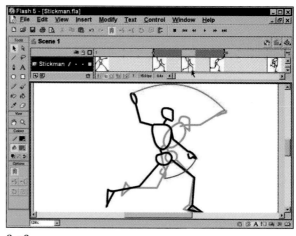

8.38

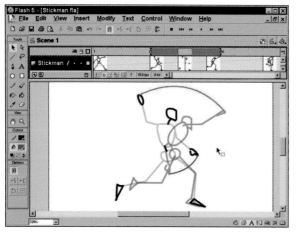

8.39

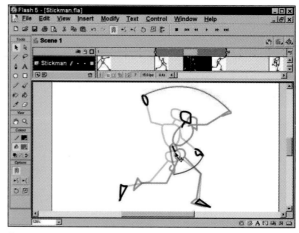

8.40

Here's something nifty: Click the icon at the far right of the timeline and select Preview (8.32). Keyframes in the timeline now show thumbnail versions of Stickman so you can see at a glance what he's doing in each frame. Resize the timeline menu until only the Stickman layer shows.

Important note: *Pay attention.* Most motion — cars falling off bridges, hammers driving nails, buildings toppling over, and so on — happens along arcs (8.33). This is especially true of human movement. When Stickman throws his pitch, his pitching hand doesn't move in a straight line from its position on frame 1 to its position on frame 5; it describes an arc. The same is true of his other hand, his head, and his feet, but it is nowhere as obvious as with his pitching hand.

So here's what to do: Draw a couple of arcs for reference, and make sure his hands move along them. Click the Add Layer button at the bottom of the time-line (8.34), or right-click the current layer and choose Insert Layer. Double-click the name of the new layer and rename it "curves."

Open the Stroke panel (Window ➢ Panels ➢ Stroke) and set the color to red (red for right), the width to 2 pt, and the style to solid. Now click the Line tool (N) and draw a single, straight line on the curves layer, running from the tip of Stickman's pitching hand in frame 5 to the tip of his hand in frame 9 (8.35).

With the red line deselected, grab it near the middle and pull up until it describes a plausible arc for Stickman's hand to follow. Grab the middle and drag left or right to alter the shape of the arc until you like it (8.36).

Change the line color to blue (blue for ... um ... left) and draw another straight line between Stickman's other hand in frames 5 and 9. Grab this line in the middle and pull down to get a curve you like (8.37).

NOTE

For finer control over movement, you can nudge selected items a pixel or two at a time with the arrow keys on your keyboard. How far the item is nudged depends on the current zoom setting.

TEMPORARY GROUPS

Sometimes lines and shapes in Flash defy your attempts to move them into place, insisting on sticking to each other and breaking apart in ways you'd rather they didn't. Here's how to stop them:

Select all the lines you want to work with (as opposed to the lines you'd rather not interact with just now) and group them. Don't worry — it's easy to break them apart later. Now move them into place. To work with the individual lines and curves, double-click your new symbol to open it up. You can still see the rest of your drawing, but the lines you're working with won't interact with them. Double-click a blank area of the stage when you're through editing. Select your temporary group and break it apart again (Ctrl+B).

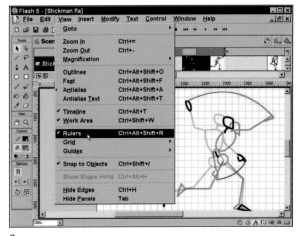

8.41

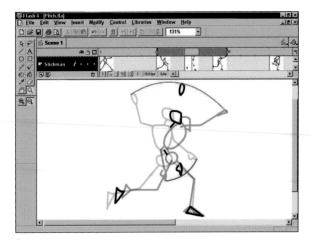

8.42

Lock the curves layer by clicking in the Hide Layer column; the dot turns to a padlock 🔒 . Scroll the timeline until you can see Stickman's layer again. Click Stickman's layer to select it as the current drawing layer.

Now for the breakdown drawing. You can start the tween either with a blank frame, or with a copy of one of the existing keyframes. For now, start with a copy. With frame 7 selected, press F6. Frame 7 is now a copy of frame 5 (8.38).

Select the lines that make up Stickman's torso and pelvis, but not his head, neck, and spine, and delete them. Likewise, select his arms and legs, but not his hands and feet, and delete them (8.39).

The torso changes shape between frames, and the arms and legs are too easily drawn to be worth the trouble of preserving. You'll draw them in last.

Select the lines that make up Stickman's head. Slide them to the right, halfway between the keyframes. (See how handy onion skin is?) Likewise, grab the small line that is Stickman's spine and move it to the midway point (8.40). (If you accidentally deleted the spine, or the neck, just draw a new one.)

If you have a hard time eyeballing positions, select View ➤ Rulers or View ➤ Grid ➤ Show Grid from the menu (8.41). (You can change grid spacing and color from View ➤ Grid ➤ Edit Grid.)

Select Stickman's pitching hand and move it halfway along the red arc. Select the other hand and move it halfway along the blue arc. You'll also want to rotate the hands so that their rotation is between that of the keyframes. Similarly, move his feet to their new halfway positions, or erase them and draw new ones if that's easier (8.42).

Time to put Stickman's body back. Start with the pelvis. If it seems difficult to get a shape halfway between the other two, at a position halfway between the other two, try this: Look at just the left side of the pelvis. Using onion skin, study it in both keyframes (8.43). Notice the shape of the space between the two curves. If you draw a line right down the very middle of this space (8.44), which is easy, it nicely tweens both the motion and the shape change of the pelvis, which sounds hard (8.45).

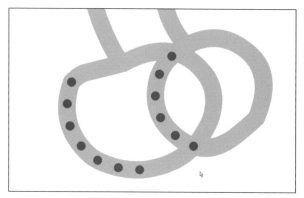
8.43

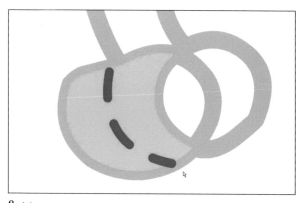
8.44

8.45

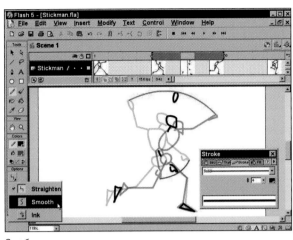

8.46

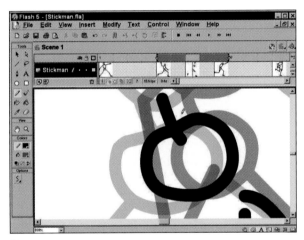

8.47

TIP

Play it, play it, play it. When developing a sequence of animated motion, do yourself the favor of bringing up the Controller (via the Window menu) and pressing those buttons often. Better yet, set Control ➢ Loop Playback, and pour through the sequence over and over again. Study it. Refine it. Mold it like clay. You may be surprised how sophisticated an animator you already are . . . and you thought you were just veggin' out and watchin' those 'toons.

Thanks to Peter Sylwester for this tip.

If the Stroke panel isn't open, open it and select 4 point, Solid, and black lines. Click the Pencil tool (Y) and set it to Smooth lines (8.46).

Draw the left curve of Stickman's pelvis. Likewise, draw the right side of the pelvis by putting a curve right down the middle of the space the two key pelvises define. Connect at the top and bottom and tweak until happy. Now that you know where to put your lines, you can probably draw the pelvis in a single curving stroke (8.47).

If you have trouble seeing what you're doing, zoom in a bit. Do the same thing up top to draw Stickman's torso, placing your new curves halfway between the keyframes' curves (8.48). Notice that Stickman's neck disappears between keyframes 5 and 9; once you

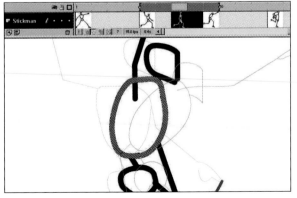

8.48

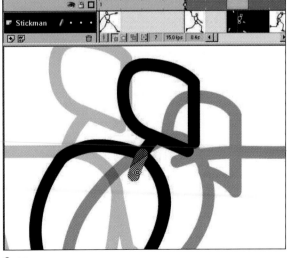

8.49

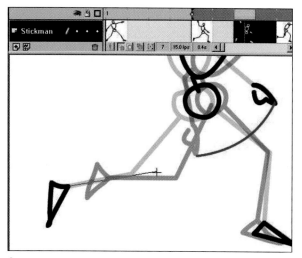

8.50

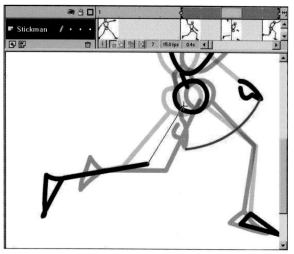

8.51

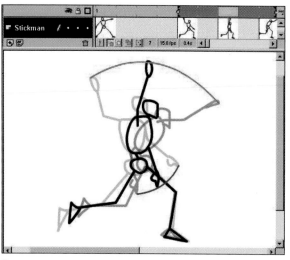

8.52

TIP

Sometimes it's a problem to work with a figure with lines that overlap other lines, like Stickman's arms and his torso. The lines tend to "stick" and "break" where they cross. One solution is to group lines (say, Stickman's arms and hands). Groups can be edited by double-clicking, and you can break them apart again (Ctrl+B) when you are done editing.

draw the torso, you'll probably have to cut off a little bit of neck sticking inside (8.49).

Time for arms and legs. Select the Line tool. Make sure it's still set to 4 pt solid black. Click at the top of one of the feet and drag the line to halfway between the two key knees (8.50). Release the mouse, and then click again to start a new line from the same spot, and drag the end to halfway between the two key "hips" (8.51). Repeat for the other leg.

Repeat the process to hook Stickman's hands to his body. As you place Stickman's arms and legs, think about how the body actually moves. The elbow of the pitching arm follows an obvious arc, so put it up near the top of the head rather than moving it in a straight line. You can eyeball it or, if you'd rather, go back to the curves layer and add another reference arc. (Actually, in this frame, I envision the pitching arm as almost totally straight.) His non-pitching arm ends below the elbow, and just needs a single line (8.52).

See? It's really not that hard, as long as you keep everything exactly halfway between two key frames.

To fill in the rest of the animation, repeat the process at frame 6, and then at frame 8. You'll probably want to set onion skin to one frame, rather than two, by clicking and dragging the onion skin marker brackets above the timeline. No use being distracted by extraneous frames (8.53).

This Stickman exercise has used a combination of techniques, but they all center around placing one line or curve between two others, something that the human eye is pretty good at.

We've looked at tweening a sequence of five frames (say, between keyframes at 1 and 5). You can apply this

8.53

technique to longer sequences, but not to *all* longer sequences. It also works with sequences of nine frames (keyframes at 1 and 9) and sequences of seventeen frames (keyframes at 1 and 17). Beyond that, the action is likely to be too far apart for effective tweening; add more keyframes.

Straight-Ahead Animation

Is tweening necessary? No. You can always animate "straight ahead." Draw the first frame, then the second, then the third, and so on. Straight-ahead animation tends to be more bold and spontaneous, but also much more technically challenging. (Onion skinning is your friend in straight-ahead animation, too.) But, if you are working your way from one preplanned keyframe to another, tweening is the only way to go.

ANTICIPATION AND SECONDARY MOTION

Remember, as you're tweening your characters moving from here to there, those realistic character movements, especially big movements, don't just happen: The character *anticipates* them with other movements. Anticipation is motion in the direction opposite the anticipated action. If a character is going to begin walking to the right, he doesn't just shoot off to the side; he

8.56

8.57

8.54

8.58

8.55

first leans back a little in the opposite direction (8.54), anticipating the action, and *then* starts walking (8.55).

If he's going to throw a heavy weight such as, say, a girl (8.56), he starts by swinging the weight in the opposite direction (8.57). This gives him the benefit of greater momentum when he finally swings and throws (8.58).

If a character is going to jump up in the air, he doesn't just rocket skyward; first he crouches down, bending his knees, and *then* jumps (8.59).

Andy illustrates another principle of character animation here, as well: secondary motion. All of him doesn't move at the same time, or in the same direction. Notice that as his body crouches, his arms go up. As he jumps up into the air, his arms swing down.

As he falls back to earth the process repeats in reverse, the arms swinging up as the body plunges down, then swinging down as the rest of the body straightens up (8.60).

In a realistic character, everything doesn't start and stop at the same time. Every body part doesn't arrive at the destination at once. Objects in secondary motion — be they hands, arms, beards, or clothing — don't move in sync with everything else; they're always just a little off . . . a little behind. Secondary motion adds an appealing texture to your animation.

8.59

8.60

CHAPTER 9
WALKING, RUNNING, AND CYCLING

M uch animated motion — walking, running, and pedaling a bike — is essentially repetitive. This chapter shows you how to set up repetitive motion cycles in Flash.

WALKING THE WALK

In all likelihood, your characters will spend a good deal of time walking, running, skipping, and riding bicycles here and there. The good news is that this gives you lots of opportunity to establish character; you can tell a lot about a character by the way he or she walks and moves. The bad news is that, when a character walks, all of it is moving: legs, arms, and head. A character simply walking from one side of the screen to the other can require 40 or 50 drawings.

BOPSEY MODELS

But Mark, you say, I'm only one guy. How can I do all that drawing? You don't have to, thanks in part to two guys named Bill Hanna and Joe Barbera (yes, that's Hanna-Barbera).

Way back in 1957, Hanna and Barbera lost their jobs directing motion picture cartoons for MGM. But, while motion picture animation was drying up, television animation was hungry for material (just like the Web is today).

TV's demand for material was far greater than motion pictures'. Instead of an hour of animation a year, Bill and Joe suddenly found themselves needing to produce an hour of animation every *week*. Necessity being the mother of invention, they perfected a new way of working, using new xerography technology and

Convincing walks are the most difficult aspect of animation to achieve, but once the art of animating a walk is mastered, it is never forgotten.

TONY WHITE, *THE ANIMATOR'S WORKBOOK*
(NEW YORK: WATSON-GUPTILL PUBLICATIONS, 1988)

© 2000, Leslie Cabarga

a technique of limited animation where animations were assembled from libraries of parts—heads, bodies, legs, and so forth—with as few new drawings made as possible. (That's why, you'll recall, Yogi Bear wears a necktie: it lets the animator slip his head in behind a separate body without an obvious seam showing.)

This technique is variously called cut-out animation, planned animation, or limited animation—although limited animation is certainly not limited to cut-outs. There's no standard name for characters built from cut-outs, but Flash cartoonist Ibis Fernandez calls them "Bopsey models," so I will too, 'cuz I like it.

This technique is certainly abused often, including by the Hanna-Barbera studios. At its worst, limited animation looks like just what they are—little cut-outs moved around into different, rote positions. Personality and expression are almost entirely eliminated; everyone moves in the same way. Performances are tepid, at best.

And yet. . . . and yet, even at its worst, limited animation is still capable of delivering a memorable cartoon; witness the enduring popularity of *Rocky & Bullwinkle*, which surely displayed some of the most egregiously sloppy animation in television history. I still own the videotapes.

Limited animation doesn't have to mean boring animation. Watch a *Ren & Stimpy* cartoon, for example, or visit John K's Web site (`www.spumco.com`) and load up a couple of episodes of the "Goddamn George Liquor Show," and you'll see some very limited animation that is definitely not boring.

Anime, too, favors extremely limited animation and still manages to be engaging and evocative (and, no, I'm not talking about *Pokemon*!).

TIP

Sometimes you want near and far, or left and right, instances of a symbol to look subtly different—a character's near and far legs, for example, or the near and far wheels on a car. Bring up the far symbol's Effect settings (Panels ➤ Effect), and use the brightness setting to make the back legs—or arms, or tires, or what have you—10 to 25 percent darker, or to change their hue a bit.

9.1

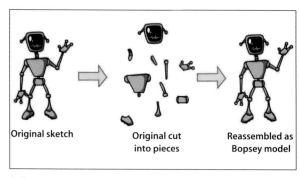

Original sketch   Original cut   Reassembled as
                         into pieces   Bopsey model

9.2

9.3

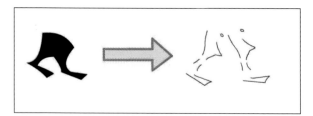

9.4

BOPSEYING YOUR BOT

Look, it's Andy (9.1). Being a robot, Andy is fairly immune to the normal cartoon rules of squash and stretch. We expect all of his parts to remain rigid and to maintain their relationships with each other. His biceps muscles don't flex, for example, when he bends his arm, because he doesn't have muscles. He's the perfect candidate for a Bopsey model.

In a Bopsey model, a character is broken into its component pieces—arms, legs, hands, and so forth. These pieces are then reassembled into a complete character (9.2).

So, basically, you draw the character, cut it apart, and then glue it back together again. By putting the parts in different positions and orientations, coupled with some judicious stretching, you can make an infinite number of poses without redrawing anything (9.3).

You can also use Bopsies as templates to "rough" out your animations, and then draw the new animation over them. For example, when I was having a hard time getting a walk cycle to come out right for Penguin, I cut his legs up (9.4) and positioned the bits to make an animation of them moving in a cycle I liked (9.5). Then I "traced" the final walk cycle over the top of them (9.6, 9.7).

To "Bopsey" a character, select each item that you will want to animate separately—arms, legs,

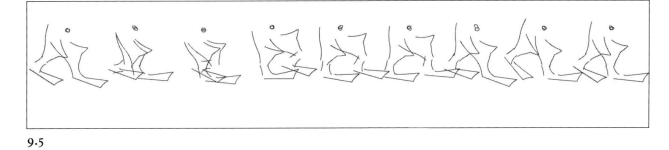

9.5

9.6

9.7

mouths, tails, and so forth. I'll cut off Andy's head (9.8). With that object and nothing else selected, choose Insert ➤ Convert to Symbol (or press F8). Give that new symbol a name, in this case, BOT head (9.9). Select Graphic behavior. It's best to give all parts belonging to a given character similar names that identify the character they go to. For example, you might name the parts BOT_Head, BOT_Torso, BOT_Upper Arm, and so forth. Even better still, you could create a new library folder for each character, and keep all of its parts in there.

Now look at your symbol. Is everything there? You may need to make small modifications, adding or extending some lines or fills that weren't completely selected, or removing some extra bits you don't want. Just double-click the symbol and edit it.

Repeat these steps until you've created a symbol for every part of your character. You'll have to judge for yourself whether you need separate symbols for the right and left arms and legs. If your character has a wooden leg, or a leg made of TV's Patrick Duffy, or if you really need the shading to be different on each side, then you'll need two of everything. In Andy's case, I've only made one hand, foot, arm, and leg, and mirrored them for the other side.

Keep these two important points in mind when you're building your Bopsey:

- **Important Point #1:** It is crucial to make sure that each part has its center in the proper place,

> ### TIP
>
> To make sure you have everything in your new symbol, move it off to one side, to make sure you indeed got all of it and nothing else. You'll often find little extra bits of line and fill lying around; odds are you won't need most of them — just select them and delete (9.10).
>
> If you use the cursor keys to move the symbol, it'll be easier to move it back into place; just keep track of how many times you press the arrow key. It's best to go in easy-to-remember 5's and 10's.

which, as often as not, isn't in the center of the object.

Here's why: symbols rotate around their centers. Draw a bone in the middle of the screen and, by default, its center is . . . well . . . in the middle. Rotate the bone, and it rotates around its center. But if that bone is, say, the thigh bone of an ani-

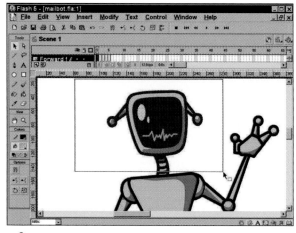

9.8

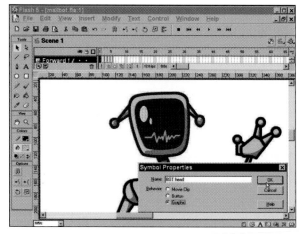

9.9

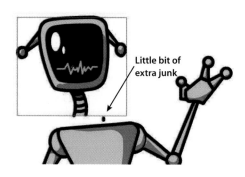

Little bit of extra junk

9.10

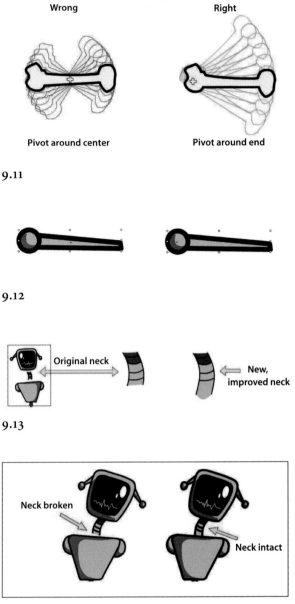

Wrong

Right

Pivot around center

Pivot around end

9.11

9.12

Original neck

New, improved neck

9.13

Neck broken

Neck intact

9.14

TIP

Sometimes you want to edit a symbol in the context of a larger scene. Perhaps you want to resize something, or adjust the position of some lines where they'll touch another symbol in the scene. Double-clicking a symbol enables you to edit it in place, in the context of the larger scene. You'll see your symbol floating in place above your scene. The rest of the scene is dimmed.

If, on the other hand, you want to edit a symbol without the distraction of the rest of the scene, right-click the symbol and choose Edit from the pop-up menu.

mated skeleton, you don't want it to pivot around its center; you want it to pivot around its top, where it attaches to the pelvis (9.11). Easily done: After you create each symbol (for instance, Andy's upper arm), edit it — either by double-clicking it or by right-clicking the symbol and choosing Edit from the pop-up menu. In the symbol editor, select everything (Ctrl+A) and drag until the desired pivot point is at the center of the symbol, denoted by the little cross (9.12).

With the pivot point properly set, you can place a symbol where you want it onscreen and then easily rotate it into position. Believe me: If you ignore this little detail, you'll spend a lot more time chasing symbols around the screen and moving them back into place every time you adjust their rotation.

■ **Important Point #2:** You will need to make most parts bigger in some way than they were on the original sketch so that you can stick them behind other parts of the model. In Bopseying Andy, for example, I've made the neck longer so that it goes down well behind the torso (9.13). That way, I can move the neck around a bit without any seams showing (9.14). If I just cut the neck out and used it, as is, any time I moved it there would be a crack showing between the neck and the chest.

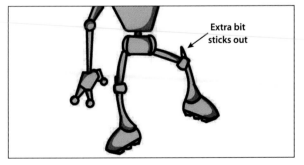

Extra bit sticks out

9.15

I've chosen to attach the neck to the head, but if I had left the neck as a separate symbol, I would have stretched it out on the top, as well, so that it went well up into the head. Make the extra "hide behind" part of your symbols larger than you'll ever need. That way, no matter how far you actually need to move it, you'll be covered. The exception, of course, is where that extra part would show: You don't want to extend the lower leg so far that it sticks out of the thigh when you bend the leg (9.15).

Now that you have your parts made, you can drag and drop them from the library onto the stage. (If the library's not open, choose Window ➢ Library.)

To keep things organized—and easy to animate—it's usually best to place each item on its own layer.

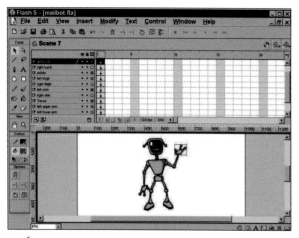

9.16

9.17

Remember that motion tweening only works on one object per layer. If you want to employ motion tweening, you'll definitely want to use separate layers (9.16).

Go ahead and take the time to label your layers—right arm, left arm, head, and so forth—so you can find everything on the first try later on.

Once everything's on the stage, you can position and rotate your elements to create whatever pose strikes your fancy (9.17).

LET'S GET WALKIN'

When a person— or a humanoid robot—walks, he (a) places his right foot in front, (b) moves his weight onto his right foot, (c) raises his body up in the air above his right foot, and then (d) pushes off with the right foot, while swinging the left foot forward to repeat the cycle on the other side (9.18).

Let's take this as the basis of our walk cycle. That gives us four frames, but we're only halfway there. The process just described is really only a half step. It starts with the right foot forward and ends with the left foot forward. You need the other half of the cycle to get back to where you started.

In a simple walk cycle, these two half-steps are

9.18

TIP

If you have a hard time selecting just the lines and fills you want, try this. Use the Lasso or Marquee tool to select all of your desired item, plus as much extra surrounding material as you need to make sure you get everything. Copy the selected material to the clipboard (Edit ➢ Copy). This time, from the menu select Insert ➢ New Symbol (or press Ctrl+F8). Give the symbol an appropriate name. In the new symbol, paste the selection from the clipboard (Edit ➢ Paste). One by one, select all the bits that should not be a part of your symbol and delete them, until only the proper bits remain.

NOTE

You can temporarily change the pivot point of a symbol by using Modify ➢ Transform ➢ Edit Center. But this transformation only applies to this one particular instance of the symbol. Other copies of the same symbol will not be affected.

exactly the same, but with the positions of the right and left arms and legs reversed. The fifth frame echoes the first frame; the sixth frame echoes the second, and so forth.

The point of a cycle is to come back to where you started. The ninth frame would be exactly the same as the first frame, but you don't have to draw it. You never draw this last frame of a cycle. In fact, if you did draw it, the animation would seem to hesitate at the end of every cycle as the two identical frames played.

As this cycle repeats, Andy's hips, and in turn his upper body and head, are alternately raised and lowered. If you traced the top of someone's head as they walked across the screen from side to side, it would be a nice curve. An even gait would produce a sine curve. Andy's a bit stiff-legged; his walk creates more of a sawtooth curve (9.19).

When designing a walk cycle, I like to start with the first pose, (a) legs scissored wide apart, the "extended position," and the third pose, (c) body raised high, the "passing position"—at the first and third keyframes. The passing position is so named because it is here that the two legs pass each other; here is where the back leg is bent the farthest.

As a bare minimum, these two poses are all you need. In fact you can get by with four frames and two

9.19

9.20

leg poses: fully extended and bent. The fully extended pose is used for both legs in the first and third frames and for the supporting leg under the body in the second and fourth frames. The bent leg pose is used for the non-supporting leg in the second and fourth frames (9.20). The second two frames are duplicates of the first two, with the positions of the left and right arms and legs reversed. Not much of a walk cycle, but it'll get you through sometimes.

Let me go a step further for Andy's walk cycle, though. It's best, although not essential, if each half-step takes an even number of frames, such as four or six. That places the key poses (for example, left foot forward and right foot forward) an odd number of frames apart, making tweening easier. We'll use the eight-frame cycle described above. At ten frames per second, that gives Andy a stride of a little more than one per second.

Alrighty, then. There's a Bopsey'd model of Andy in the movie Andy Walk.FLA. Load it up. I've already positioned all of his parts in frame 1 (9.21). (You're welcome.)

I've put in a reference line on another layer below the walk cycle elements. This is the ground line; the bottom of Andy's feet will be touching this line in every frame. Don't be shy about using reference lines, arcs, and circles. They are a huge help, and Flash makes them really easy to erase when you're done.

As you saw before, because each half-step takes four frames, the fifth frame is the same as the first, but with the right and left arms and legs reversed, so make a copy of the first keyframe at frame 5, and reverse the limbs. Right-click frame 1 in the Andy layer and select Copy Frames. Right-click frame 5 in the Andy layer and select Paste Frames.

Now, you've probably already noticed that, despite my admonitions about putting all the different parts of your characters in their own layers, this version of Andy has all of its parts in a single layer. Well, rules are made to be broken, as long as there's a good reason. Here's my good reason: I'm going to swap their order around as I work on the walk cycle; the right leg will become the left leg and vice versa. This entails swapping which parts are in front and which parts are behind, as you go, which you can't do easily if they are all on different layers.

You change the order in which objects on the same layer are stacked—which objects are behind which other objects—with Flash's Arrange command. With frame 5 selected, select each part of Andy's right arm and leg and use Ctrl+Shift+↓ (or Modify ➤ Arrange ➤ Send to Back) to send them to the bottom of the stack. The right arm and leg are now behind the body, instead of in front of the body. He looks a little funny (9.22).

Likewise, select each part of his left arm and leg and use Ctrl+Shift+↑ (or Modify ➤ Arrange ➤ Bring to Front) to move them to the top (9.23). You might

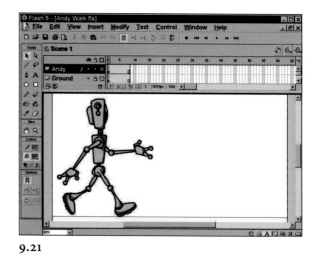

9.21

9.22

9.23

find it easier to Shift+click to select all the right-hand parts, or all the left-hand parts, and then move them *en masse*.

Use the < and > keys, or drag the playhead, to bounce back and forth between frame 5 and frame 4; you should see the arms and legs swap places (9.24).

Notice that the arms swing in the opposite direction from the legs: The right arm is forward when the right leg is back, and vice versa. This is true of all humanoid characters, including humanoid animals such as Bugs Bunny and Daffy Duck.

Select frame 3 and create a new keyframe there (F6). Rearrange Andy's parts until he is standing upright on his right leg, with his left leg bent up under him, somewhat like a stork. Position his arms near his body, halfway between their extremes. This is the passing position; Andy's arms and legs are both passing each other (9.25).

9.25

Now I have three keyframes, with one frame between each pair, a perfect arrangement for a little tweening. (If, say, your character's arms are all one piece from the shoulder to the hand, then you can use motion tweening and have Flash use motion tweening to compute the rotation of the arm from extreme to extreme. Because Andy is cut up into smaller pieces than that, I'll tween him manually.)

Select the second frame. This frame of the walk cycle is called the "recoil position." In this frame, the forward foot takes up the weight of the body, and the knee flexes. Andy has a very stiff-legged gait so his knee hardly bends in the recoil position (9.26). A character with a springier step would bend down much farther in the recoil position (9.27). In fact, it is usually the lowest point in the walk cycle — the upper body and head are closest to the ground. Depending on how bouncy your character's walk is, the forward leg can actually bend up, in the opposite direction, in

9.26   **9.27**

9.24

9.28

the recoil position, while the lower leg bends more drastically at the knee. Use onion skinning to help with positioning but, rather than worrying overmuch about tweening everything exactly halfway between the keyframes, concentrate on making a good pose.

Select the fourth frame and create a new keyframe (F6). This is what I call the "toppling" or "push-off" position. At this point in the step, the character is actually toppling forward—if you don't get his other foot around in time, he'll fall right on his face! The center of gravity is well forward of the supporting foot. The supporting foot is rolling forward onto the toe or the ball of the foot. The character is pushing off with the supporting foot, driving the body upward and forward. This is usually the highest point in the walk cycle—the upper body and head are farthest from the ground. The right arm is coming up in front, and the left arm is reappearing behind the back (9.28).

Whew! Now make sure playback is set to looping (Control ➤ Loop Playback), and watch that bad boy walk. (Press Enter, or press the Play button ⏩ on the playback controller.) At this point, the walk cycle should look pretty good. If you squint a bit, you can pretend that it's a full walk cycle, instead of only half of one. If you spot any problems—the arms seem to jerk around, or the legs don't bend enough, for instance, or you just don't like the "personality" of the animation— now is the time to change it. Edit the individual frames until you're happy with the half-step.

TIP

You can temporarily change the center and pivot point of any group or symbol for use in any particular scene. Perhaps the skeleton's thigh bone pops loose and flies across the scene; in that case, it should spin around its center. With the symbol or group selected, choose Modify ➤ Transform ➤ Edit Center from the menu. You can now drag the center to whatever point you wish—including outside of the boundaries of the symbol.

This change only applies to the current scene; it won't affect the symbol's center point in other scenes.

Now to finish up, *muy pronto*. Hold down the Ctrl key and click and drag from frame 2 to frame 4 to select all three frames. Click and hold on those frames; the cursor becomes a closed fist with a plus sign on it ▣. Continue holding down the mouse button and drag those three frames to the right, to create duplicate keyframes at frames 6, 7, and 8.

Select frame 6 and, just as before, move all the pieces of Andy's right arms and legs to the back (Modify ➤ Arrange ➤ Send to Back), and move his left arms and legs to the front (Modify ➤ Arrange ➤ Bring to Front). Repeat the process on frames 7 and 8. You're done! Press Play to watch Andy walk.

You can change this walk cycle a bit in several ways. The most obvious is probably to add additional frames, lengthening the cycle and adding extra bits of personality. I would probably start by adding a new frame between frames 1 and 2, and then another between frames 3 and 4.

You might want to move the supporting foot back behind the center of gravity a bit, making your character lean forward a bit.

As I mentioned before, you can accentuate the actions at frames 2 and 4, giving your character more knee bend ("flexion") in the recoil position, and rising up higher or leaning forward farther in frame 4, the push-off/topple position.

Experiment with how your character's arms swing. How far forward? How far backward? How much does the elbow bend? Note that the arm bends more when it swings in front of the body; it stays relatively straight when it swings behind the body. Remember that the arms swing in the opposite direction of the legs.

You can also play around with how the upper body and head tilt as the character walks. Generally, the body leans the farthest forward around the recoil position, as weight is transferred to the forward foot, and leans the farthest backward (or the least forward) around the passing position. The faster the walk or run, the farther the body leans forward of the center of gravity.

USING THE WALK

All this cool walk cycle work doesn't do much for us unless we actually have Andy walk somewhere. The

> **TIP**
>
> When doing fast runs, minimal walk cycles, and other animation cycles that play quickly with very few frames — say, five or less — try to avoid having two or more frames with identical silhouettes. Don't have the legs pass in exactly the same position going both ways, for example, or the eye will confuse them when the animation plays back.

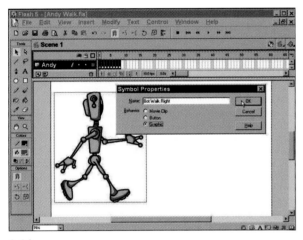

9.29

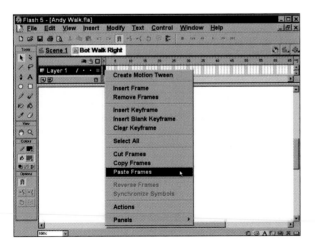

9.30

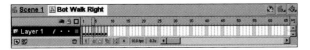

9.31

best way to do that is to convert Andy to a symbol, and then move that symbol around using motion tweening. Here's how to do this:

1. Hold down the Ctrl key and click and drag from the first frame to the last, to select every frame on the Andy layer. Right-click the selected frames and choose Copy Frames.

2. Choose Insert ➤ New Symbol (*not* Convert to Symbol) from the menu. Name the new symbol something like Bot Walk Right. Under Behavior, select Graphic (9.29).

3. In the new symbol, right-click the first frame and choose Paste Frames (9.30). The new symbol is now a copy of your walking robot.

4. Click the Scene 1 tab above the timeline (9.31) to return to the main scene.

5. Create a new scene (Insert ➤ Scene).

6. Open the library (Ctrl+L, or Window ➤ Library). Drag your new walking robot symbol onto the left side of the stage.

7. Click Frame 30, and press F6 to make a new keyframe. With the playhead at frame 30, grab Andy and move him to the far-right side of the stage.

8. Ctrl+click and drag from frame 1 to frame 30, selecting all 30 frames. Right-click the selected frames and choose Panels ➤ Frame.

9. Preview the animation. Andy walks across the stage.

Notice that Andy's feet seem to slide backward as he walks. This means he is moving across the screen too slowly to keep up with his feet. Drag the last keyframe to the left so that he moves across the stage more quickly.

If the feet seem to "skate" across the ground, the movement is too fast. Drag the end position keyframe to the right, so he takes longer. If you don't feel that Andy has enough room to move around in, make the movie wider (Modify ➤ Movie).

RUN CYCLES

This basic walk cycle has an infinite number of variations. With a little adjustment, you can transform a walk into a run, a skip, a strut. The happier, the more

confident, the character is, the farther he thrusts his chest, the higher his nose and chin (if he has them) point into the air, the wider he swings his arms to and fro. Conversely, the less confident he feels, the farther back he draws his chest, the more he humps his shoulders, the more his head droops forward.

The most common variation on the walk is probably the run (9.32). As a character runs, he tips forward. The faster he runs, the farther forward he tips. A character in a flat-out run assumes postures impossible to maintain in a simple walk; he'd fall over flat if his momentum didn't keep him up (9.33).

The faster a character runs, the farther back and higher up the back foot is when the front foot contacts the ground in the extended position. The faster a character runs, the farther back under the body the front foot is when it contacts the ground in the extended position (9.34).

Whereas, in a walk cycle, one foot is always on the ground, a running man, like a running horse, lifts both his feet from the ground at the same time. The feet both come off the ground during the extended position — the point where the feet are the furthest apart and the legs are scissored wide open (9.35) and the head and pelvis are at their highest point above the ground.

CARTOONY MOTION

Of course, not every cartoon character moves in a realistic fashion. Cartoons don't have to mimic the real world — that's why they're cartoons in the first place. Penguin's walk cycle involves only his feet (which are a separate symbol) and his swinging arms. The niceties of realistic motion are almost totally missing here.

Other walk cycles are even less realistic. Characters in *South Park* cartoons simply bounce up and down as they move across the screen; there's not even any leg motion. Ed Beals' "The Last Hula Doll" (9.36) features menacing skeletons with a wonderful, totally unrealistic walk cycle with their legs spinning in complete circles around their hips. It bears no resemblance to any kind of real-world walking, but it looks great in the context of the rest of the cartoon, which is highly stylized (9.37).

However your characters move, cycles will save you tons of animation and give you more time to spend with your friends and family.

HIERARCHIES AND NESTED ANIMATIONS

But Mark, you plead, that's still too much work. Isn't there a way to make it even easier to work with Bopsey models? Hang on to your hats: Yes, there is! With hierarchies.

A *hierarchy* is basically a branching tree. Big companies are hierarchies, with one president directing a handful of vice presidents, who in turn direct even more managers, who boss everyone else around.

Hierarchies are a way of organizing things. Our hierarchies are a way of organizing Bopsey models

9.32   9.33   9.34   9.35

9.36

© 2000 Ed Beals

9.37

© 2000 Ed Beals

for easy animation. By grouping all of the symbols together, you can keep all the parts together — so that the hand stays attached to the arm, and the feet stay attached to the legs, for example — and still position your model however you wish.

IT STARTS WITH AN ARM

This sounds pretty complicated, but it's really not that hard once you get used to working with hierarchies. Load the file Arm FK.FLA, and save it under a new name. It's one of Andy's arms (9.38), a Bopsey model with three parts.

When you create a hierarchy group in Flash, you work from the outside in, from the bottom to the top, from the children to the parent. In this case, you work from the hand back to the shoulder.

Select Andy's hand and then his forearm and group them (Ctrl+G). The forearm is referred to as the "parent" of his hand; likewise, the hand is the "child" of the forearm. When the forearm moves, it takes the hand with it. Choose Modify ➤ Transform ➤ Edit Center and drag the group's center point to the middle of the elbow joint (9.39).

The upper arm is the parent of the lower arm group so select the new lower arm group and the upper arm and group them to create an arm group. Again, adjust the group's center, moving it near the end of the upper arm (9.40). With this new group selected, select the Rotate tool and spin the arm around a bit; it should pivot around the shoulder.

Double-click the arm group. This temporarily breaks the last group apart so you can select just the forearm and hand. You can also select just the upper arm, but don't; you'll rarely want to select a parent symbol without its children. Select the grouped forearm and hand and rotate them to a new angle (9.41).

Every time you double-click an item, you move one level deeper into the hierarchy. Every time you double-click outside of a group, you move one level higher within the hierarchy.

Double-click outside of the symbol a few times, or click the Scene 1 tab above the timeline to leave nested symbol-editing mode.

A FULL HIERARCHY

Before you set up a hierarchy, you need to stop and think about how the hierarchy will work. What will

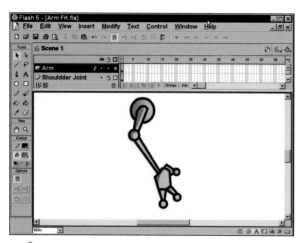

9.38

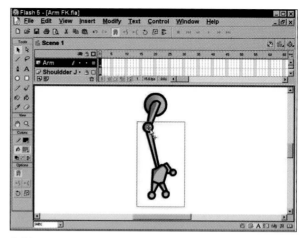

9.39

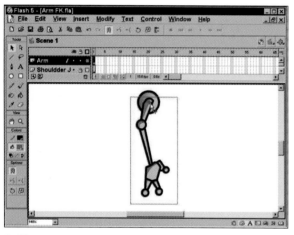

9.40

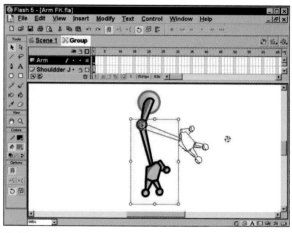

9.41

9.42

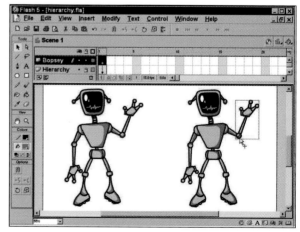

9.43

be parented to what? Should the master node be at the feet? Or at the head?

When animating human or human-like figures, remember that virtually all large body movement originates in the pelvis. The legs are said to be the children of the pelvis; that is, when the pelvis moves, the legs move. The spine and chest, or torso, are also children of the pelvis. The arms are, likewise, children of the torso. So, in one direction, the hierarchy of movement runs from pelvis to spine to chest to upper arm to lower arm to hand (9.42).

You follow roughly this same hierarchy when you group your Bopsey. Load the file Hierarchy.FLA, and save it under a new name. The first bot has been grouped into a hierarchy. The second bot is still broken into individual parts; he's been left as an exercise for the student. (You're welcome.)

To build a hierarchy, you work from the outside in. Select Andy's right hand and his right forearm and group them (Ctrl+G), just as you did for the severed arm in the last example. Choose Modify ➤ Transform ➤ Edit Center, and move the center of the new group to the center of the elbow joint (9.43). Select this new group and the upper arm, and group them together (Ctrl+G), giving you a single group for the entire arm and hand. Again, choose Modify ➤ Transform ➤ Edit Center, and move the center of the arm group to the middle of the shoulder (9.44).

Repeat the process with the left hand and arm, and then for the legs and feet, starting at the feet and

TIP

You can save a lot of menu clicking by adding a keyboard shortcut for Modify ➤ Transform ➤ Edit Center — or almost any Flash command you use often. Choose Edit ➤ Keyboard Shortcuts, and navigate your way through Modify ➤ Transform ➤ Edit Center under Commands. Press the plus sign to add a new shortcut, and press the key combo you'd like to attach to the command (9.45).

Keyboard shortcuts must include the Ctrl key.

9.45

working up to the upper leg (9.46). Remember to edit the center of every group as you create it.

Select both leg groups and the pelvis and group them to make a lower body group. Move the center to the middle of the pelvis (9.47).

Select the head, and then the neck. Group them and move the center to where the neck joins the chest. Select the head and neck group and the chest and

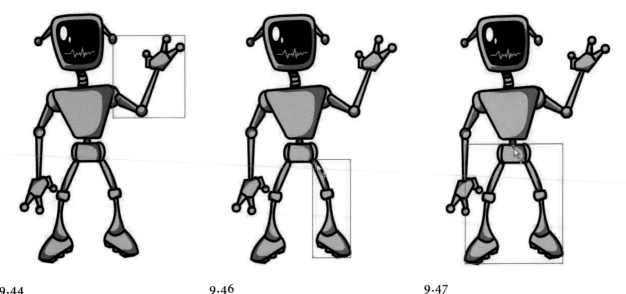

9.44   9.46   9.47

group them. Move the center to where the "spine" joins the pelvis (9.48).

Select both arm groups, and the head and chest group, and group them to make an upper body group. Again, move the center to where the "spine" joins the pelvis.

Last step: Select the upper body group (the arms, chest, and head), and the lower body group (pelvis and legs), and group them all into one final group, comprising all of the components (9.49).

Whew! It's a bit of a pain to set up, but the advantage of all this hierarchical grouping is that all your bits and pieces remain firmly locked together. Move the pelvis

9.48

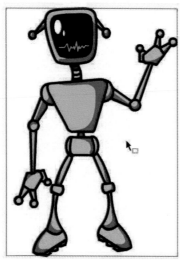

9.49

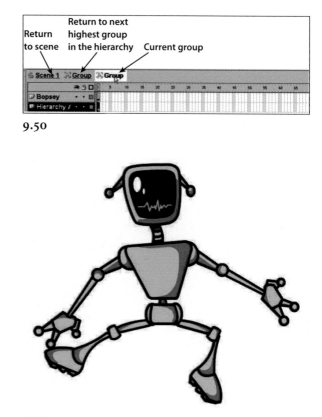

9.50

9.51

and the whole body moves. Twist the upper leg to a new position; the lower leg and foot automatically follow along. Your character becomes a poseable doll. To edit any particular part of the character, just double-click it until it is selected. Every time you double-click, you move one step farther down the hierarchy.

Now let's pose him. Double-click Andy's legs; he breaks into an upper and lower group. Double-click the legs again and he breaks into a pelvis and two legs. Rotate the right leg to a new position. If you go too far, breaking a group down too far, double-click some empty space outside the character to "back up." You can also click the next to last Group tab above the stage to back up one level (9.50).

Click the left leg group once to select it. Rotate it until the thigh is in a new position. To bend the left leg, double-click the lower leg to break the leg into upper and lower groups. Select the lower leg and rotate it into its new position (9.51). Enjoy!

CHAPTER 10
FACIAL ANIMATION

Facial animation, including lip sync, is often the most intricate activity in a cartoon. In fact, in very simple cartoons, it is sometimes nearly the *only* animation.

MAKING MULTIPLE MOUTHS AND SUCH

One trick to fast facial animation in Flash is to use libraries of symbols — eyes, mouths, even entire heads — and swap individual symbols in and out as you animate. Follow these steps:

1. When you make multiple instances of a particular item — say, a number of different mouth shapes — *do not* draw them all from scratch. Rather, start by creating a single instance, such as Mouth Default (10.1).

2. Now, instead of drawing the next mouth or whatever from scratch, duplicate that default symbol by right-clicking on the symbol's name in the library and choosing Duplicate Symbol from the pop-up menu. Give the symbol a useful name, such as Mouth Smiling (10.2).

3. Don't delete the old shapes. Rather, set all the existing layers to Guide (Modify ➤ Layer). Remember that Guide layers don't show up in your final animation; they're just there for reference. Lock these Guide layers so you can't accidentally alter them. You may want to switch them to outline mode so it's easier to see your work (10.3).

4. Create new layers for your new symbol and draw its elements (10.4). Copy and paste any elements you need from the Guide layers into your

[An] animator has on enormous range of facial expressions. He often studies these expressions in a mirror so he will be better able to draw them. Every expression is based on four factors: the eyebrows, the eyes, the eyelids, and the mouth/cheek area. All affect the expression and they must all work together.

PRESTON BLAIR, *CARTOON ANIMATION*
(LAGUNA HILLS, CA: WALTER FOSTER PUBLISHING, 1995)

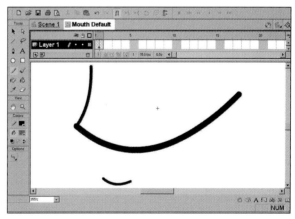

10.1

10.2

new layers. Use Edit ➤ Paste in Place to drop them exactly in the same place.

Under no circumstances should you reposition anything from one symbol to the next, unless that movement is a necessary part of the symbol. That is, if you want symbols for Eyebrows Raised and Eyebrows Lowered, then it's okay for eyebrows to move up and down between them. But you don't usually want the eyes and nose moving around within the face.

Why? As you'll see in a bit, you can easily swap symbols around while you're animating but only if you're careful to keep everything properly aligned. If you draw each mouth "more or less" in the middle of the page, when you try to swap them later, they will jiggle unattractively.

To that end, it's often helpful to include elements that won't be part of the finished symbol, just to give you a reference. If you're creating mouths, for example, it can be handy to include the nose, or the outline of the head, to aid you in fitting the mouth properly within the face (10.5). You might even want to add extra reference lines, the eye line, or the center line of the face. Because they're on Guide layers, these extra elements don't appear in the final animation anyway.

ONE STEP BEYOND

It's often handy to take the idea of extra, guide parts to the next level:

1. Build the entire face with all its separate parts—ears, noses, eyes, glasses, hair, and so on—on the main stage.
2. Select every frame on every layer and copy them.
3. Create a new symbol called, say, Eye. Paste the copied frames into the new symbol.
4. Adjust the face so that its center is where you want it to be, probably the neck somewhere.
5. Now, turn every layer into a Guide layer (Modify ➤ Layer and set Type to Guide) *except* for the layer holding the eye, or whatever part you wish to start with (10.6).
6. Select your new symbol in the library, right-click it, and choose Duplicate. Give the new symbol a name such as, say, Ear.

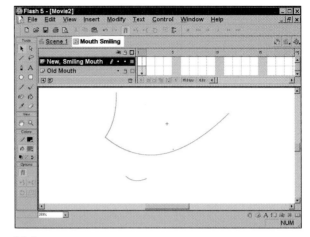

10.3

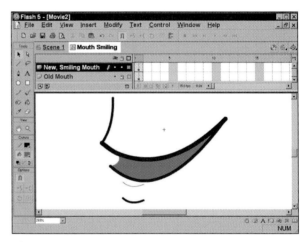

10.4

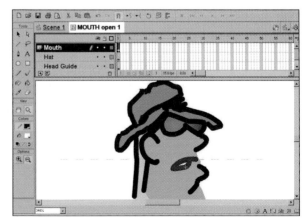

10.5

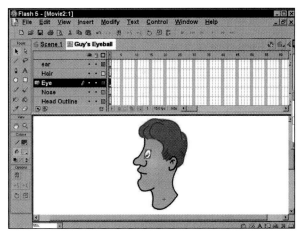

10.6

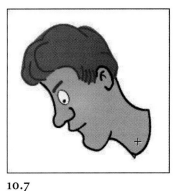

10.7

10.8

NOTE

You can embed sound — such as dialogue — into a symbol, but that sound only plays in the final movie if the symbol is a movie clip. Sound embedded in a regular graphic symbol does not play in the movie.

7. Edit the Ear symbol, but this time make every layer a Guide layer *except* the Ear layer.

You get the idea. It doesn't really matter whether you start with the ear or the nose.

The advantage here is that every part of the face shares the same center. You can build your face (or body, or airplane, or what have you) on separate layers but the parts all snap together on their common center and, when you rotate them, they all rotate around the same center. You can grab your eyes, glasses, hair, ears, nose, and so forth, rotate them all individually by the same amount on separate layers, and they all stay lined up when you're done (10.7) and properly attached to the rest of the body.

Once you have a library of different eyes, mouths, and so on, swap them around at random (10.8). You'll be amazed at the variety of expressions you can obtain with only half a dozen of each.

SWAPPING SYMBOLS

Once you have a library of mouths — and other bits — it's easy to swap them, one for another. Open the file Fisherman.FLA, and save it under a new name. This is a little snippet from my cartoon about a fisherman (10.9). The fisherman only has a few mouth shapes — he isn't a very expressive speaker.

Look for the layer called Voice. You'll see that Flash displays a small copy of the actual sound waveform on the timeline. Right-click frame 10 of the Voice layer, the beginning of the keyframe containing the sound clip, and choose Panels ➢ Sound to bring up the Sound panel (10.10). Note that this sound is set to Sync: Stream. You almost always want your voice tracks set to stream. Flash tries to keep the rest of the movie in sync with a streaming sound. If the anima-

10.9

10.10

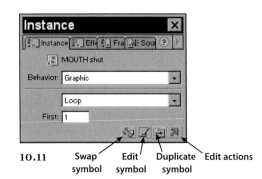

10.11   Swap   Edit   Duplicate   Edit actions
        symbol   symbol   symbol

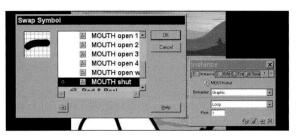

10.12

TIP

Break long bits of dialogue into smaller pieces. It gives you more freedom in adjusting your animation's timing, and allows the processor to "rest" during silences.

tion lags behind the sound, Flash skips frames to keep them synched up.

Streaming sounds have another useful feature that helps in setting up lip-sync: you can "scrub" streaming sounds on the stage. That is, you can grab the playhead and drag it back and forth to hear the sound backward and forward, slow or fast, listening to when individual sounds and silences happen. Try it now. Cool huh?

Alrighty. Select the layer named Mouth. Move the playhead to frame 10 and insert a new keyframe (F6). This is the frame in which the fisherman begins to speak. Now it's time to get him a new mouth.

With the playhead still on frame 10, click the fisherman's mouth once to select it. Right-click the mouth and choose Panels ➤ Instance (10.11). At the bottom of the Instance panel are four little buttons. Click the first of these buttons, the Swap Symbol button, to bring up the Swap Symbol panel (10.12). From here, you can replace the current mouth symbol with any other symbol in the library.

You can see how handy it is to give all the mouths similar names and put them in their own folder; it saves you scrolling through the entire library looking for the mouth you want.

TIP

Take the viewer's eye away from the minimal mouth animations with the old magician's trick of misdirection: Give viewers something else to look at. In "Fishin' Ain't So Bad," I gave the fisherman a cigarette to smoke. As he talks, the cigarette bounces up and down in his mouth, lending motion, emphasizing the dialogue, and drawing the eye away from the cartoon's minimal facial animation.

Select another mouth symbol. (Flash *should* give you a preview of the new mouth, but it doesn't always. If you don't like the new mouth, you can always swap it out again for another one.) Double-click the new symbol, or click OK, to perform the swap. The fisherman opens his mouth (10.13).

Any mouth (or other symbol) you swap in inherits whatever scaling, rotation, and transformation the original symbol had. Even if you've scaled the fisherman's head up or down, or flipped him left for right, the new mouth drops into place perfectly. This is why it's so important to build all your mouths, eyes, and so on so that they are centered in the same place.

Go through the scene, adding new keyframes and swapping in new mouths until you are happy with

---

TIP

Put your thumb under your chin and say the dialogue slowly and distinctly. Notice when your chin moves down. These are the big accents. You really need to catch these.

10.13

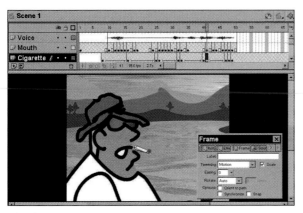

10.14

SOUND SYNC

Event: An event sound plays when the playhead reaches its starting keyframe. Event sounds always play all the way through, even if the movie stops. An event sound must be played from the beginning. If the movie jumps to the middle of an event sound, the sound won't play. You can use the same event sound — say, birds chirping in the background — as many times as you want without paying any size penalty: Flash only embeds a single copy of an event sound.

Stream: Flash tries to synchronize streamed sounds with the animation. If playback falls behind, the Flash player skips frames to catch up. Stream sounds stop if the animation stops. You can jump to the middle of a streamed sound and the sound plays from that point. If you use the same streaming sound multiple times, Flash embeds a copy of the sound file for each time it is used in the movie, potentially inflating your file size very quickly.

Start: Start is the same as Event, unless the sound is already playing, in which case Flash starts another copy of the sound.

Stop: Stops the sound from playing.

---

the result. Remember that you can scrub back and forth to check the synchronization of the sound with the mouth movement.

For extra credit, add some more keyframes to the Cigarette layer, and move the cigarette around in the fisherman's mouth as he talks (10.14). This technique works to swap in different heads, eyes, hats, wings . . . whatever you want.

LIP SYNC AND JAW SYNC

Lucky for you, Flash cartoons aren't expected to have very precise lip sync. In fact, as is often the case, less is more. You're better off with three or four distinct mouth shapes, which change relatively infrequently, than with a dozen or more similar mouth shapes that change precisely with the dialogue.

TIP

As a rule, avoid Shape Morphing's Angular Blend option; stick to Distributive Blending.

South Park uses only a few rude mouth shapes, which are shared by almost every character on the show. Still, the lip sync works and gives the impression of following the dialogue closely because those few mouth shapes are sufficiently different and expressive, and because they fall on the right beats.

The Cartoon Network's Johnny Bravo is an excellent study in the use of a few strong poses and mouth positions to put across a story. Johnny often delivers long lines of dialogue ("Hey look, Mister. Don't force me ta whip ya right here!") using only two or three mouth shapes, properly timed. Of course, it helps that the series affects a stylized look, and that Johnny always talks out of the side of his mouth like a bad Elvis impersonator.

PHONEMES AND EXPRESSIONS

Phonemes are the basic sounds that make up spoken language: "Sssssss" and "Ooooo," for example. English comprises around 44 phonemes . . . depending on what part of the country you're from. Certain phonemes dictate certain mouth positions. Say, "eeeeeeeeeeeeeeeee" and notice how your mouth changes shape, how your lips open up, how your upper teeth become exposed. Say "rrrrrrrrrrrrrrr" and notice how your lips purse. The cheeks stay put or go up, possibly impinging on the eyes. The top lip can slide up to reveal the upper teeth. The jaw can

move up and down—a little or a lot. Some sounds require virtually no jaw movement. Lips can purse or stretch wide.

In cartoon animation, there are only about nine standard mouth shapes, depending on who you ask. All other mouth actions are composed of either in-betweens or a combination of the basic nine. Fellow Flasher Ibis Fernandez has an informative article on cartoon phonetics. Give it a read at `www.ibisfernandez.f2s.com/pages/17.htm`.

Many books include charts showing the mouth positioned for various phonemes. I've found these to be less useful than I initially expected. In my experience, you're better off building a good library of mouth shapes for your character, in a variety of expressions, and then browsing through it later for the mouth that "looks right" at any given keyframe (10.15). Add to the library any time you need a new mouth.

Buy a little pocket mirror to keep at your workstation. Recite the lines you're animating while watching your mouth in the mirror. Does your chin move noticeably? Do your lips purse outward? (Give Grandma a big kiss!) Do they pull back to reveal your teeth? Do your cheeks hold still? Or pull up and outward (Smile!)?

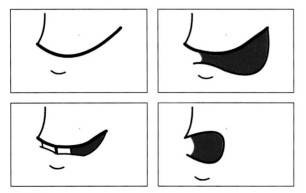

10.15

10.16

© 2000, Dave Jones, www.transcience.com

R's and w's entail a distinctive pursing of the lips. If you're going to put extra effort into some mouth shapes, do it here. Don't overdo lip sync. Dialogue that is over-animated looks odd. The vast majority of Flash cartoons delivers dialogue with the benefit of only a very few mouth shapes.

And remember, if you're publishing in Flash SWF format, there's no way to guarantee precisely what rate your animation will be played back at. Don't spend hours meticulously perfecting lip sync that won't play back reliably anyway. The exception to this rule is when you are transferring your animation to video or film, which *do* have guaranteed playback rates.

Generally speaking, there's no sound unless the mouth's open. Bang the mouth open on the vowels and you're 90 percent of the way there.

SMOOTH MOVES

You can make wonderful, believable head movement with simple motion, coupled with scaling and rotation. Let's take a look at a character from Dave Jones's wonderful "Teetering" (included on the CD-ROM that accompanies this book). Here, the girl's head turns— a simple movement (10.16).

This printed sequence doesn't really do the cartoon justice, so load up "Teetering" from the Movies folder and watch it now. Notice how round and three-dimensional the characters' heads look when they move, despite being made of the simplest circles and lines.

Jones has made every element into its own symbol, and kept every symbol on its own layer (10.17). Good for him! This makes it easier to move each ele-

ment individually, and Jones makes great use of the capability.

For example, take away everything but the outline of the head, and you can see that its motion is a simple skewed rotation. Viewed by itself, it doesn't look very 3D at all (10.18).

Likewise, the hair on her head is simply moved, stretched, and skewed (10.19). As the girl's face rotates, the hair on the right side of her head (on your left) comes toward you. The hair moves

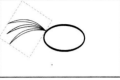
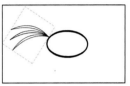
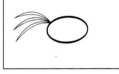
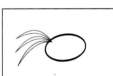
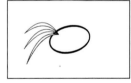

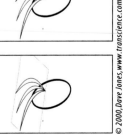

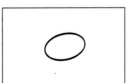
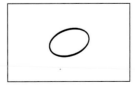
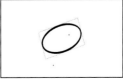

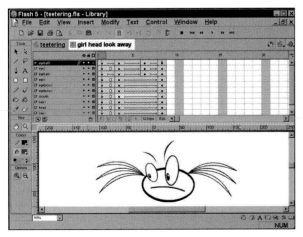

10.17

© 2000, Dave Jones, www.transcience.com

10.18

10.19

© 2000, Dave Jones, www.transcience.com

NOTE

Shape hints don't show up unless the layer containing them is the currently selected layer. Otherwise, you won't see anything.

from left to right. Jones scales it up to almost twice its vertical height and also skews the hair to point downward rather than to the side. It looks narrower as the eye sees it from the side rather than the front.

Here's the point: nothing is redrawn here. The same hair symbol suffices for the entire animation. In fact, every symbol used here is used elsewhere as well, making it, in effect, free.

In fact, as you might have guessed, both pigtails are actually the same symbol, as are both eyes. This helps keep the animation very small. Teetering runs three minutes and yet weighs in at under 300K, including 30K of sound. Jones has created an effective, evocative animation with a very small byte size by using simple motion tweening, scaling, and skewing on a collection of reusable library symbols — themselves merely lines and circles.

Don't get me wrong: I'm not saying that because the shapes are simple and the operations are basic, that it was *easy* to make this animation. Far from it. But, because the shapes and techniques employed are so basic, it's easy to see just how a given effect is accomplished.

NOTE

Remember that if you're having trouble seeing what's going on where different lines join, you can switch to outline mode. In outline mode, the thickness of the lines doesn't obscure your view. If the outline color is hard to see — and it usually is — choose Modify ➢ Layer and change the outline color to black.

SHAPE TWEENING SIMPLE LINES

Flash's shape tweening sometimes seems to have a mind of its own. Follow these simple rules to stay in control, and save yourself a lot of grief:

1. Break your character up into its separate components and put each of these on a separate layer.
2. Drag all of the components around to assemble the first keyframe of the movement.
3. Create another set of keyframes, maybe 10 frames down the track.
4. Drag all of the components around to assemble the final keyframe of the movement.
5. In-between every thing that moves between the two endpoints (using shape tweening for shapes and motion tweening for symbols).

See if it works. If it works, then do the following:

6. Increase or decrease the number of frames between the two endpoints to get the timing right.

7. You can alter the ease in and ease out property of the tweening to make the movement more realistic (giving the character weight).

If it doesn't work ... because it just doesn't look right, do this:

7a. Add another set of keyframes in the middle and reposition the components so that they look the way you want them to. Check the movement again. Keep adding sets of keyframes until you are happy with the way it looks. (More complicated movements may require a lot of sets of keyframes.)

If it doesn't work ... because the lines do funny things (flipping etc.), do this:

7b. You can add a shape hint to one of the ends of the line for both keyframes of the movement. (Look in Modify, Transform for this.) Check it again and see if it works. Keep adding shape hints to points on the line until it does.

Thanks to Dave Jones, www.transcience.com.au.

TIP

Your characters' eyes shouldn't just slide from side to side when they move; rather, they should follow a shallow curve. Eyes that move in a straight line seem to slide unrealistically (10.20).

SHAPE MORPHING DO'S AND DON'TS

For the very smoothest animation of heads and other body parts, without having to draw hundreds of frames by hand, you'll want to explore Flash's shape tweening. Revisit Chapter 2, which discusses the importance of controlling the lines and curves that make up your shapes. This is nowhere more important than when you are planning to employ shape tweening.

Shape tweening, as the name implies, is similar to motion tweening except that it changes the actual shape of the object. You can change a star into a circle, one letter into another, and so on. You can also change a smile into a frown, or a straight arm into a bent one.

The shape tweening part of Flash isn't especially smart; it's easy to confuse it. Shape tweening can produce some wonderfully smooth animation effects, but it can also produce a jumbled mess (10.21). Which is okay, if you don't mind, but in character animation, you usually mind.

This jumbling can even occur when shape tweening occurs between two similar shapes (10.22).

The most likely culprits are little bits of line, almost impossible to see,

that can be left behind by the normal process of drawing and painting in Flash.

Let's take a look at the shape of Penguin's head (10.23). If I zoom way, way in on the tip of Penguin's beak, you can see a hint of the problem (10.24). There's a weird little "wart" sticking up near the tip.

If I switch to outline mode and zoom in to the maximum 2,000 percent, you can see, sure enough, that there's an extra little loop there (10.25). This is what's messing up the morph.

The easiest way to fix this problem is to select and cut out the entire area in question, and then reattach the remaining line segments to get a clean join.

These little bits and snips and invisibly small loops occur all the time in Flash when you join lines together. The more lines you're bringing together, the more likely they are to occur. They aren't usu-

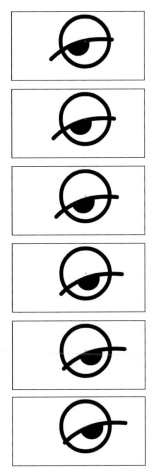

10.20

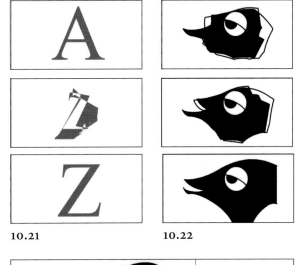

10.21

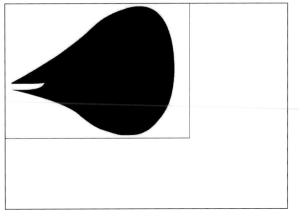

10.22

10.23

TIP

The nose should always be pointing in the direction a character is looking. Otherwise the character is going to look very strange.

ally a big problem, although they add a little bit to your file size, but when you are doing shape tweening, they can be deadly!

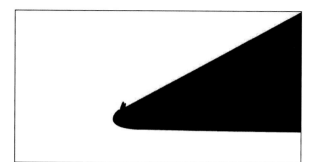

10.24

TAKE A HINT

Sometimes, no matter how carefully you build your characters, no matter how you curse, Flash just won't perform your motion tween the way you want it to. It's time to give it a hint. Shape *hints* identify the same point in both the beginning shape and the ending shape, telling Flash, in effect, *this* goes *there*. Here's an example: I've added three shape hints to Penguin's face to keep Flash from growing confused (10.26).

Once in place, shape hints turn either yellow, if they are on the beginning keyframe, or green, if they are on the ending keyframe. A shape hint that's red has not been properly positioned (10.27).

To add a shape hint, choose Modify ➤ Transform ➤ Add Shape Hint. Click and drag the shape hint to the appropriate point on your shape. Shape hints usually work best when you butt them at corners where lines meet.

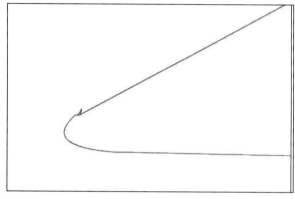

10.25

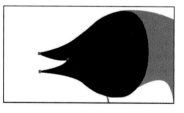

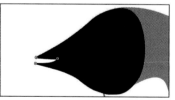

10.26

SMOOTH SHAPE MORPHING

The animations of Flasher Vaughn Anderson feature smooth, lifelike motion. Where Mr. Jones primarily uses motion tweening in his facial animations, Mr. Anderson achieves his patented facial animation via a combination of motion tweening and clever shape morphing.

NOTE

Grace shows us, again, that the eyes always lead the head (in voluntary motion, anyway). Grace's eyes look to the side before she turns her head (10.28).

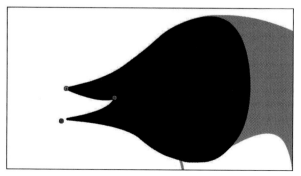

10.27

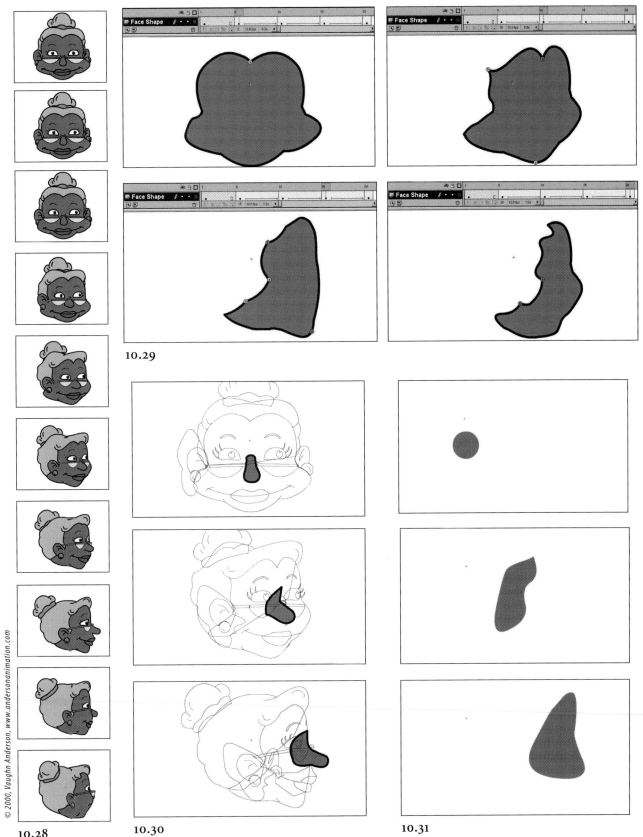

10.29

10.28

10.30

10.31

© 2000, Vaughn Anderson, www.andersonanimation.com

NOTE

It's easy to become so enamored of Flash's various flavors of morphing that you spend much more time trying to set up a morph than you would need to draw a couple of in-between frames.

Here's Grace, again (10.28). (You'll find this animation on the CD-ROM, as grace_st_43_a_va.SWF.) Grace has the look of frame-by-frame animation, but achieves it with careful keyframing and tweening.

Here, for example, is the shape of Grace's face (10.29). You can see that the motion derives from three shape tweens.

By building the shape out of a few carefully controlled lines, Vaughn is able to get shape tweening to work reliably. You'll notice that he's had to use very few shape hints.

Sometimes lines need to appear and disappear, and sometimes shape tweening produces weird artifacts

TIP

Play it, play it, play it. When developing a sequence of animated motion, do yourself the favor of bringing up the Controller (via the Window menu) and pressing those buttons often. Better yet, set Control ➤ Loop Playback, and pour through the sequence over and over again. Study it. Refine it. Mold it like clay. You might be surprised how sophisticated an animator you already are. And you thought you were just veggin' out, watchin' those 'toons.

Thanks to Peter Sylwester for this tip.

and "extra bits" that you can do without. Consider Grace's nose (10.30). At the beginning of the turn, it is almost completely outlined. But by the end of the animation, only part of the nose is outlined; the rest blends seamlessly into her face.

How'd Vaughn do that? With a little cheat called a "cover." A *cover* is a little blob of color that masks something ugly in your cartoon.

The cover goes on a separate layer, above the offending item, and hides the naughty bits from view. This is the cover for Grace's nose, for instance (10.31).

It is the same color as her skin and, therefore, effectively invisible. Its shape tweens right along with the nose, hiding progressively more as the tween unfolds. The effect is that it hides the extra lines, making for a lovely combined morph (10.32). Look again at Grace (10.28) to see how nicely this works. You can use this technique for more than faces; it can hide unwanted lines anywhere in your animation. Don't be afraid to use covers in any situation, morph or non-morph, where you need to hide certain bits from view.

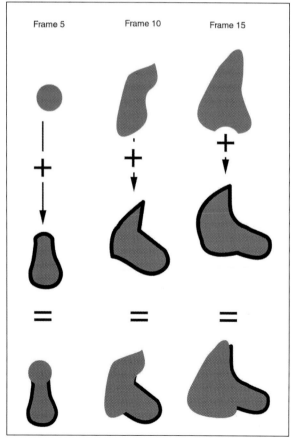

Frame 5   Frame 10   Frame 15

10.32

CHAPTER 11
LAYOUT, STYLE, AND CAMERA MOVES

You've storyboarded, designed your characters, and worked out their basic animations . . . now it's time to fill in some actual scenes. To fill in some backgrounds, drop in some characters and watch the whole thing go.

THINK

The first step in staging a scene is to . . . think. Why is this scene here? What purpose does it serve within the larger cartoon? Are you establishing a setting? Building tension? Why are your characters here? What are they doing, and why? How can you best put across the important ideas and business? If you've storyboarded your animation, award yourself a gold star because you will have already given these questions a lot of thought.

Be clear in your own mind about every scene's purpose. If this scene doesn't add something definite to your cartoon, if it doesn't move your story along, drop it.

Look for opportunities to get depth and perspective and avoid too many scenes in a row that are flat-on.

FRANK THOMAS AND OLLIE JOHNSTON, *THE ILLUSION OF LIFE: DISNEY ANIMATION* (NEW YORK: HYPERION, 1995)

Call it composition, call it layout, call it design — it all adds up to one vitally important point: you've got to put your picture together so that it's pleasing to the eye and it gets its message across clearly and interestingly.

STAN LEE AND STEVE BUSCEMA, *HOW TO DRAW COMICS THE MARVEL WAY* (NEW YORK: SIMON & SCHUSTER, 1984)

> **TIP**
>
> How your characters relate to each other and to their environment is of paramount importance. Keep your eye out for potential shots that show viewers the size of your characters, and their sizes relative to each other.

© Vaughn Anderson 2000

When you're laying out the scene, make sure you leave yourself enough room to accommodate all the action you'll be animating.

BACKGROUNDS

Now is the time to finalize decisions on your backgrounds, as well. What does this background need to establish? The background is as important as the characters in establishing the style of your cartoon. What look are you striving for? Realistic (11.1)? Highly stylized (11.2)? Intricate (11.3)? Simple? No background at all (11.4)?

11.3

© 2000, Peter Richardson

11.1

Copyright 2000, Wish Tank Studios, LLC

11.2

© 2000, Ed Beals, www.edbeals.com

BITMAPPED BACKGROUNDS

A common misconception is that vector images consume less memory than bitmapped images. This is not always the case.

For "Lovely St., Kickin' n Streamin'," we wanted a softer feel for the backgrounds. The only way to really achieve the look we were going for was to use a bitmapped image.

When we sit down and look at the overall show, we carefully go over the storyboards and see where we can "trick" the audience. Where can we reuse animation or backgrounds? Figure this out early and you'll be able decide where you can really put the juice.

In "Kickin' n Streamin'" there are only three backgrounds. By using the backgrounds in creative ways — blurred, close-up, and cropped — we're able to keep the final file size down and still make our audience believe we have a number of separately painted backgrounds. Hopefully, they'll forget they are watching a Flash movie (11.5).

Thanks to Bryan Byers of Wish Tank Studios.

LINE WEIGHTS AND COLORS: SEPARATING FOREGROUND FROM BACKGROUND

In almost every case, you want to use color and line to visually separate your characters and other important foreground objects from the background. You want this (11.6). Not this (11.7). Cartoons generally use thicker, heavier lines to outline the characters than to outline the background elements.

11.4 © 2000, Tobias Wolf

11.6

11.5 © 2000, Wish Tank Studios, LLC

11.7

Movement can also break a foreground character away from the background. A character that is in constant motion is fairly easy for the eye to track. (Of course, let it sit still for a moment and it might blend back in, again.) Less obvious, perhaps, is that a character who holds still against a constantly moving background also "pops out." The fisherman in "Fishin' Ain't So Bad" barely moves at all as he delivers his long monologue on hunting and fishing. The lake in the background behind him, on the other hand, is in constant motion — the reflected colors of the sunset sky twisting as the lake's surface ripples (11.8). (The lake

11.8

surface is a 22-frame animation that I created in Photoshop and then brought into Flash as a bitmap sequence.)

> **NOTE**
>
> Gradient fill backgrounds are surprisingly CPU-intensive. Dropping a gradient fill in behind your scene can really slow the playback.
>
> Thanks to Vaughn Anderson for this note.

STRONG POSES AND SILHOUETTES

Don't just drop your characters into a scene; pose them. As much as possible, make a character's every pose a strong pose. Even moving from keyframe to keyframe is, in essence, moving from pose to pose.

What is a strong pose? First and foremost, a strong pose is easy to *read:* it's easy for the viewer to interpret the pose. Here, for example, is Andy preparing to pull a stable operating system out of a hat (11.9). This pose is terrible; it's jumbled up and hard to interpret. Granted, in the middle of a cartoon it would be clear to viewers what's going on — they would have seen Andy pick up the hat; they'd see his hand waving and so on — but that's no excuse for a crappy pose. (Walt Disney would never have set still for it; I'll guarantee you that!) Here's a much clearer pose of the same action (11.10).

The best way to judge how well a pose reads is in silhouette. The silhouette of the first pose is clearly inscrutable (11.11). The silhouette of the second pose reads very well in silhouette (11.12).

Always build poses that are clear, even in silhouette (11.13). Strive to make your whole cartoon so clear that viewers could follow the action even if the entire cartoon was rendered in silhouette.

Beyond being easy to read, strong poses are visually interesting — they have drama.

SCENE SILHOUETTES

Scenes have silhouettes, too: patterns of light and dark, of figure and background, that define how the viewer "reads" the entire image (11.14). Pay attention

> **TIP**
>
> Don't forget, amid the myriad technical details of putting together an animation, to, as Frank Thomas and Ollie Johnston put it in *The Illusion of Life*: Disney Animation, "put the juice in it." Concentrate on the individual actions, timing, and expressions that give life to the action.

to every scene's silhouette. Can the eye easily pick out the major props and characters? Is the layout clear? Do viewers know what they're looking at?

Some cartoon characters (11.15), because of their design and construction, can do very little posing in and of themselves. It is even more important with these characters to pay attention to your staging — where everything is onscreen, how the characters and background work together, where the viewer's eye is directed (11.16).

11.9

11.10

11.11

11.12   **11.13**

11.14   © 2000, Wish Tank Studios, LLC

11.15   © 2000, Ed Beals

NOTE

It takes a viewer several seconds to comprehend a new scene. Wait a bit before you start flinging things around.

11.16   © 2000, Ed Beals

TIP

Here's a quick way to check how well your layout "reads" in silhouette: Squint at it. Squint your eyes, more and more, until you can barely make out the broad shapes and colors of your image. Is the pose still (relatively) clear? Is your eye still drawn to the intended focal point? Do the foreground characters stay visibly separate from the background?

CAMERA MOVES

After a lifetime in a video-saturated environment, you and I have learned the language of camera moves and editing techniques. You can tell that two people are talking to each other, even if you only see one at a time. You can tell that someone's being followed, or that two cars are going to collide, or that a bomb is about to explode, just by the way the scene is framed and lit, the way the camera moves, the way the action is cut together.

People understand and expect certain conventions in a movie. In Flash, there is no camera, but you can, and probably should, use the same techniques to tell your story.

NOTE

No matter what kind of camera move you are emulating, begin and end on a well-composed shot.

THE CUT

The most basic editing tool of them all is the cut. In a cut, one piece of animation is replaced by another piece of animation on consecutive frames.

You can create cuts in a number of ways:

- By creating a keyframe and replacing the objects in the scene (as in a cut from one character to another) (11.17)
- By creating a keyframe and moving or scaling objects (as in a cut to a close-up) (11.18)
- By creating a keyframe and starting and stopping different animated symbols

TIP

When you're animating a conversation, the natural place to cut is at the end of a line of dialogue. Experiment with cutting just *before* the end of the dialogue so that we still hear the first character speaking, but we already see the second character.

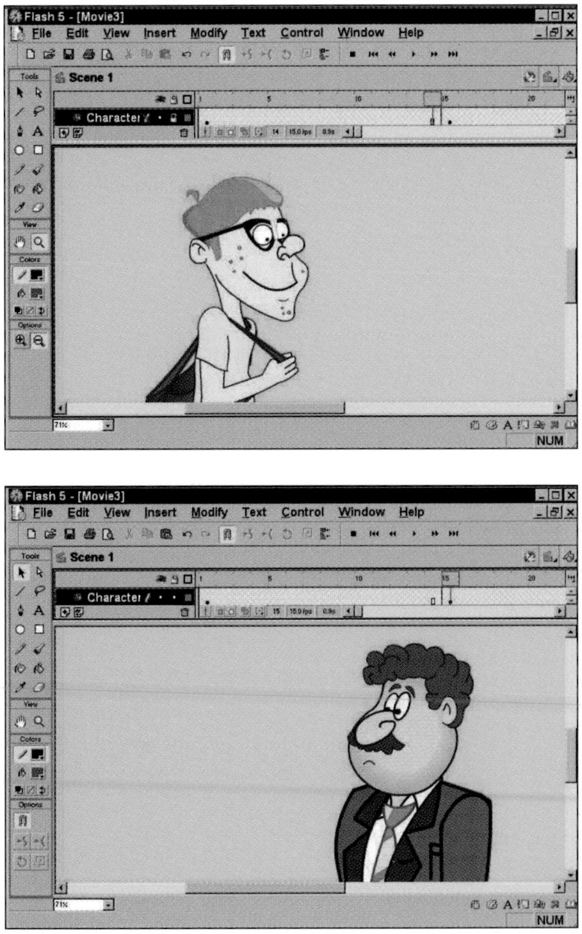

11.17

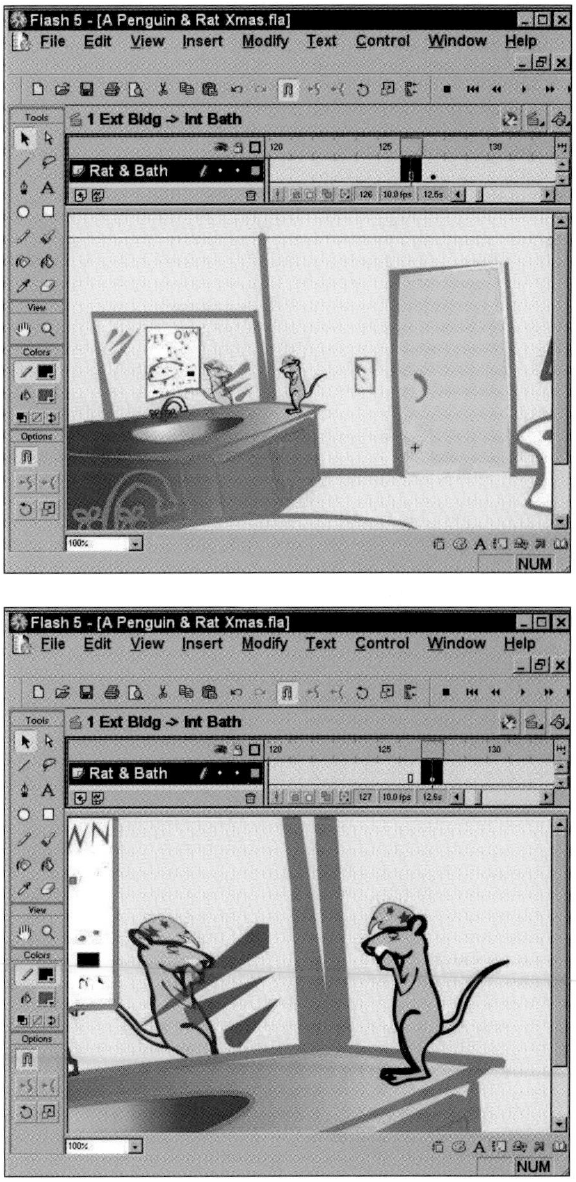

11.18

The beginning of a new scene is a natural place for a cut. If you build your actions in different scenes, then Flash automatically cuts between them on playback.

> **NOTE**
>
> **As a rule of thumb, cut on the action — the gun firing, the hand closing on the gun, the chicken laying an egg, whatever — especially when cutting from a wide shot to a closer shot. The exception to this is that when you are cutting from a close shot to a wider shot, it's usually best to cut just before the action, on the "anticipation."**

THE PAN

In a pan shot, the camera stays in one place and pivots, either left and right for a horizontal pan, or up and down for a vertical pan.

Horizontal Pan

In a horizontal pan, the camera stays in one place but rotates to the left or right. Think of a shot of a character speaking that turns to reveal an audience listening.

In a Flash cartoon, you usually fake a horizontal pan by moving all of the elements in a scene across the stage, sideways, simultaneously.

It's often easiest to construct the entire scene as a symbol and then move that symbol across the main stage with motion tweening. In this scene, the camera pans across the mall to reveal Penguin shopping. The entire scene, including the background and foreground elements, and Penguin, is a single, multilayer, animated symbol (11.19). Moving it across the stage emulates a horizontal pan (11.20).

Tilt Shot

In a tilt shot, or *vertical pan*, the camera stays in one place but tilts to point up, or down. Think of a shot that begins looking across the Grand Canyon, and then slowly tilts down to the Colorado River far below. You usually treat a tilt shot just like a horizontal pan and move all the elements in your scene simultaneously, but this time up or down.

Due to atmospheric haze, items outdoors get progressively lighter as they get farther away. In a cityscape, for example, buildings far away would appear lighter — more washed out — than closer buildings (11.21).

Panning Perspective

Simply sliding scene elements around does not mimic the change in perspective that occurs when you use real camera pans. This loss of perspective isn't a problem with shorter pans when, for example, you might pan down a wall to a mouse hole. However, it's noticeable in a long pan such as when you might pan up the side of a tall building or rocket ship. We expect a tall building to look larger at the bottom, nearer the camera, and smaller at the top, farther from the camera.

Imagine, for example, a camera 20 feet off the ground, looking down at the entrance to a high-rise office building. The camera then tilts up to take in the building's peak high above. At the beginning of the shot, looking down, perspective renders the bottom of the building smaller because it is farther from the camera (11.22). In the middle of the shot, as the camera lens comes parallel to the wall, the building doesn't show any perspective (11.23). At the end of the shot, as the camera tilts up, the perspective appears to taper the building toward the top, high above the camera (11.24). At first, the building appears to taper toward the bottom, then not to taper at all, then to taper toward the top.

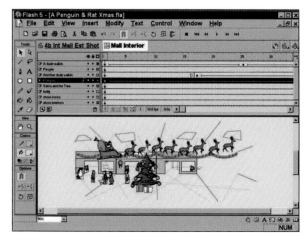

11.19

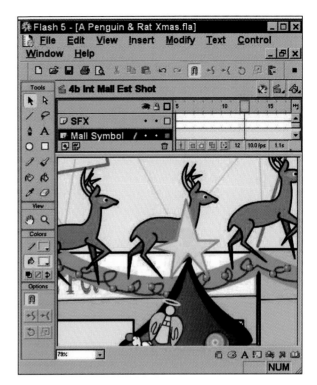
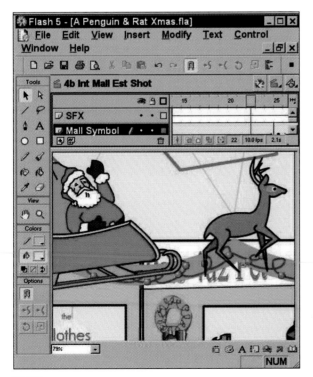

11.20

11.21

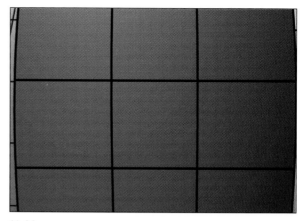

11.23

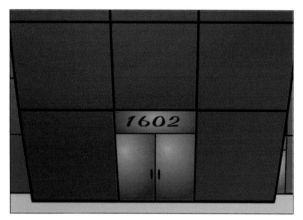

11.22

To achieve this effect, animators build their backgrounds with predistorted geometry to fool the eye into seeing the shifting perspective you'd see with a physical camera.

Here is a drawing of a simple skyscraper that tapers at the bottom, straightens out in the middle, and tapers again at the top (11.25). When you view all of the skyscraper at the same time, it looks weird. However, if you pull it slowly through the scene from bottom to top, allowing only a slice to be visible at any given time, it successfully mimics the shifting perspective we'd expect to see from our hypothetical tilt pan if we shot the skyscraper with a real camera.

The same technique can be employed for wide horizontal pans, as well (11.26).

Parallax

Hold out your arm and put up a finger (no, not that finger). Look past your finger at a faraway wall and move your head from side to side. See how your finger seems to move from side to side in relation to the wall? That's *parallax:* an apparent change in an object's position arising from a change in the observer's position. The closer an object is to you, the more pronounced the parallax shift.

Perhaps we are following Penguin as he drives along a country road. There are tall weeds on both sides of the road (11.27). As the shot progresses, the weeds nearer the camera appear to go by faster than the weeds behind the car.

The foreground goes by faster than the background because the camera can see less of it. The closer objects are to the camera's lens, the less of them the camera sees (11.28).

You can usually achieve an adequate parallax effect with only two moving layers, a foreground and a background, but the more different layers you combine, and the more skillfully you manipulate them, the more realistic the effect becomes.

Swish Pan

In a swish pan, the camera moves rapidly from one position to another, blurring the scene in between. Swish pans are sometimes used as transitions from one scene to another.

11.24

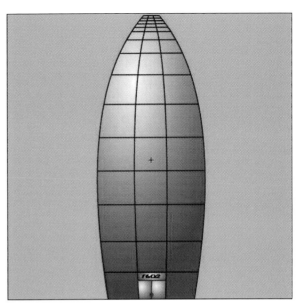

11.25

11.26

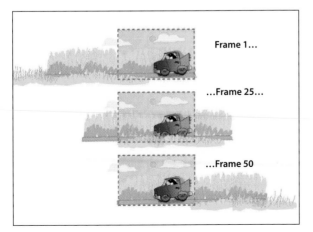

11.27

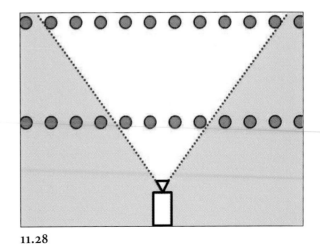

11.28

SPACEMAN BOB'S SMOOTH PERSPECTIVE

This is a scene in my cartoon "Who is Spaceman Bob?" where a spaceship flies through the city and then the camera pans down to the interior of the park.

I made each piece of the city on a different layer. The farther a city section is from the camera, the lighter I made the brightness (Panels ➤ Effects ➤ Brightness). The farthest layer back was about +80 percent. This gives the illusion of atmosphere.

I set the entry keyframe positions, and then added a new keyframe about 80 frames down, and then set the last frames. The closer the city section is to the camera, the faster and farther it moves, thus giving the impression of depth with a large pan. The

secret to having this move fast and smooth is setting the quality to low (File ➤ Publish Settings ➤ HTML).

Another trick: Using ease in and ease out makes the camera movement much smoother. Add a keyframe halfway between the beginning and ending keyframes. If your first keyframe is frame 1 and the last is frame 20, add a new keyframe at frame 10. Then add an ease in of –100 to the first tween (frames 1 to 10) and an ease out of 100 to the last tween (frames 10 to 20).

I use this technique a lot to create fluid and natural movements. Animation tends toward techno-servo-robotic movement without proper easing (11.29).

Thanks to Vaughn Anderson.

11.29   *© 2000, Vaughn Anderson, www.andersonanimation.com*

11.30   *Copyright 2000, Vaughn Anderson, www.andersonanimation.com*

To achieve a swish pan in Flash, you'll have to blur the background yourself in another program such as Photoshop, and then import the blurred background into Flash (11.30) and motion tween it moving sideways.

THE TRACKING SHOT

In a tracking shot, the camera stays focused on the main character as it moves through the scene. A tracking shot might fall along with the coyote as it plummets into a canyon, or fly alongside a rocket as it blasts into orbit, or even follow a character walking through a house.

In the real world, a tracking shot requires that the camera be mounted on wheels, or a crane, so that it can move along with the characters it's following.

In a Flash cartoon, of course, the characters don't go anywhere unless you move them so it isn't really necessary to track them. Instead, you leave the characters in the middle of the screen and move the rest of the scene — background and foreground — around them.

In this scene of Penguin driving his car (11.31), the car stays put while the background and foreground move from left to right, using simple motion tweening between two keyframes. Notice that the background is much larger than the movie frame because it has to continue moving through across the frame for the entire duration of the scene without showing an edge. The extra, off-screen parts do not show up in the final rendering.

DOLLY AND TRUCK SHOTS

In a Flash cartoon, you usually emulate a horizontal dolly or truck shot — in which the camera, mounted on wheels, rolls next to or through the action — by moving all of the elements in a scene sideways, simultaneously, just like a horizontal pan.

11.31

11.32

Dolly in and dolly out shots, however, require a little more sophisticated setup to pull off. As the camera pushes in through the scene, for example, parallax comes into play; objects seem to get larger and, if they are off-center at all, to move to the side. If you dolly in on a pair of trees, for example, they should not only grow bigger, but also move apart (11.32). Nearer objects are affected most; the farthest objects are affected the least.

Long dolly in shots are often used to establish a scene, such as pushing through a forest of trees to reveal a castle, for example.

CROSS-CUTTING AND INTER-CUTTING

Cross-cutting and inter-cutting both involve jumping back and forth between action happening in two different places that, together, make up the scene.

Cross-cutting is a device to increase tension; it usually builds toward a climax. Think of any battle scene in the movie *Braveheart*. As the two armies run toward each other, the camera shows first one army, then the other, then the first again. As the men race toward each other, the cuts grow quicker until the armies finally collide in the middle of the field. That's cross-cutting.

Inter-cutting, on the other hand, is just a device to move the story along. It's significantly less dramatic and doesn't necessarily build toward a climax. An inter-cut scene might jump between the two people having a phone conversation, for example, or between a wife working late at the office, and her husband sitting alone at home.

The easiest way to build a cross-cut or inter-cut scene in Flash is to build each half of the scene as its own animated symbol. Use keyframes to make each symbol appear and disappear as called for; one symbol should be disappearing as the other is appearing;

TIP

As long as the camera only slides sideways — left and right, up and down, in and out — and doesn't tilt or rotate, the sky shouldn't change at all. The sky is too far away for any changes in perspective to be visible.

11.33

> **TIP**
>
> You may find it easier, sometimes, to build complex symbols, such as those comprising entire scenes, on the main stage. Create a new, temporary scene to work in. When the scene is complete, select all frames on all layers, copy them to the clipboard, create a new symbol, and paste those frames into the new symbol to create a symbol copy of your scene. Now delete the temporary scene.

IRIS IN AND OUT

Want to Iris in or out? I use two different methods:

1. I make a screen-sized Background symbol with a small hole in it. I use motion tweening to zoom in until the hole is big enough (or zoom out until it's small enough).
2. I create a symbol with a number of frames (approximately 10) of a hole growing larger (or smaller). By placing this symbol in the movie timeline and using "play once" . . .

Voila!

Thanks to Xeth Feinberg, creator of Bulbo. Check out his work at www.bulbo.com.

they shouldn't overlap, nor should you leave any "dead space" with nothing on the screen.

Here's my favorite method: Drag each symbol onto its own layer. Create a keyframe on each layer, everywhere that the action will cut to that layer's symbol. For example, imagine that Andy and Penguin are playing "chicken," hurtling toward each other in cars (11.33). Penguin first appears on frame 1, and then on frame 19, frame 31, frame 40, and frame 46. Andy appears on frame 10, frame 26, frame 36, frame 43, and frame 49. (You already worked your timing out in the animatic, right? Right? Good.)

Next, you need to remove the symbol that should not be visible in the shot at each keyframe. In the example, you'd insert blank keyframes (F7, or Insert ➢ Blank Keyframe) on the Bot car layer everywhere there's a keyframe on the Penguin car layer, that is, frames 1, 19, 31, 40, and 46. Inserting a blank keyframe clears that layer of all objects, up to the next keyframe. Likewise,

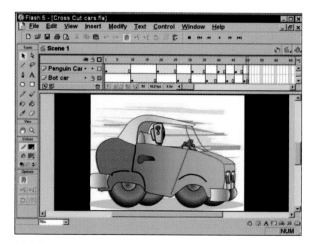

11.34

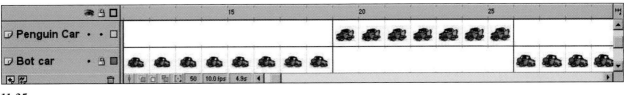

11.35

you'd insert blank keyframes on the Penguin car layer, everywhere there's a keyframe (not a blank keyframe) on the Bot car layer. The resulting timeline looks like a checkerboard (11.34). You can clearly see which layer is visible at which frame. To see even more clearly how the scene is cut, choose Preview from the Frame View pop-up menu 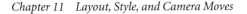 (11.35).

In this example, each symbol is 50 frames long, as is the scene. When the scene is on frame 3, or 17, or 46, the symbol playing is also on frame 3, or 17, or 46; there is a one-to-one correspondence between the scene timing and the symbols' timing, but it needn't be so. You can "cheat" the timing, if you want.

The Penguin symbol plays for the first nine frames, but when the Andy symbol appears at frame 10 of the scene, it doesn't have to play frame 10 of its animation. It could start playing at the beginning, at frame 1. When the Penguin symbol picks up again on frame 19, it could start playing, not from frame 19, but from frame 11 or 12. The effect is that the symbols don't play back, or don't play back at full speed, when they're not visible. Real movies use this technique *a lot*; it stretches out the action. To change which frame a symbol plays from, move the playback head to the desired keyframe, right-click the symbol, and choose Panels ➢ Instance. Type in the new frame in the First field.

Of course, you probably don't want to waste time and effort building a lot of complicated animation into the parts of a symbol that will never be seen onscreen.

ZOOMS

The purpose of a zoom is to focus the viewer's attention on a detail of the action (zoom in) or to reveal the context of the action (zoom out). If you have a lot of objects in the scene and want to do a simple zoom, consider building the entire scene as an animated symbol, and then using motion tweening to resize that symbol.

If you build your elements on different layers and zoom them at different rates and to different extents, you can create a dolly in shot. Zoom the nearer elements more and faster; zoom the farther elements less and slower.

CHAPTER 12
INTERACTION, PART I

One of the advantages of Flash as a cartooning tool is its capacity for interactivity. This chapter shows how to make Flash animations interactive, with the addition of buttons, menus, and simple scripting.

BUTTONS

Your primary method of interacting with Flash animations is through buttons of one flavor or another. Buttons can be wired up to cause a number of actions when you click them, such as starting and stopping animations, and jumping from place to place within the animation.

You may have a button pop up at the very end of an animation, for example, to give the viewer the option of playing it again. If the viewer clicks the button, the animation jumps back to the beginning and begins playing.

Joe Cartoon's Frog in a Blender (12.1) uses an array of buttons disguised as power settings; as you push different buttons, the animation jumps to different scenes of the frog being blended.

USING BUTTONS

Buttons are easy to create and set up in Flash. You can create one now. Open the file Skip Actions.FLA, and save it under a new name. Press Enter to preview the animation. The robot skips across the screen (12.2). Let's add a Play button and make the animation wait until the viewer presses Play before running (or skipping, as it were).

© 1999 The Joe Cartoon Co.

If we can dispel the delusion that learning about computers should be an activity of fiddling with array indexes and worrying whether X is an integer or a real number, we can begin to focus on programming as a source of ideas.

HAROLD ABELSON

12.1

© 1999, The Joe Cartoon Co.

STOP!

Left to its own devices, the animation plays as soon as it is loaded. First and foremost, you need to add a Stop command to stop the animation from playing as soon as it loads.

The scene has three layers: Robot, Button, and Actions. Double-click the first frame in the Actions layer to bring up the Frame Actions panel. This is where you see all of the commands—called ActionScript— that are embedded in your animation. At the moment, there are no commands at this frame. At the top of the panel (12.3) is a button that resembles a plus sign ⊞. Click and hold this button and select Basic Actions ➢ Stop from the pop-up list of commands (12.4).

The Stop command appears in the ActionScript window (12.5). Leave the Actions panel open, but move it out of your way. Notice that the keyframe at frame 1 of the Actions layer now has a little *a* in it. This shows us that frame 1 contains some ActionScript—our Stop command.

Test the movie now (Control ➢ Test Movie). Sure enough, as soon as the animation loads and begins to play . . . Bang! It stops. In fact, nothing seems to happen at all.

ActionScript can be included in any keyframe, but it's a good idea to put your actions on a separate layer; it makes them easier to find and edit later. Remember: Separate layers are your friends.

GO!

Now that you've got the animation stopped, you have to get it started up again. For that, you need a button.

Select the Rectangle tool and give it a green fill color. Select the Button layer, and click and drag on the stage to create a button-sized green box (12.6).

12.2

That's your button. (You can pretty it up later, if you want.) Select the entire button-to-be, and choose Insert ➢ Convert to Symbol from the menu. Name the new symbol Button, and select the Button option under Behavior (12.7). Click OK to create the button.

Nothing much seems to happen, but our box is now a button. Double-click the button to edit it (12.8).

Button symbols come prefurnished with four labeled keyframes: Up, Over, Down, and Hit. The model for a Flash button is a simple push-button, like a doorbell. It's up by default. To activate it, you push it down.

The Up frame represents the button is in its default, up position. This is what the button looks like when nothing is happening. When the mouse cursor passes over the button, it displays the Over frame. When the viewer clicks the button, it displays the Down frame.

The Hit frame defines the area that Flash recognizes as your button. Sometimes you want to use a small graphic, or some text, as a button; but you don't want to make it too hard for the viewer to actually get a piece of it with the mouse cursor. You can draw another, larger shape in the Hit frame. If the viewer clicks anywhere inside of this area, Flash counts it as a button click. Color doesn't matter in the Hit frame.

Your green box is already in the first, or Up, frame. If you don't do anything, the button works just fine, but it won't animate; it won't respond visibly to the viewer clicking it. Whether or not the button is animated has no effect on how it functions as a button; any actions we set up the button to perform works just the same, animation or no.

Now give your button some simple animation. Select frame 2, the Over frame, and press F6 to create a new keyframe. Select the Paint Bucket and set its fill color to a very light green. If the button is still selected, it is automatically filled with this new color. If not, click inside the button with the Paint Bucket to fill it.

Select frame 3, the Down frame, and insert a keyframe (F6). Use the Paint Bucket to fill the button with a darker green. Select frame 4, the Hit frame. You can leave this one alone because the "hit area" of your button is the same size and shape as the button itself. (You can make it larger, or smaller, if you want to.) Although you're only using one layer, buttons can have multiple layers, just like any other symbol.

> **NOTE**
>
> If you are unable to select a button you created, make sure Enable Buttons is turned off (Control ➤ Enable Buttons).

Move the playhead back and forth across the keyframes to make sure the button changes colors like you want it to.

Note that when you edit the button symbol, you are only editing the way the button looks. Wiring it up—

controlling what the button actually does when the viewer clicks it or passes the mouse over it—happens back on the main stage.

Click the Scene 1 tab above the timeline to return to Scene 1 (12.9).

Wiring It Up

Finally, you have to tell your button what to do. Select the Arrow tool and right-click the button. Choose Actions. Click and hold the Plus button ➕ and select Basic Actions ➤ On Mouse Event from the pop-up list of commands (12.10). As you can see from the bottom of the dialog box, you can wire the button to

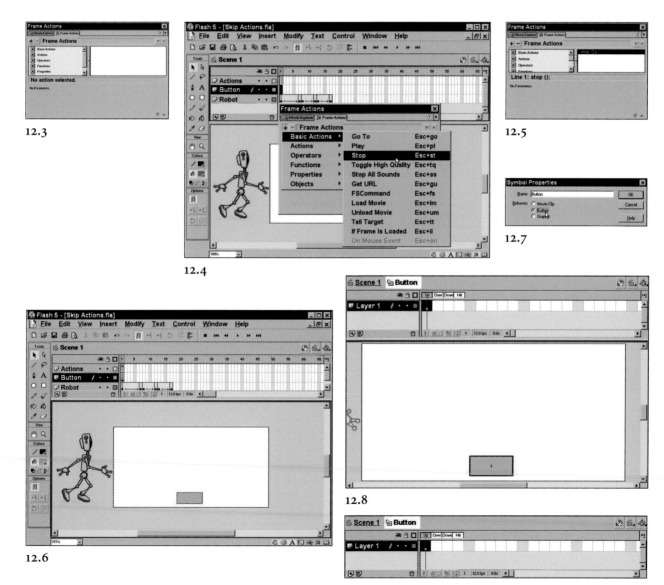

12.3

12.4

12.5

12.7

12.6

12.8

12.9

respond to a variety of different events. Release should be checked by default; if not, check it now. This tells Flash to activate the button when the viewer clicks and releases your button.

Click and hold the Plus button again. This time, select Basic Actions ➢ Go To from the pop-up list. Leave Scene set to <current scene>. Leave Type set to Frame Number, and enter **2** in the Frame box. Make sure the option "Go to and Play" is checked at the bottom of the dialog box (12.11).

You've told Flash, upon the viewer releasing the button, to go to frame 2 and begin playing.

Close the Object Actions panel. Flash doesn't always recognize buttons and actions in Preview mode. To better test the animation, turn it into a Flash movie. Choose Control ➢ Preview Movie.

It works! Notice that the button changes colors as the mouse cursor passes over it, and as you click it, just like you told it to.

A couple of things worth noting. The Button layer is only one frame long. As soon as we click the button and jump to frame 2, the button automatically disappears. Likewise, the Robot layer is empty on frame 1; the robot doesn't appear until frame 2. Save your file under a new name and close it.

PLAY IT AGAIN, SAM

You can use this same technique, with a few variations, to allow the viewer to watch your cartoon again.

Open the file Play It Again.FLA, and save it under a new name. This simple animation has four scenes:

TIP

To give your buttons more sophisticated animations, use movie clips. Movie clips play on their own timeline; even a multiframe animation plays in a single keyframe in another symbol.

A movie clip may be an animation of a character jumping up and down, for instance. Place this movie clip in a keyframe at the Over frame of your button, and the character jumps up and down as long as the mouse cursor is over the button.

The opening titles, the animation, the closing credits, and the Play It Again menu. Choose File ➢ Publish Preview ➢ Default (or press F12) to watch the movie.

To make this movie work properly, we need to stop it when it gets to the Play It Again menu, and wire up the button to restart the animation when the viewer clicks it.

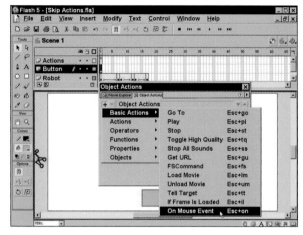

12.10

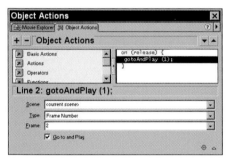

12.11

12.12

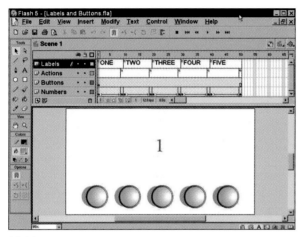

12.13

12.14

12.15

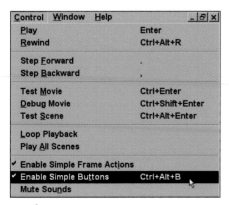

12.16

NOTE

Buttons still work, even if the animation has been "stopped."

Go to the "Play it again" scene (12.12). This scene is only one frame long, but that's enough for your purposes. Right-click the first frame of the Actions layer and choose Actions from the pop-up menu. As you did in the previous example, click the Plus button ⊞, and choose Basic Actions ➤ Stop from the pop-up list (12.13). This command stops the animation as soon as it reaches this scene.

Leave the Actions panel open and select the Play button. Click the Plus button and choose Basic Actions ➤ On Mouse Event. Make sure Release is checked. Click the Plus button again and select Basic Actions ➤ Go To.

This time, you want Flash to jump to a different scene from the current one. Choose the Animation scene from the Scene drop-down box. Leave the frame set to 1. Make sure "Go to and Play" is checked at the bottom of the panel.

Now the animation stops at this scene and waits for the viewer to click the Play button, which sends the viewer directly back to the cartoon. (Viewers get to skip the opening titles the second time around . . . unless you don't *want* them to.) Choose Control ➤ Test Movie to test the animation.

USING BUTTONS AND LABELS TO JUMP AROUND A SCENE

You can use buttons to jump around within a single scene, too. If you're going to be jumping to more than one or two frames, especially if those frames are not the first or last frame, it's a good idea to use labels. A label is just a name, a tag that you attach to a keyframe.

Load the file Labels and Buttons.FLA, and save it under a new name. Notice that the Labels layer has five keyframes, each with a label (12.14). Right-click the first keyframe in the Labels layer and choose Panels ➤ Frame. Notice the label, ONE, in the Label box (12.15). Go ahead and close the Frame panel.

Under the Control menu, make sure that "Enable Simple Frame Actions" and "Enable Simple Buttons" are both selected (12.16). Click the stage and press Enter to preview the animation. Click each of the five buttons at the bottom of the stage in turn.

You can drop this invisible button over an existing element in your animation — say a cloud or house that's already part of your background — turning this element into a button, after the fact, without redoing any art. Or you can hide it in some obscure corner or undifferentiated area of the sky if you want the viewer to have to search for hidden buttons. Check out John K's "Goddamn George Liquor Show" (www.spumco.com) or "Weekend Pussy Hunt" (www.icebox.com) for some examples of hidden buttons within cartoons . . . although it may take you a while to find them! Here's how it works. On the Numbers layer are five simple, keyframed animations, each 10 frames long. On the Actions layer are five keyframes, each with a Stop command. They stop the playback at the end of each number animation.

On the Buttons layer are five stock buttons from the Flash library (Windows ➤ Common Libraries ➤ Buttons). Turn off Enable Buttons (Control ➤ Enable Buttons). Right-click the right-most button and choose Actions. This is the button that fires the animation of the number five.

Click the line of ActionScript that says gotoAandPlay ("FIVE") to select it (12.17). Notice that Type is set to Frame Label. Instead of the action in the button

TIP

You can make "invisible" buttons by leaving all keyframes blank except the Hit keyframe; the Hit keyframe defines the size and shape of the button, but doesn't actually render onscreen.

jumping to a particular frame number, it jumps to the frame labeled FIVE.

You can see on the timeline that the label "Five" is attached to a keyframe at frame 40; so this command jumps the animation to frame 40. You can drag that keyframe labeled "Five" to any frame in the scene and the button jumps to that new frame automatically.

If, on the other hand, you use a frame number, you'd have to change the scripting to point to the new frame.

Using labels also makes it easier to remember what your actions do when you go back to work on a piece after a hiatus of several weeks. An action that jumps to "Smile" or "Wave hello" is much easier to interpret than an action that jumps to frame 117, or frame 21.

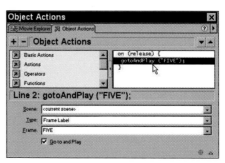

12.17

TIP

To create a link to your e-mail or your Web site within your Flash animations, first create a button. Right-click the button and select Actions. Choose Basic Actions ➤ Get URL. Type in the Web address you want the button to load (for example, www.markclarkson.com). When viewers click this button, their default Web browser fires up and loads the page. To have a button send e-mail, replace the Web page address with your e-mail address (for example, mailto:mark @markclarkson.com). Remember to add the prefix mailto: to your e-mail address.

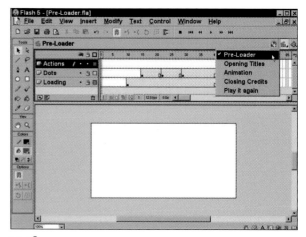

12.18

You place labels on any layer, at any keyframe — even keyframes that already contain actions and objects — but, as with actions, it's a good idea to place labels on their own separate layer. It makes them easier to read and to move around.

LOADING ANIMATIONS

Flash *streams* over the Internet. That is, it starts playing before the entire file has been downloaded to your computer. Streaming is a great technology, but you can run into trouble if the viewer's Internet connection is slow, or stalls. If the animation doesn't come down from the Internet fast enough to keep up with the playback, your animation stalls and stutters.

Some stalling here and there may be acceptable to someone waiting for the elements of a Web page to load, but it ruins a cartoon. The favorite way to circumvent this problem is with a *pre-loader*. A pre-

loader is a special scene that stops the movie and keeps it from playing until most or all of it has been downloaded to the viewer's computer. When the desired amount of movie has been downloaded, the pre-loader starts it playing.

Sound familiar? You're right: Building a pre-loader is not that different from building a Play It Again button. The difference here is that the pre-loader doesn't immediately stop the movie in its tracks; it stops it from playing past a certain point until the entire movie has been downloaded. The pre-loader is in the first scene in your movie. That scenes *loops* — that is, it plays over and over — until the entire movie is loaded. All it takes is two keyframes.

Let's put a pre-loader on the Skippy the Robot movie that we just added a Play It Again button to. Open the file Pre-loader.FLA, and save it under a new name. This is exactly the same as the Play It Again file, but I've added a new scene to the beginning and called it "Pre-Loader." Select the Pre-Loader scene (12.18). This is a simple animation. As it plays, the word "Loading" appears, followed by one, two, and then three dots. Press Enter to preview it.

Select the Actions layer, and create a new keyframe at the last frame, frame 40. Double-click the new frame to bring up the Actions panel. Click the Plus button and select Simple Actions ➤ Go To from the pop-up menu.

On the right, leave Scene set to <current scene>. Make sure the Frame Number is 1, and that "Go to and Play" is checked at the bottom (12.19). When the play-

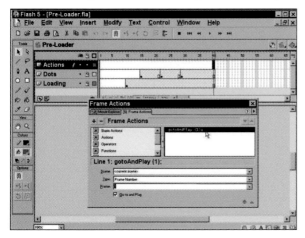

12.19

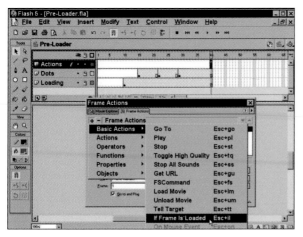

12.20

> **NOTE**
>
> Although placing labels on a separate layer certainly makes them easier to read, I personally recommend placing the label in the actual keyframe with which you want it to associate. If the keyframe happens to change, the label still remains with it. You can also keep a written record of where all your frames and actions and labels are located as a quick reference while working in Flash.
>
> Thanks to Ibis Fernandez for this note.

head gets to the end of the scene, this action makes it jump back to the beginning again. Simple enough.

Leave the Actions panel open.

One more step. Flash has a command to allow you to check whether a given frame has been downloaded from the Internet, or loaded from your disk. You'll use that to make sure the entire animation has been downloaded before it starts playing.

Create a new keyframe at frame 39 — the next to last frame — on the Actions layer. Double-click this new keyframe to bring up the Actions panel. Click the Plus button and select Basic Actions ➤ If Frame Is Loaded (12.20). Which frame is loaded? Why, the last frame in the animation.

Choose the last scene, "Play it again," from the Scene drop-down box. Leave the Frame Number at 1. Click the Plus button again and select Basic Actions ➤ Go To from the pop-up menu. Choose Opening Titles from the Scene drop-down box. Leave the Frame Number at 1. Make sure "Go to and Play" is checked.

So, what is this code doing? *If* the first frame of the last scene has been loaded into memory — that is, if the entire movie is downloaded and ready to play — we jump to the opening credits and begin playing the movie. If the first frame of the last scene has *not* been loaded into memory, the playhead moves on to frame 40, where the Go To command sends it back to the beginning of the scene again.

TIP

Make use of natural pauses in your movie to allow Flash to stream smoothly. Here is advice from Ibis Fernandez: "One of the tricks I use is to make an invisible movie that, when placed on any keyframe, causes the animation in the main timeline to pause for a certain number of seconds. This is helpful in segments where a character stops to think about something, or where you just pause to add a bit of drama to the sequence. Aside from the aesthetic effect, this pause gives the processor a chance to rest and catch up. It's also a good way to stream more frames without the user knowing it." (Ibis's movie clip "Pause" is included on the CD-ROM that accompanies this book.)

BETTER PRE-LOADERS

A pre-loader doesn't have to be a boring "please wait" screen. Some cartoonists give viewers a game to play, or a simple animation to watch, while they wait for the main animation to download.

If you have opening credits, you can "hide" a pre-loader in the credits. Instead of stopping the animation immediately, let it begin playing through the opening credits. Depending on the size of your animation and the length of your credits, Flash can download enough of the animation while the credits play to allow for smooth playback. If you don't have many credits, you can stop the movie until it's halfway down, and then begin the credits.

You can use a series of pre-loaders. Scene 1 may be a very simple "please wait" screen that stops the animation until Scene 2 is completely downloaded, and then jumps to Scene 2. Scene 2 may be a short animation, or a simple game, which repeats until the rest of the movie is downloaded.

Choose Control ➤ Test Movie to test the movie. It's really hard to tell if the pre-loader is working with such a short movie. In fact, it's hard to see if the pre-loader is working with any movie that you're testing from your hard disk; even multi-megabyte animations load before the pre-loader has played once. But, trust me, it works.

You don't trust me? Okay — you can see for yourself. Make sure the VCR controls are enabled (Window ➤ Toolbars ➤ Controller), and select Control ➤ Test Movie. When the movie begins playing, stop it with the VCR controls. From the main menu, choose View ➤ Show Streaming. Playback is now artificially slowed; the animation plays back as though it were streaming from the Internet. You can change the simulated download speed under the Debug menu. I recommend 28.8 as a rule of thumb.

Your pre-loaders can be as simple, or as complex, as you want. Instead of a simple bit of text, you can have animated characters, or sweeping clock hands, or whatever you want. The whole trick lies in those two keyframes on the Actions layer. How you fill in the rest is up to you. Of course, if your pre-loader grows too ornate, it may need a pre-loader of its own!

CHAPTER 13
INTERACTION, PART II

Buttons are a great start, but you can make Flash jump through all sorts of hoops, and greatly increase your animations' level of interactivity, by sprinkling it a little ActionScript. Read on to find out how.

BASIC ACTIONSCRIPTING

ActionScript is Flash's own little programming language. Don't let that worry you if you're not a programmer; as an animator, you've got the option of using very little ActionScripting—or even none at all.

You've already played a little with ActionScripting in the previous chapter to make a simple pre-loader, and to make a "play it again" button for your movie. ActionScript is a powerful, full-blown programming language, but I won't be going into most of it in this book. Luckily, ActionScripting a cartoon is a lot less complicated than ActionScripting a Web store.

USING VARIABLES

A variable is like a box. You can put whatever you want in there, then look inside to examine the contents. A variable is just a place to put your stuff until you need it later. A variable might hold the current time, or someone's name, or the number of times an animation has looped. They're called variables because their contents can vary. A variable holding the current time, for instance, would change constantly to reflect the new time. A variable holding the number of

If you begin with Basic Actions and then add a little code here and there, before you know it, you've got a lot of control over what's happening on the stage.

BILL SANDERS, SANDLIGHT PRODUCTIONS;
WWW.SANDLIGHT.COM

©2000, Vaughn Anderson

©2000, Vaughn Anderson

times an animation has looped would grow by one ("increment") every time the animation looped.

Variables are your friends.

LOOPS AND RANDOM FUNCTIONS

Let's take a look at a variable in action. Load the file Bugs Background.FLA, and save it under a new name. Watch the movie (Control ➤ Test Movie). This is a nighttime background with eight lightning bugs blinking serenely in the grass. There is one problem with this, though; the lightning bugs are all blinking in sync. That doesn't look very realistic, or even very good.

This scene can be fixed in a several different ways. You could make eight different lightning bugs, with each one blinking at a different rate, for example. But an even more pleasing effect is if each lightning bug blinks more or less at random. Besides, I hate to make eight symbols where one will do. Again, there are

many ways to accomplish this; let's look at one that's fairly similar to the pre-loader from the last chapter.

Close the preview window.

Click and hold the Edit Symbol button (or open the library with Ctrl+L) and choose the Random Flashing Light symbol (13.1). Here's what's going on: Random Flashing Light uses the Glow symbol, which is a simple green gradient blob. I used Flash's motion tweening to fade in the background color at frame 1, to its own green gradient color at frame 4, and back to the background color at frame 8, making it seem to *blink*. (Fading to and from the background color is easier on your processor, and therefore faster, than fading to and from transparency.) Because the movie's frame rate is 15 frames per second, this blink lasts about half a second.

The blink stays off from frame 9 to frame 45, about two and a half seconds. The stage is empty at this point. At frame 45, the animation automatically loops back to the beginning and the symbol blinks again.

But we want to add a random delay, so that the blink stays off for a different amount of time with every loop. Here's how:

First, dump the fixed pause. Click frame 45, and drag it to the left to frame 9 to select all of the blank frames. Press delete to eliminate the frames from 9 to 45 (13.2).

Control+drag (hold down the Ctrl key and drag) from frame 1 to frame 9 to select all the remaining frames. With those frames selected, click and drag them to the right until the final keyframe is at frame 15 (13.3) This leaves a gap of seven blank frames before the blink — about half a second. We're going to tell Flash to play these blank frames in a random amount before blinking.

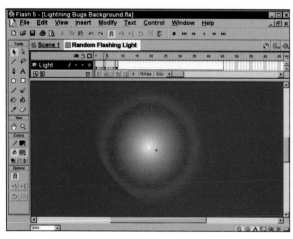

13.1

13.2

13.3

Click the New Layer button ⬚ below the timeline to add a new layer. Label it *Actions*. Now you're ready to drop in a little code. On the Actions layer, right-click the first frame and choose Actions from the pop-up menu (13.4).

Click the Add Action button ➕ (the plus sign) and choose Actions ➤ Set variable. Ta-da! You've created a variable. This variable keeps track of how many times Flash has looped through those first seven blank frames. Every variable needs two things: a name and a value. Give the variable a name. In the name box, type **LoopCount** (13.5).

In addition to a name, every variable needs a value. LoopCount's job is to keep track of the number of times to loop through the blank front frames. Its initial value is the number of times you want to loop.

For example, if you wanted Flash to loop ten times, you'd type **10** in the Value box below the variable's name. But you want it to loop a *random* number of times, to give you a random delay. Luckily, Flash comes equipped with a function that comes up with random numbers. (A function is just a little bit of software that does a particular job.)

Check *Expression* to the right of the Value box. This makes it explicit to Flash that you're putting in a number, rather than text. In ActionScripting, there's a big difference between the *number* 398 and the *text* 398.

Click in the Value box to make sure Value is selected. Click the Add Action button and choose Functions ➤ Random (13.6). If all has gone well, what you see should be similar to the figure (13.7).

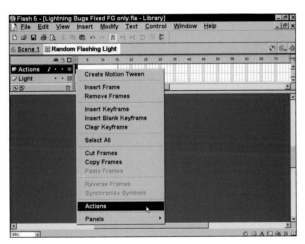

13.4

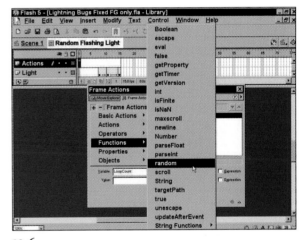

13.6

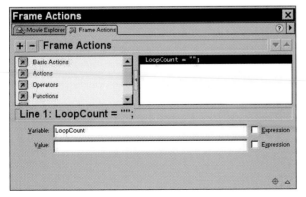

13.5

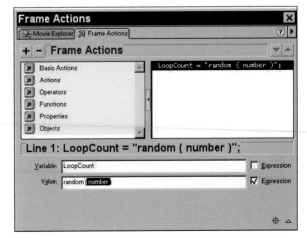

13.7

The random function needs to know how big a random number you want. A random number between 0 and 10? Between 0 and 1,000? Replace the word *number* in the random function with 16 (13.8). The random function now returns one of 16 whole numbers in the range of 0 to 15. The random function always returns a number between 0 and one less than the number you type in. (Counterintuitive, yes, but the programming types don't want to make it too easy on the rest of us.)

Alrighty. Now Flash knows how many times to loop. Time to put in the loop itself.

Move the playhead to frame 2 and press F6 to insert a new keyframe on the Actions layer. With the new frame selected, open the Frame Properties panel (Window ➢ Panels ➢ Frame, or Control + F.) Type the word **loop** in the Label box (13.9). This is the beginning of your loop.

Move the playhead to frame 7 and insert a new keyframe on the Actions layer. This is the end of the loop. Here you have Flash check to see if it's looped enough times. If it has, tell it to go on to the *blink* frames. If not, send it back to frame 2, the frame you labeled *loop*, to do it again.

Right-click the new keyframe at frame 7 and choose Actions to bring up the Actions dialog. Click the Add Action button and choose Actions ➢ set variable. In Variable, type **LoopCount** (or whatever name you gave the variable in frame 1). In Value, type **LoopCount – 1**

Watch your spelling and capitalization (13.10). Check the Expression box to the right of the Value. Every time Flash hits this statement, the value of LoopCount is reduced by one ("decremented"). LoopCount counts down from whatever random number it was assigned, for example 7,6,5,4,3,2,1.

If LoopCount hasn't reached 0 yet, we need to play through the blank frames again.

Let's tell Flash to check and see if LoopCount has reached 0 yet. Click the Add Action button again and choose Actions ➢ If (13.11). In Condition, type **LoopCount > 0**

If LoopCount is greater than 0, you want Flash to loop back again. Click the Add Action button and choose Basic Actions ➢ Go To. Choose Frame Label from the Type drop-down list, and select the label loop from the Frame box (13.12).

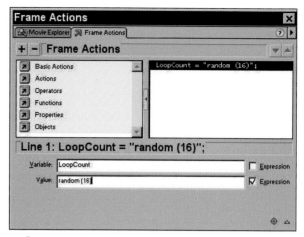

13.8

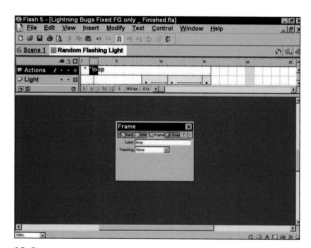

13.9

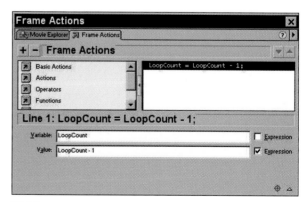

13.10

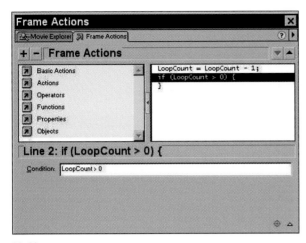

13.11

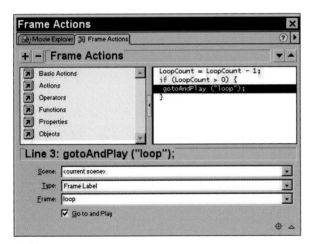

13.12

> **NOTE**
>
> If the random function returns a zero, Flash still plays through the blank frames once. After decrementing, LoopCount would be –1, but that's okay because –1 still isn't greater than 0, so Flash still ignores the body of the If statement. Whether the random number function returns a 0, or a 1, Flash plays through the blank frames one time. Because this is not exactly rocket science, that works fine for us.

The ActionScript should read:

```
LoopCount = LoopCount-1;
if (LoopCount>0) {
  gotoAndPlay ("loop");
}
```

So if, after being decremented, LoopCount is still greater than 0, we send Flash back to the frame labeled *loop* (frame 2). If LoopCount has reached 0, the body of the If statement (the part inside the curly brackets) isn't executed, and Flash moves on to frame 8, and the light blinks.

The loop runs, at most, 15 times. Because the loop is 6 frames long, and the movie runs at 15 frames per second, the pause lasts from about half a second (once through the loop) up to 6 seconds (15 times through the loop).

Perhaps it goes without saying, but this random looping technique can be used for more than blank frames. You can loop over frames containing actual animation—characters blinking or jumping or scratching or what have you—just as easily. In fact, because the blank frames are, in a sense, *wasted* in this example, this technique is actually more appropriate to situations where you want characters to actually "do something" a random number of times.

You should be aware that this method might yield different results on different systems, depending on the processor speed. A very fast computer might make it through a loop faster than a very slow computer. For blinking bugs in the background, this is no big deal. For a time-critical animation such as lip-synching, or a real-time clock, it would be a very big deal, indeed.

LOOPS AND GETTIMER

Let's take a look at another way to get random—or non-random—timings in your Flash cartoons. This method, which uses actual elapsed time to time the pauses, is more accurate than the previous "random number of loops" example. The easiest way to measure elapsed time is with another Flash function, called getTimer.

Open the movie Bugs with Heros.FLA, and save it under a new name. This movie uses the background animation from the previous section, but adds two large, detailed lightning bugs — and a little grass — in the foreground (13.13).

A special, detailed character that is seen in close-up is sometimes referred to as a *hero*. The two large lightning bugs are the hero bugs. A hero doesn't have to be a character; it can be a spaceship, or a leaf . . . any drawing with extra detail for close-ups.

Play the movie by choosing Control ➤ Test Movie. The large bugs blink at random, just like the little background bugs, but their wings move all the time, and in sync. Let's make bugs rattle their wings at random, using the getTimer function. Sound like fun? You betcha!

Click the Edit Symbol button 🔲 and choose Lightning Bug Parts ➤ Wings from the drop-down menu (13.14). This is a simple looping animation; after a brief, three-frame pause, the wings flutter twice, using simple motion tweening.

Let's add the random pause. You're going to check the current time, add a random pause of up to 10 seconds to it, then wait until the time has expired before allowing Flash to move on to the wing movement.

Insert a new layer 🔲 and name it Actions. If you look at the other two layers, you notice that frame 4 is the first frame where the wings actually move. Let's label this frame so you can jump here when it's time for the wings to move. With the Action layer selected, move the playhead to frame 4 and insert a new keyframe with F6. Right-click the new keyframe and choose Panels ➤ Frame. In the Frame panel, type **Move Wing** in the frame label field (13.15). Go ahead and close the Frame panel.

Now for the actual actions. With the Action layer selected, move the playhead to frame one and insert a new keyframe with F6. Double-click the new keyframe to bring up the Actions panel. Click the Add Action button ➕ and choose Actions ➤ set variable. Give the variable the name, `time` (13.16).

Now to set the variable, `time`, to the current time.

Flash has a function, called getTimer, which measures the time since the movie began playing, in thousandths of a second (milliseconds). Now, we don't really care how long its been since the movie started playing; in fact, it will be a different time every time you call the getTimer function. But we need to find out what time it is now, at the beginning of the animation, so we measure how much time has elapsed.

TIP

When you get good at ActionScripting, you can choose Expert Mode (Control+E) and just type the ActionScript right in. This can be faster, because you don't have to choose ever action from a menu; but it's more prone to errors — misspellings and so forth — as well.

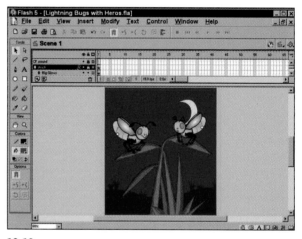

13.13

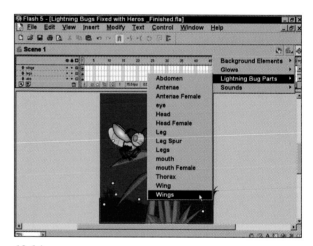

13.14

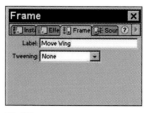

13.15

Click the Actions panel's Value field. Click the Add Action button and select Functions ➤ getTimer.

Remember that getTimer gives times in thousandths of a second. If a movie has been running exactly 60 seconds, for example, the current time would be

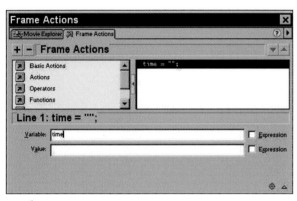

13.16

13.17

13.18

60,000 — 1,000 × 60 seconds. To add 1 second to a time, you'd add 1,000. To add 10 seconds, you'd add 10,000.

Let's add a random pause of up to 10 seconds. In the Value field, after getTimer(), add a plus sign, then click the Add Action button and choose Function ➤ Random. Give the random function a value of 10,000, which translates into a pause of between 0 and 10 seconds . . . well . . . between 0 and 9.999 seconds, but close enough. Make sure the Expression box to the right of the Value field is checked.

You should wind up with this (13.17):

```
time = getTimer ()+random (10000);
```

In fact, if you're feeling brave, you can just type the whole thing into the Value box, and skip all the pop-up menus.

The variable `time` is now set to a time somewhere up to 10 seconds in the future.

Move the playhead to frame 2 and insert a new keyframe on the Actions layer (F6). If the Actions dialogue is not already open, double-click the new keyframe to bring it up. Click the Add Action button and choose Actions ➤ If. In the condition box, type **time < getTimer()**

Click the Add Action button and choose Basic Actions ➤ Go To. Choose Frame Label from the Type menu, and choose Move Wing from the Frame drop-down box. Make sure "Go to and Play" is checked (13.18). So, if enough time has elapsed — if the current time is greater than the value assigned to the `time` variable — Flash jumps directly to frame 4, the frame labeled *Move Wing*.

Add a new keyframe at frame 3. In the Frame Actions dialogue box, click the Add Action button and choose Basic Actions ➤ Go To. Choose Frame Number from Type, and type **2** in the Frame field. Make sure "Go to and Play" is checked.

So, if enough time has elapsed, Flash moves on to frame 4, Move Wing. If not, the action at frame 3 sends it back to the previous frame, frame 2, to check again, over and over until enough time has elapsed.

Test the movie and watch for a while. Sure enough, the lightning bugs wiggle their wings at random.

TELL TARGET

Tell Target is just a way of passing instructions to and from movie clips, to tell them what you want them to do. Movie clips can, for example, start and stop playing independent of the main timeline. Tell Target is a way of telling them when to stop, and where and when to play.

THE PSYCHIC GOLDFISH

Load the file Pam's Goldfish.FLA, and save it under a new name. This is an interactive animation designed and built by my 12-year-old daughter, Pam, just to show you that this isn't really so hard (13.19). You can find it on the CD-ROM.

Goldie, the psychic goldfish is based on the venerable Magic 8-Ball: you ask her a yes or no question and she replies. In truth, as with the original Magic 8-Ball, the answers are generated at random. Try it now (Control ➤ Test Movie). Type in your question and then click the Ask button (13.20).

Myriad ways exist to build this application, but Pam chose to do it thusly: the movie is divided into two scenes. In the first scene, you ask your question; in the second scene, Goldie answers.

Goldie swims in circles until you press the ask button, then she consults briefly with the spirits (13.21) and renders up her answer (13.22).

Pretty simple but the following factors are required for it to work:

1. Goldie has to know when the Ask button's been pressed, and keeps swimming until then.

2. The box in which viewers type questions has to disappear after a question has been asked.
3. The text, "I'm consulting the spirits," has to appear after the question is asked and then disappear again when the answer is given.
4. Because Goldie appears in a fixed position in the second scene, where she gives her answer, she must continue swimming in the first scene until she reaches that position.

Most of these use techniques we've discussed previously. The new part comes between Step 2 and Step 3. How can the "Consulting the Spirits" text appear just as the viewer clicks the Ask button? The answer is, we have the Ask button *tell* the text to appear, using the Tell Target command.

13.20

13.21

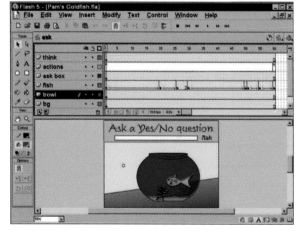

13.19

Close the preview window.

Double-click frame 1 of the actions layer to bring up the Frame Actions panel. Here, Pam's setting the variable SkipScene to 0 (13.23). As long as SkipScene equals 0, the movie won't jump to the next scene.

Leave the Actions panel open and select the last keyframe on the actions layer (13.24). Here she checks to see if SkipScene is still equal to 0. If it is, then she jumps back to frame 1, and the animation loops. If it

isn't then the movie continues on to scene 2.

But how does SkipScene get set to other than 0? Let's look.

Click the Edit Symbols button and choose the

13.22

Ask Box symbol (13.25). This symbol comprises the colored dialog box, the prompt, the text input field, and the Ask button. It is two frames long; the second frame is blank.

Select the Ask button—the text "Ask" at the box's lower-right corner.

If you closed the Actions panel, bring it up again by right-clicking the Ask button and choosing Actions from the pop-up menu (13.26).

Remember that you can wire up buttons to perform many different actions. Let's look at what this one does.

When the user clicks and releases the button—on (release)—it sets the variable called SkipScene to 1. Remember that this is the variable from the main timeline that controls whether the movie skips ahead to the second scene or not.

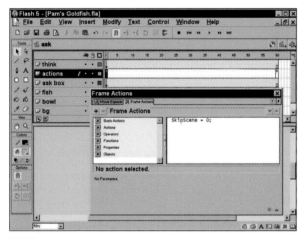

13.23

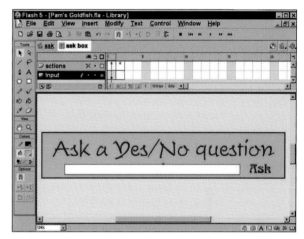

13.25

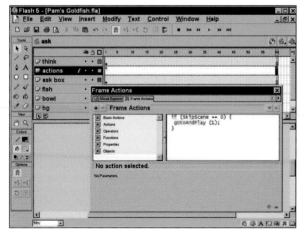

13.24

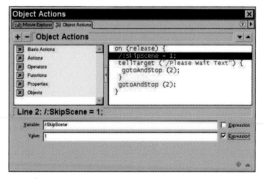

13.26

TIP

To create a text field viewers can type in, open the Text Options panel (Window ➢ Panels ➢ Text Options) and choose "Input Text" from the drop-down menu.

You should notice that the line referring to the variable refers to it as `/:SkipScene`, with an extra `/:` in front of it. This notation is telling you that the variable isn't in the Ask Box symbol; it's in the main timeline. More on this later.

The next line is the much-anticipated TellTarget command:

```
tellTarget ("/Please Wait Text")
```

Here's what this means: somewhere in Pam's movie is a movie clip symbol named "Please Wait Text." The next command given, `gotoAndStop(2)`, is directed to that symbol, rather than to the main timeline. That is, the symbol named Please Wait Text jumps to frame 2 and stops playing.

As you might have guessed, this symbol is the very one that displays the message "I'm consulting the spirits." Its frame 2 holds the text; its frame 1 is blank. When the movie starts, it stops on frame 1, the blank frame, and waits for the Ask button to tell it to jump to frame 2 and display its text.

Finally, the Ask Box symbol itself jumps to frame 2, the blank frame, making itself disappear from the screen.

So this one button is actually sending commands to three different places:

- It is setting a variable (SkipScene) back on the main timeline.
- It is commanding the symbol named Please Wait Text to jump to its second frame and display its text.
- It is telling the Ask Box symbol which contains it to jump to its own second frame.

Click the Ask tab above the timeline to return to the main timeline. A small white circle appears, suspended in midair to the left of the fishbowl (13.27).

This is the handle of a symbol that is currently invisible, in fact, the notorious Please Wait Text symbol, which doesn't show itself until Ask Box tells it to. Right-click the small circle now, and choose Panels ➢ Instance from the pop-up (13.28). You'll notice that this is actually the *Thinking* movie clip, but that this instance is named Please Wait Text. There could be many different copies of this movie clip, each with its own name. We only need one, but — in order to use Tell Target — it needs an instance name.

13.27

13.28

NOTE

You must specify a unique instance name for any movie clip referred to by a Tell Target command. Double-click the little circle to edit the symbol (13.29). It's two frames: the first is blank and the second displays the text. A `Stop()` command in the first frame of the actions layer stops the symbol from moving to frame 2 until it's told to.

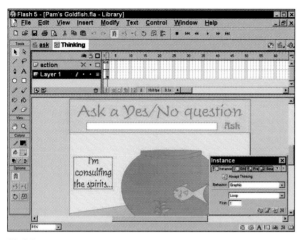

13.29

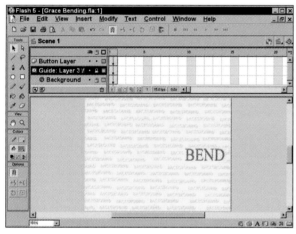

13.30 *© 2000, Vaughn Anderson, www.andersonanimation.com*

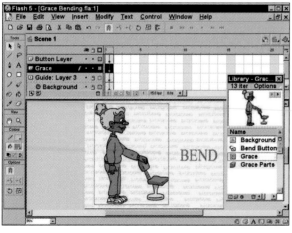

13.31 *© 2000, Vaughn Anderson, www.andersonanimation.com*

MY OWN LITTLE TELL TARGET

It's a little hard to really get the idea just looking at someone else's movie. It's time for your own little Tell Target project.

Close any open movies. Load the file, Grace Bending. FLA, and save it under a new name (13.30).

Insert a new layer, and name it *Grace*. Open the library (Windows ➤ Library).

With the Grace layer selected, find the movie clip symbol called "Grace" and drag it onto the stage (13.31). Test the movie (Control ➤ Test Movie). Grace blinks, even though the movie's only one frame long, because she is a movie clip, and animates on her own timeline.

Close the preview window.

Now, Grace has a frame labeled "Bend" (13.32), and if you jump there, she bends her knee and stretches a bit, to limber up from a long day sitting at the keyboard. How to get her to jump there? Sounds like a job for Tell Target.

Remember that you can't access a movie clip with Tell Target unless you've given that movie clip an instance name. Right-click Grace and choose Panels ➤ Instance. Type Grace's name in the Instance Name field (13.33). Close the instance panel.

Someone's left a button lying around—the word Bend—so you might as well use that to trigger Grace's exercise. Right-click the button and choose Actions from the pop-up (13.34).

In the Actions panel, click the Add Action button ➕ and choose Basic Actions ➤ Tell Target (13.35). Click once in the Target field at the bottom of the panel. At the bottom of the Actions panel is a little cross inside of a circle ⊕; this is the Insert a Target Path button. Click this to bring up the Target Path panel (13.36). If yours looks different, select Notation: Slashes and Mode: Absolute at the bottom of the panel.

> ### NOTE
>
> **Grace appears in the book courtesy of talented Flasher, Vaughn Anderson,** `www.Anderson Animation.com`**. There's more of Vaughn's oh-so-smooth Flash animation on the CD-ROM that's included with the book.**

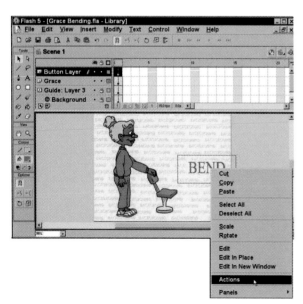

13.32

© 2000, Vaughn Anderson, www.andersonanimation.com

13.33

13.34

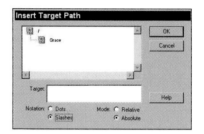

13.35

13.36

13.37

13.38

The Insert Target Path panel's top shows a hierarchical tree of all movie clips in the scene. In this case, there's only a single movie clip and the main timeline (denoted by a slash "/") (13.37). However, more complex animations might have any number of instances to choose from.

Select the instance of Grace (13.38). The next command we add is addressed not to the main movie timeline but rather to the movie clip symbol named Grace. Click the Add Action button and choose Basic Actions ➤ Go To.

As I already told you, to get Grace to bend her knees, you need to jump her to the frame labeled "Bend" in her timeline. Select Frame Label from the Type drop-down menu (13.39). Type the word **Bend** in the Frame field (13.40).

When the viewer clicks and releases this button, the button tells the movie clip, Grace, to jump to its frame labeled "Bend."

Close the Object Actions panel and Test the movie (Ctrl+Enter). If you spelled everything right, Grace should stretch those ligaments when you press the button (13.41).

We've been using buttons, but any keyframe on any timeline, be it the main timeline or that of a movie clip, can send commands to any movie clip or to the main timeline, via Tell Target. Movie clips even can talk to each other. You might, for instance, set up the lightning bugs in the earlier example so that when the abdomen movie clip blinks, it tells the wing movie clip to flutter.

LOADING AND UNLOADING MOVIES

Flash movies can load other Flash movies from the Web or a drive on your computer.

Why would you want to do that? You might make a standard movie interface and load different movies into it (13.42), so that viewers can watch all the movies they want, but only have to download the interface once. Or you might build a very complicated menu system that only loads certain elements as they are needed. Or you might think of all sorts of other groovy uses.

It's really pretty easy to do. Close any open movies and open the file, Load Movie.FLA. Save it under a

13.39

13.40

13.41

13.42

NOTE

Loading a movie clip on a level that already holds a movie clip causes the newly loaded movie clip to overwrite the older movie clip.

new name. This movie is essentially the same as the movie from the last exercise with one big difference: Grace isn't in the library this time. You're going to load her from your drive.

Create a new layer and name it Actions (13.43).

Double-click the Actions layer's first frame to bring up the Actions panel. Click the Add Action button and choose Basic Actions ➤ Load Movie.

In the URL field, type **Grace.swf** (13.44). This is the name of the Flash movie you're going to load. Leave *Location* set to Level, but change the level number from 0 to 1 (13.45). For this example to work, the file Grace.swf must be in the same directory as your movie.

A few words about levels and loaded movies. Levels are similar to the layers on the main timeline: movies on higher levels eclipse movies on lower levels. A movie on Level 2, for example, eclipses the movies on Level 1 and Level 0 (13.46).

The main timeline is always on Level 0. Because you're loading Grace into Level 1, she comes in *on top of* the movie that's already on the main timeline. The main timeline contains a simple background graphic, and Grace loads in on top of that background graphic (13.47).

If, on the other hand, you loaded Grace on Level 0, she would *replace* the background graphic (13.48).

Click the Add Action button and choose Basic Actions ➤ Stop to stop the movie so it won't end-lessly load new copies of Grace.SWF.

NOTE

To Unload a movie from memory, use the Basic Actions ➤ Unload Movie command. Refer to the movie by the level on which it's loaded.

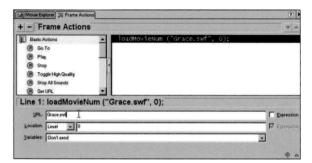

13.43

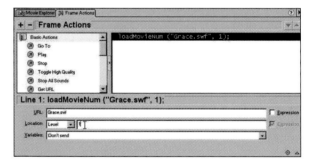

13.44

13.45

13.46

© 2000, Vaughn Anderson, www.andersonanimation.com

13.47

13.48

TIP

The main advice I can give is to slowly learn the code. If you begin with Basic Actions and then add a little code here and there, before you know it, you've got a lot of control over what's happening on the stage. Features such as collision detection and user interaction are greatly enhanced by ActionScript.

Thanks to Bill Sanders, SandLight Productions, for this advice.

With the Actions panel still open, select the Bend button. Click the Add Action button and choose Basic Actions ➤ Tell Target. Under Target, type **_level1** (13.49).

Remember that Tell Target refers to each instance by its name. Loaded movies go by the name of the level you loaded them into. Because you loaded Grace on Level 1, her instance name is `_level1`, with a preceding underscore. If you'd loaded her on Level 2, her instance name would be `_level2`.

Click the Add Actions button again and choose Basic Actions ➤ Go To. Set Type to Frame Label, and type **Bend** in the Frame field (13.50).

This is the same code as in the last example, except that Tell Target now refers to a movie loaded on Level 1, instead of referring to an instance name.

Close the Actions panel and test the movie. It should work just as it did before.

13.49

13.50

CHAPTER 14
MAKING A MOVIE

You've sketched, scanned, and storyboarded. You've built beautiful backgrounds. You've designed, drawn, and animated your characters. You've tweened, squashed, and stretched until every movement looks just right. Now it's time to put the whole piece together in finished form — so you can share it with the world and receive the wealth and glory that is your due. Read on.

PUBLISH SETTINGS

You have to make some important decisions when it comes time to publish your work. One of the first decisions is what version of Flash you use to publish in.

VERSION 4 OR VERSION 5?

While you can, in theory, choose to publish in any version of Flash from 1 to 5, the real choice is between Version 4 and Version 5. If you publish your cartoon in Flash 5, any viewers who don't have the current version of the Flash player won't be able to watch it. If you use any of Flash 5's new programming features, then you have no choice but to publish in Flash 5 but, otherwise, consider publishing in Flash 4 to expand your potential viewing audience. Select the Flash player version from the Flash tab of the Publish Settings panel, or choose File ➤ Publish Settings (14.1).

READING THE SIZE REPORT

If you're going to publish your animations on the Web, then size is very important. The bigger your car-

After each step of the process, watch the movie and look for places where you can cut out slow parts or tighten the action and dialog up. Invariably there will be things you'll cut to improve the pacing. From the first rough animation to the final version of the movie, it's just a succession of revisions and refinements.

JANET GALORE, HONKWORM INTERNATIONAL, INC.

14.1

toon is, the longer it takes to download and the less likely it is that potential viewers will stick around long enough to see it.

Flash provides several tools, however, to help you root out oversized sounds, graphics, and effects . . . to see just where you're spending all those bytes. The first tool is the size report.

To generate a size report, open the Publish Settings panel (File ➤ Publish Settings) and select the "Generate size report" option on the Flash tab. Make sure the Flash Type is selected on the Formats tab, and then press the Publish button. Flash generates both your animation (the SWF file) and a size report. The size report is a text file; it has the same name as the Flash SWF file, with the word "Report" grafted on to the end. If your cartoon's name is Psychic Pigs, the size report is called Psychic Pigs Report.

> **NOTE**
>
> If you are publishing your animation as a Windows or Mac executable, then you needn't worry about what version of Flash player, if any, your viewers have installed; the published executable includes the Flash player.

14.3

FRAME BY FRAME

Here's the first page of the size report from a cartoon (14.2). The first column is the frame number. The last column is the page number. If you only have one scene, then the page number and the frame number are the same; if you have more than one scene, then the page number starts over with every new scene.

The meat of the report is in the middle. The second column gives the bytes taken up by a particular frame. In this report, the first frame is almost 5K. An animated graphic, a background, and some text first appear in this frame (14.3). The next seven frames, in contrast, are only two bytes each; there's nothing new appearing in these frames. The third column gives the total accumulated bytes for the movie, so far. This number just goes up and up.

PAGE BY PAGE

Skipping ahead a bit, we come to the next part of the size report, the scene-by-scene rundown (14.4).

> **NOTE**
>
> If you select HTML on the Format tab in the Publish Settings panel, Flash publishes a Web page with your Flash animation embedded in it. It's a start, but Flash's default Web pages are pretty lame. You'll want to pretty it up a bit in a Web page program such as Adobe Pagemill or Macromedia Dreamweaver.

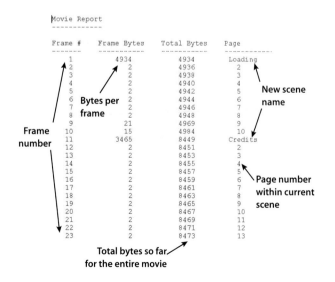

14.2

```
Page                          Shape Bytes    Text Bytes
----------------------        -----------    ----------
Loading                                57             0
Credits                              5197          1102
1 Ext Bldg -> Int Bath               3434             0
2 Int Kitchen                           0             0
2B Int Kitchen - CU calendar            0             0
2c Int Kitchen P Boggles                0             0
2d Int Kitchen P turns 2 cam            0             0
2e Int Kitchen Pt II                    0             0
2f P turns from Cal                     0             0
2G Int Kitchen P runs out               0             0
BLAK 2 sec                              0             0
3 Int Den                               0             0
3 Int Den Search Page CU                0             0
4a Ext Mall                            66             0
4b Int Mall Est Shot                    0             0
Est Shot - Pet Shop - still             0             0
Int Mall - Pet Shop                     0             0
Int Mall - Penguin Dreams               0             0
Meanwhile Bumper                       59            60
```

14.4

```
Symbol                        Shape Bytes    Text Bytes
----------------------        -----------    ----------
Music Credits                          39           330
Santa-Chimney                           0             0
Den BG color plate                     42             0
NiteCap Side                          332             0
Nite Cap                              418             0
PJ's                                  313             0
HollyWrap                               0             0
Present for Rat                       102             0
Present Tears Open                    726             0
Yamakitti                            3466             0
Penguin's Backside                    558             0
Bits&Bytes sign                         0           210
sw10                                  252             0
sw9                                   196             0
sw8                                   202             0
sw7                                   438             0
sw6                                   182             0
sw5                                   103             0
sw4                                    88             0
sw3                                   312             0
sw2                                   369             0
```

14.5

14.6

```
Bitmap                     Compressed   Original   Compression
----------------------     ----------   --------   -----------
Wrestling.jpg                   96969    2249600    JPEG Quality=50
NewsArticle.gif                 24615     267000    Lossless
Holly.bmp                        5139     160000    JPEG Quality=50

Tweened Shapes: 14977 bytes
```

14.7

Although the first column is labeled "Pages," each row actually represents an entire scene. There are columns for shape bytes — that is, graphics — and text bytes. You'll notice that many of these scenes report no byte size at all. That's because this section only reports "extra" bytes: bytes that are not part of symbols. If a scene is made up entirely of symbols from the library, then it reports no shape bytes. If some of your scenes have large numbers of shape bytes — as does the scene here named Credits — you should investigate replacing some groups, shapes, and lines with symbols.

SYMBOL BY SYMBOL

Skipping ahead farther, you come to the symbol breakdown (14.5). Here you'll see the size of every symbol in your library. The Yamakitti symbol (14.6) is a whopping 3K, which makes it a place to invest some time optimizing shapes. That's one of the advantages of turning everything into a symbol: you get an accurate byte count in the size report. You can tell just how big your character's moustache is, how many bytes his left arm contributes to the final file size, and so forth. If you just draw things on the stage, or make them into groups, then their contribution to the file's final size is folded into the shape bytes in the Page section of the report; you can't tell what's big and what's small.

Notice that some symbols report a size of zero bytes; these symbols are, themselves, made from other symbols so they are free as far as file size is concerned.

> **TIP**
>
> Armed with information from the size report, you can adjust the JPG compression for each bitmap individually. Double-click the bitmap icon in the library, which brings up the "bitmap properties" menu. Deselect "Use document default quality," and you will be able to select an export compression for that particular image.
>
> Thanks to Janet Galore at Honkworm International, Inc. for this tip.

14.8

14.9

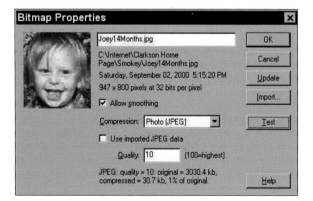

BITMAPS

The next section reports any bitmaps used in the animation and shows their compression settings and byte size, both before and after compression (14.7).

JPG versus PNG

Flash compresses any bitmaps in your animations to save file space. You can choose between two types of compression: lossy (JPG) and lossless (PNG).

JPG (pronounced *jay-peg*) compression is called *lossy* because, in the process of shrinking your image, it throws parts of it away. At low compression settings, the loss is virtually undetectable (14.8). At higher settings, it becomes quite pronounced. JPG compression can reduce a photo by almost any amount, provided you're willing to put up with progressively worse *artifacting*— the rectangular blobs and lines that emerge as JPG compression squeezes more and more info out of the image (14.9).

PNG (pronounced *ping*), on the other hand, is *lossless*; it retains all image information. Lossless PNG compression, in my experience, reduces a photograph by about 35 to 55 percent.

Set your global bitmap compression on the Flash tab of the Publish Settings panel (File ➢ Publish Settings). Depending on the size and quality of the JPGs used, a global setting of anywhere from 20 to 60 is appropriate.

You can test the results of different compression settings without publishing the movie. Double-click a bitmap in the library, deselect "Use document default quality," and try out different Quality settings. Results are displayed in the preview window (14.10).

SOUND BYTES

Near the bottom of the report, you come to the sound section (14.11). The settings and resulting byte size for every sound in the animation are provided here.

> **NOTE**
>
> To hear sounds as they will sound when published, you must test the movie (Control ➢ Test Movie) or publish it. Sounds are not previewed accurately on the Flash stage.

TIP

In vector-based animation, sound usually takes up the bulk of the data stream. There's a tradeoff between larger overall file size and quality of sound. I opt for a slightly larger file size so that the sound quality is commensurate with the sound you usually hear in vector-based "Webisodes." This is typically MP3 sound at 20 or 24 kbps mono, best quality.

Yet another great tip from Janet Galore, Honkworm International, Inc.

```
Stream sound: 22KHz Mono 24 kbps MP3
Event sounds: 22KHz Stereo 24 kbps MP3

Sound Name                    Bytes      Format
----------------------        --------   --------
meow robot.wav                  2043     22KHz Mono 24 kbps MP3
ClosingMusic.wav              191817     22KHz Mono 24 kbps MP3
paper rips.wav                  3837     22KHz Mono 24 kbps MP3
P eureka.wav                    4929     22KHz Mono 24 kbps MP3
worldpeace.wav                161553     22KHz Mono 24 kbps MP3
boxtop falls.wav                2199     22KHz Mono 24 kbps MP3
P maybe rat a kitten.wav        9219     22KHz Mono 24 kbps MP3
vwoop.wav                       7113     22KHz Mono 24 kbps MP3
crowd.wav                      63351     22KHz Mono 24 kbps MP3
keyclick.wav                     873     22KHz Mono 24 kbps MP3
ChairScrape.wav                 1341     22KHz Mono 24 kbps MP3
DoorSlam.wav                    2745     22KHz Mono 24 kbps MP3
P ididnt say anything.wav       6411     22KHz Mono 24 kbps MP3
P favorite breakfast.wav       13743     22KHz Mono 24 kbps MP3
Newspaper 2.wav                 1263     22KHz Mono 24 kbps MP3
Newspaper 1.wav                 1341     22KHz Mono 24 kbps MP3
CatClockTickTock.wav            5163     22KHz Mono 24 kbps MP3
Stirring.wav                    2589     22KHz Mono 24 kbps MP3
alarm.wav                      15303     22KHz Mono 24 kbps MP3
IntroMusic.wav                 26925     22KHz Mono 24 kbps MP3
```

14.11

Notice that streamed sounds and event sounds can be given different encoding and different resolution and bit depths. Event sounds are often encoded at a lower quality — either lower bit depth (kHz), lower quality (kbps), or both — than are streaming sounds. In this cartoon, they are both given MP3 encoding at 22 kHz, and 24 kbps, but event sounds are encoded in stereo (doubling their size) while the streaming sounds are only in mono.

To change your sound settings, choose File ➤ Publish Settings, and adjust the bit rate and quality for event and streaming sounds on the Flash tab (14.12). Set the bit rate and quality as low as you can while still getting adequate sound. Unless you have some overarching reason not to (such as client demands), encode all of your sounds using MP3 encoding.

You can override the default settings for individual sounds (14.13) by double-clicking that sound in your library and selecting new compression settings.

FONT SIZE

The last part of the report provides the number of bytes taken up by the text in your animation (14.14). The Characters column shows what characters from that font are in your cartoon. Each character is, in effect, a symbol. For example, if your movie includes the text "flummox" in Times New Roman, Flash stores the curve information that makes up those particular letters — f, l, u, m, o, and x — in that font. You can use those letters, in that font, as many times as you want

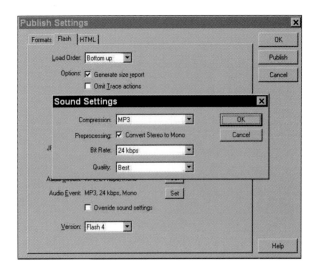

14.12

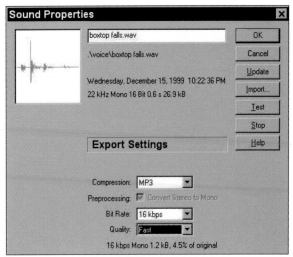

14.13

```
Font Name                  Bytes     Characters
----------------------     -------   ----------
Arial Black Bold Italic     439      ETdehn
Arial Bold Italic          2227      ":ABCIJMRYabcefghiklmnorstuwy
Cadellinis Bold Italic     1157      aeimnrt
Quixley LET Bold Italic    2269      19ACEPSVWabceghilmnorstuy
Aachen BT                  2956      %&'()04BHKLNSacdefgilmnorstuwz
Mini Pics L'il Stuff        607      V
LcdD                       1102      ,BMabegity
Gorilla BT Italic          2816      iKLPeginostuv
Plover                     2398      '?ACFGILPQSTWadefghiklmnorstuvwy
SloganD                    1889      ()AFdeghilnorstw
StopD                       808      GPefginorstu
Mini Pics Red Rock          692      %
Odessa LET                 1279      CHehlorst
Viva BoldExtraExtended      701      24Pestu
Jokerman LET Bold           347      AlM
BellBottom Bold            1724      'BSfnstu
Pump Demi Bold LET         1071      iCacefhinostw
First-Grader               2665      12345DLSaefghinopsty
Raphael                    3097      .0123456789CMaehilmnrstwy
Arial Bold                 1312      -.3BHPRTbeiklmosuy
Times New Roman Bold       1842      ABDEGILYdfimorst
Times New Roman            4264      &+,.ABCDEFMPRSTVacdefghiklmnorstuvwx
Bard                       3044      .12489BSTWaeilrst
Serifa BT                  1269      EFKacehilmnostx
```

14.14

with no additional size penalty. The more fonts you use, and the more characters you use per font, the larger the resulting animation. If you use the word "flummox" in three different fonts, Flash must store three times as many sets of curves, so try to avoid using a lot of different fonts. (You'll notice that I didn't follow my own advice in this cartoon!)

BANDWIDTH PROFILER

In addition to the size report, Flash provides another tool to help you spot where your bytes are going to cause problems on download and playback: the bandwidth profiler. The bandwidth profiler gives you a graphical display of your movie.

With your movie loaded, choose Control ➢ Test Movie. Once the movie starts, choose View ➢ Bandwidth Profiler. The bandwidth profiler profiles your movie in several different ways.

NOTE

Viewers needn't have your fonts installed on their system to watch your cartoon. However, if anyone else needs to open and edit the FLA file of your cartoon, then they'll need any fonts used in that cartoon installed on their system — or Flash substitutes other fonts that are available. Results can range from okay to disastrous. If you must share FLAs with animators who don't have the right fonts, break text apart (Modify ➢ Break Apart).

TIP

One way to control spikes is to preload specific symbols before you need them in the data stream. Test the movie and look for a spot in the data stream before the scene that doesn't have much going on. Make a note of those frame numbers. Then go back to the main timeline and drag a few bitmap elements into those frames, in a layer that is beneath everything else so the bitmaps won't be visible in the frames. Then test the movie again to see the results. This way, you can spread out the symbol data before it's needed, and when the Flash player comes to the big scene, it will already have some or all of the symbols it needs.

©2000, Janet Galore, Honkworm International, Inc.

WHAT IS STREAMING?

One of Flash's key features is the capability to stream data. This simply means that your animations begin to play without waiting for the entire file to arrive. Regular broadcast television is a streaming medium: The six o'clock news begins playing on your TV at 6:00; your TV doesn't wait to receive the entire half-hour broadcast before it begins to play.

Flash's streaming is predicated on the faith that the animation will continue arriving from the Web, or wherever, quickly enough to keep up with the playback. As long as it takes about a second for each second of animation to make its way to the Flash player, the movie plays back smoothly. If it takes two seconds — or even 1.1 seconds — for each second of animation to arrive on the viewer's computer, then there's a problem; the animation stutters and freezes. The Flash player does not show any given frame until all of the assets in that frame — graphics and sound — are available.

You can assume that someone with a dial-up modem can download about 2K (2,000 bytes) every second.

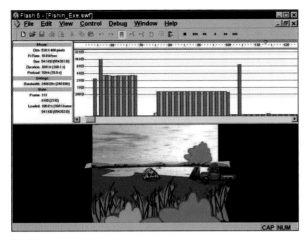

14.15

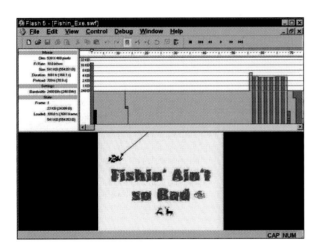

14.16

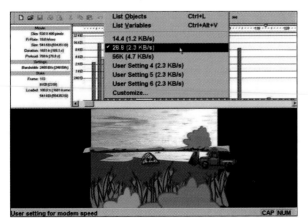

14.17

NOTE

Test your cartoon on as many different machines and browsers — including different versions of browsers — as you can before you publish it. Try to make sure it runs well no matter what browser your viewer may be running, even on a slow machine. Quite a few P-133s are still out there.

FRAME BY FRAME

Choose View ➤ Frame By Frame Graph from the menu. The frame-by-frame graph shows you the amount of data in each frame (14.15). This is the same information you get in the first section of the size report, but rendered in a nice graph instead of stodgy text.

STREAMING GRAPH

Choose View ➤ Streaming Graph for another look at the data (14.16).

The streaming graph helps you pinpoint frames that contain too much data to stream and play smoothly. Under the Debug menu, set the profiler to the slowest connect speed at which viewers may be downloading your animation (14.17). I recommend 28.8. Any frames that contain too much data to stream and play smoothly at that speed results in peaks that rise above the red line in the center of the graph.

The higher the spike, the worse the hiccup.

Frames are represented by alternating light and dark areas. In some cases, the data for a single frame will download while several frames play. In other cases, the data for several frames may download while a single frame plays back. By the end of the movie, all frames will likely have downloaded, leaving

NOTE

If you export your movie as a series of bitmaps, choose a full-color, uncompressed format such as BMP or PNG. Avoid JPGs and GIFs, as they compress the images, which may alter the look of your cartoon.

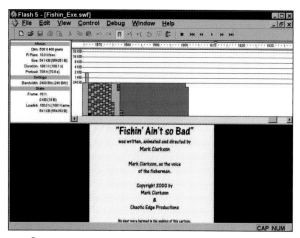

14.18

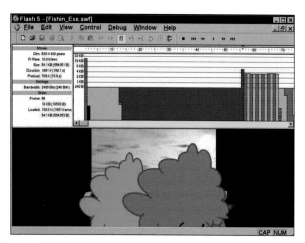

14.19

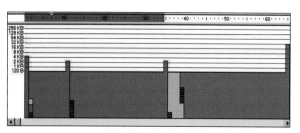

14.20

NOTE

If you are making an animation that will be exported to a video format from Flash, avoid using movie clips. Unfortunately, only the first frame of a movie clip is exported to AVI or QuickTime. The good news is that movie clips can easily be changed to animated symbols.

Thanks to Janet Galore, Honkworm International, Inc.

the graph blank for the last several frames of playback (14.18).

Click any dark or light area in the graph to display the frame of animation it represents (14.19).

As long as no spikes are sticking up above the red line, the animation streams smoothly from the Internet at the connection speed you've set. As you saw in Chapter 12, you can tell Flash to preload all or part of your animation before it begins playing. This effectively eliminates the problems with streaming playback.

SHOW STREAMING

The third profiler option, Show Streaming, plays your animation back as though it were streaming down from the Internet at the selected speed, letting you see how long it will take viewers to download your cartoons, and how well they'll play back.

The green bar at the top of the graph fills in as more and more of the animation is "downloaded" (14.20).

OPTIMIZING BITMAPPED MOVIES

Optimizing the data stream is much more important in bitmap-based movies than in vector-based movies. Each bitmap image used will make a spike in the stream of data. If these spikes are not minimized and accounted for in preloading, they will make the playback of the movie over the Internet pause for the image to load or, worse, the frame the image is loaded on may be skipped, and the image will not appear in the movie!

© 2000, Janet Galore, Honkworm International, Inc.

BROADCAST COLORS

Not every color that your computer can produce will be accurately reproduced when your animation is transferred to videotape, or viewed on a television. If you are planning to transfer your work to video, avoid highly saturated colors, especially reds. Pure red (at or near RGB 255,255,255) will "smear" when viewed on a television. Also avoid pure black and white values. The standard values for broadcast black and white are RGB 16,16,16 and RGB 235,235,235, respectively. Professional video production equipment can perform color correction — making your animation video safe after the fact — but working with video-safe colors from the beginning makes things easier. A Flash color palette of video-safe colors, called Video Safe.clr, is included on the CD-ROM that accompanies this book. If you stick to the colors on this palette, you should be okay.

The Show Streaming option enables you to test the performance of your preloader, if you have one, under Internet speeds.

But viewers can still encounter some hiccups on playback. Certain Flash features are especially CPU-intensive. That is, your computer must work extra hard to perform them.

Alpha transparency fades, color fades, and, surprisingly, gradient fill backgrounds can all slow down playback, as will anything that causes large areas of the screen to be re-rendered with every frame. If more than one is happening at once, slower machines start to chug and stutter.

VIDEO OUTPUT

Want Mom to see your cartoons on TV? Flash exports your movie as AVI or QuickTime files, or as a sequence of bitmaps. Any of these can be pulled into video-editing software. AVIs and QuickTime movies can be published with sound. If you prefer to work with bitmap sequences, you have to add sound in your video-editing software.

You can pick up add-in cards for as little as $100, which will allow you to output to video from your computer. That's fine if you want to pass your cartoons around to your friends and relatives, but if you want to produce high-quality tapes, you need to pick up a high-end card, cables, and VCR, as well as a nice, fast audio/video-rated hard drive (to make sure it can play back long animations without stuttering) and lots of RAM.

Until you're sure you're ready to go into the video production business, look for a service bureau — a company whose business it is to transfer your files to videotape — and have them do the work for you professionally.

CHAPTER 15
SELLING YOUR WORK

Finally, after all that hard work, your cartoon's finished. It's a thing of beauty. All your friends love it. And now you want to turn it into bucks? I'm shocked. Shocked! It used to be about the art, man.

Ah, well. I'll do what I can to help. Read on.

THE ENEMY OF GOOD ENOUGH

The first step to selling your cartoon is to get it out there. There's a saying that "*perfect* is the enemy of *good enough*." There's a tendency among all creative types — musicians, poets, novelists, animators — to hold onto their work forever, to keep reworking it, tweaking it, fiddling with it, forever, to say, "I want to make it a little bit better before I show it to anyone." Hell, look at George Lucas who spent *decades* mooning about what he wished he'd done differently with his hugely successful *Star Wars* films, eventually spending millions to change details and add eye candy before *finally* going on to make another film.

Now, far be it for me to suggest that you shouldn't be critical of your own work, that you shouldn't strive for perfection — you should. But you don't achieve perfection in a particular cartoon; you build toward it over a body of work, by making every cartoon better than the last. And you can't do that if you spend eternity working on that first cartoon.

My own work is a good case in point. If I'd known how much exposure "Fishin' Ain't So Bad" was going to get — about 125,000 people have watched it on AtomFilms.com; it has appeared on Blockbuster's Web site; and it's included on the bonus CD-ROM

Boys, never, never, never, never give up!
SIR WINSTON CHURCHILL

© R. Brad Yarhouse

© R. Brad Yarhouse

that accompanies this book — I'd probably still be working on it, trying to make it "good enough" to publish. Instead, I threw it together in just four days to amuse myself and my friends. Then, because it was done, I figured I had nothing to lose by submitting it to AtomFilms, which, much to my surprise, bought it. The cartoon's bigger than it needs to be and there are countless details that bug me every time I watch it. But I was much better served by sending it out, flawed as it was, and moving on to other work.

Again, I'm not suggesting that you should publish work that you're not proud of, or that you try to sell your work when it's still in a rough, unfinished form — unless you have a previous understanding with the buyer. But nothing is ever perfect; you'll probably never be completely satisfied with any work you do. Don't use that as an excuse to stall forever.

There are thousands of first novels, songs, poems, paintings, and cartoons out there, hidden away in

drawers, closets, and shoeboxes full of floppies. In most cases, that's where they belong, but the authors will never know until they let their work out into the world for others to see, to criticize and, possibly, to embrace.

Get it out there. You're never going to sell your work while it's sitting on your hard disk.

GOTTA GET A WEB PAGE

If you don't have a Web page, get one now. Your Web page is your identity, your home on the Web, your store, your advertising brochure, your resume, and your best friend. (Well, okay, maybe not your best friend.) Your Web page is the face you show the world. When people see your cartoons and want to see more of your work, learn more about you, or contact you to offer rich contracts, your Web page is where they'll go (15.1).

Make your Web site look as clean and professional as possible. If you don't know where to start, cruise the Web for other sites that appeal to you and borrow inspiration from them. I like the old-fashioned cartoon look of Bulbo.com (15.2).

Have a Web presence. You can even build your entire Web site in Flash (15.3), wiring up buttons to jump from scene to scene or, more commonly, to load new SWF files instead of Web pages. Even a very simple, one-page Web site is better than nothing.

Get an e-mail account. People can't hire you if they can't get in touch with you.

DOUG ARNEY, ATOMFILMS

The same rules apply to Flash that apply to any content: the style and the storyline must be of good quality. Since Flash cartoons tend to be short, I look for a strong punch line . . . a strong climax.

Stylistically, a lot of Flash cartooning looks the same. To be able to get outside of that, to extend it, to make your work more stylistically appealing, that gets points in my book.

File size is also key. Nobody wants to wait around — it's all instant gratification. For the moment, anyway, the shorter the better. If the file is big, if it's going to take forever to load, that's kind of a turnoff. I'd talk to [the animators] and say, "Is there anything you can do to cut this down? Can you break it into two episodes?"

I don't typically buy anything before it's finished, unless you have a pilot episode done and have scripts or treatments for other episodes. I definitely want to see at least one episode in finished form, to see how you work within the medium, before I just take your word for the storyline.

Thanks to Doug Arney, Animation Acquisition Specialist, AtomFilms.com.

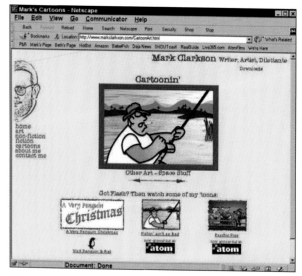

15.1

VIRAL MARKETING

At first, no one's going to know who you are, and it's up to you to spread the buzz. Your best, cheapest option is *viral marketing*. Viral marketing isn't about selling colds and flus; it means promoting your work with software, screensavers, games . . . anything that people will want to copy and pass around.

15.2   © 2000, Xeth Feinberg and Mishmash Media

15.3   © 2000, The Joe Cartoon Co.

15.4   © 2000, The Joe Cartoon Co.

Joe Cartoon is a prime example of the success of viral marketing. His early cartoons were passed around as e-mail attachments in the tens of thousands, and each and every one had a link back to his Web site. It wasn't long before everybody with an e-mail account had heard of Joe Cartoon, and now he drives a Humvee (15.4). (I drive a '72 Buick, so draw your own conclusions.) Only on the Internet. Of course, for Joe's viral marketing to work out, the cartoons had to be *funny*; people had to *want* to pass around copies to their friends. Joe Cartoon's viral downloads were in the form of executables so they didn't require the recipients to have a Flash player installed on their systems. (Of course, executables are a bit bigger than Flash SWF files.)

As a viral marketer, you can use anything and everything — games, desktop wallpaper, executable versions of your cartoons — anything people can download and pass around to their friends and relations. Make sure everything includes a link back to your Web site.

MONDO MEDIA

If you're coming to me with a realized cartoon, either it should be exactly what you want it to be — the execution, writing, production values, everything — or it should be a very fast teaser for same.

If it needs work, you're giving people a taste of something that's not really what you have in mind. It's better for you to show something that's less complete, but true to the vision that you have.

With Flash, more than with other types of animation, you really have to focus on the writing — on what is underneath the animation. You can't make up for the lack of writing, lack of story, lack of thought, with 24 frames a second and a bunch of squash and stretch. The more you try to do that, the more you compromise the reason you use Flash in the first place, which is to make an efficient, small-sized animation that can be transferred via the Web.

Thanks to Philo Northrup, Director of Groove Content Acquisition, Mondo Media, Inc.

I like screensavers. Screensavers are little software toys, and people are always looking for new ones (15.5). A number of programs allow you to turn Flash animations into screensavers . . . even interactive screensavers. I use FlashJester Creator from 3rd Eye (15.6). You can snag a demo version at `www.flashjester.com`. There are a number of programs that make screensavers from your SWFs, including Grooveware's Screenweaver, and MacSourcery's ScreenTime, demos of which are included on the CD-ROM that accompanies this book.

NETWORK, NETWORK, NETWORK

How do you meet the people who can give you that all-important first break? Time and time again, when I ask Flash animators how they got into the business and how they first began selling their work, the answer begins with "Well, I knew this guy . . . ."

Most animators I know got their first business through someone they worked with in a T-shirt shop, or someone they met in a college multimedia class, or

a landlord, who is also a part-time video producer. The point is that you never know where your break is coming from, where you're going to meet the person who'll make a difference in your career.

Get away from your computer once in a while. Meet people. Take classes. Go to conferences. Be active on message boards. Let everyone and his mother know that you are a Flash animator. Be alert for opportunities; you never know where they're coming from.

MAKING THAT CALL

If there's someone you want to work with, give him or her a call. When Flasher Meredith Scardino wanted to work with an independent film producer, she approached Bill Plympton, whose work she admired.

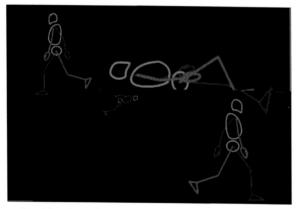

15.5

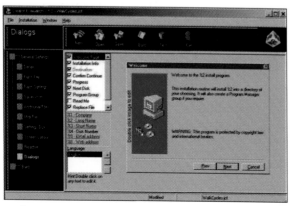

15.6

ED BEALS

Ask yourself "Why do I want to make Flash cartoons?" If it's because you like working with computers and it sounds like fun, then learn all you can about all aspects of the software. Be the person who knows everything about Flash.

If you see Flash as a way to tell a story, then focus on the aspects of the program that help you tell your story better. If 3D effects or mouse trails don't add anything to what you are trying to do, don't worry about them. If you need to tell a story that has five possible endings for the viewer to choose from, then learn how to make it work. But remember, just because you can do something does not always mean you should.

Don't try to second-guess what your audience wants. Tell stories to please yourself.

When you see or read or hear a story you like, figure out why. Deconstruct it. Absorb it. Learn from it.

Take a course in creative writing if you like, or go fishing, or learn to play the banjo, or take up gardening . . . do something that gets you away from the computer. Do and see things; it will inspire you and infuse your stories with life.

Thanks to Ed Beals, www.edbeals.com.

> ## CORY WYNNE, ATOMFILMS
>
> **If it's a great idea — if it's great storytelling, great writing — I don't care if it's stick figures scribbled on a napkin. The writing is the most important thing. Strong characters and strong stories are important . . . if you can establish those things then you're part of the race.**
>
> **The best advice I can give you is to get out there and do your own damned research — know the market, know who the players are . . . what they offer, what's different from one site to another, what their businesses look like. The more savvy you are as a creator, then the better off you're going to be, the better terms you're going to get, the stronger relationship you're going to build.**
>
> **Thanks to Cory Wynne, Senior Content Manager, AtomFilms.**

The timing was right: Plympton was becoming interested in putting his work on the Web. Meredith got the gig of transferring Plympton's work into Flash form. You can see the results on AtomFilms.

You have nothing at all to lose except a little money on your long-distance bill. The worst someone can do is say no.

SELLING YOUR WORK ON THE WEB

You've finished the cartoon. It's killer. It's published on your Web site and your friends love it, but you want to show it to the world. And you want to get paid for it. How do you make the sale? Luckily for you, the Web is still hungry for content, and it's much, much easier to get someone to look at your work, publish it, and pay you for it on the Web than on, say, TV. I've conceived, animated, pitched, sold, and gotten a check for a cartoon within a month. But don't just go out, willy-nilly, sending every cartoon to every online site.

"Know who we are and what we do before you approach me," advises Cory Wynne, Senior Content Manager at AtomFilms. Different sites have different criteria, different styles, and different needs. Watch everything on the site; know whom you're approaching and what they're buying before you pitch your work. AtomFilms is looking for sophisticated, adult material. They love to push the boundaries in content and in form. Don't pitch them kiddy cartoons with cute elves; and don't approach CartoonNetwork.com with your series on lesbian angst.

SELLING YOUR WORK TO ADVERTISERS

If your viral marketing efforts are getting you ten thousand hits a day on your Web site, it may be time to seek out banner ads. In fact, they'll probably seek *you* out. Banner ads aren't really selling your work; they're using your work to sell viewers' eyeballs to the advertisers, or at least to rent them, but you still get paid. There are some Flash cartoonists out there right now making a living off of banner ad revenue.

Invent other ad revenue possibilities. Approach businesses about doing cartoons for their Web sites, or about incorporating their ads into your cartoons. John K. ("The Goddamn George Liquor Show," and others) is experimenting with incorporating sponsorship in his cartoons — billboard advertising may appear in a cityscape, for example.

KEEPING AT IT

No matter what happens, no matter how many times you're rejected, no matter what your friends say, keep at it. Write, draw, animate. Make cartoons that entertain you, and keep making them until they find their audience.

Your technical skills — working with layers, wrestling with shape tweening and alpha fades — are ultimately less important than your writing and drawing skills. Buy a pencil. Draw and sketch. Write down ideas. Regale your friends. Keep at it and you'll keep getting better. It's inevitable. It's work but, luckily for you, it's fun work, and you want to do it, anyway. Right?

Be true to your own vision and, above all, as Winston Churchill said, ". . . never, never, never, never give up!"

I'll be looking for your cartoons.

Peace,

APPENDIX
ABOUT THE CD-ROM

The CD-ROM at the back of this book contains bytes and bytes of fun and useful stuff: chapter files for the book, some great Flash cartoons, a digital copy of this book, and free and demonstration software to get you started making your own Flash cartoons. Here's how to get at them.

Insert the CD into your CD-ROM drive. On the Mac, a CD icon appears on your desktop. Under Windows, you probably need to double-click the My Computer icon on your desktop to find the CD icon.

Double-click the icon to open the CD-ROM. Depending on your platform, you will see one of two independent partitions, one for the Mac and the other for the PC. If you own Virtual PC on the Mac, you can check out the PC half of the CD from inside Windows.

The most important item you'll find on the CD is the Chapter Files folder. Within this folder are separate folders for each chapter. For example, you'll find the example files for Chapter 13 in the folder called "Chapter 13." Most of these files are referred to within the chapters, so you'll know what they are by the time you need them. If you're overly curious or impatient, you can double-click them now and see what they do. It's OK; you won't hurt anything. If some folders seem to be missing, don't worry: not all chapters have supporting files. While it isn't strictly necessary, you'll probably want to copy the Chapter Files folder to your hard drive. It makes them easier to work with. Just make sure you remember where you put them.

The coolest items on the CD are the animated movies. You'll find them, appropriately enough, in the Movies folder of the CD. The movies comprise a wide variety of work to inspire you: some short, some long, some interactive, some funny, some beautiful, some indescribably bizarre. Something here will surely blow your feathers back. Enjoy. Each animator's work is contained in its own folder. My cartoons, for example, are in the folder "Mark Clarkson." Most of the folders include a shortcut to the animator's Web page. Double-click this icon and your default browser should take you there, to enjoy more of that animator's work.

Those of you who can't be bothered to fiddle with old-fashioned paper-based technology will be happy to find a complete digital version of this book on the CD, rendered in Adobe Acrobat format, in the folder called Flash 5 Cartooning PDF. You need to install Acrobat to access this copy of the book. Installation instructions are in the Adobe Acrobat folder.

© 2000, Greg Kelly

You'll also find free and demonstration software from a variety of vendors, including a trial of Macromedia Flash 5; a demo of Sonic Foundry's Acid — the easiest way to make music for your cartoon, even if you lack all musical talent; screen saver makers from Grooveware and MacSourcery; Paint Shop Pro for working with bitmaps; and SoundForge for massaging sounds.

CD TECHNICAL SUPPORT

If you have any problems getting the CD to work with your computer, it's very likely that some of your settings files or drivers are not working properly. For assistance, call Hungry Minds' technical support hotline at 1-800-762-2974. You can also call this number if your CD is damaged.

INDEX

Numbers

101 Dalmations, 4
3D motion, 119-120

A

accents, determining in dialogue, 155
action, cutting on, 172
ActionScript
  collision detection and user interaction, 205
  getTimer( ) function, 195-197
  loops and random functions, 192-197
  Tell Target, 198-203
  variables, 191
Adjust Curve tool, 19
advertisers, selling cartoons to, 221
anchor points, 38
Anderson, Vaughn, 162, 176, 201
Angular Blend option, 156
animatics, creating, 101-110
animations. *See also* cartoons; movies
  adding buttons to, 181-186
  arms, 72
  balance, 79-80
  basic construction steps, 75-77
  bitmaps, 80-81
  Bopsey models, 133-138
  breaking into frames, 122-128
  building pre-loaders for, 187-188
  changing stacking order of, 140-141
  dialogue. *See* dialogue
  ears, 72
  easing in and out of, 100, 122-123
  emotions of, 144
  exporting from Flash to video format, 214
  facial expressions, 156-157
  full, 4
  gestures, 79-80
  hands, 74
  heads, 70, 72, 157-162
  hierarchies, 145-148
  interactions in. *See* interactions in
    animations

jumping around scenes, 185-187
keyframes, 95-100
layers in, 70, 72
legs, 72
limiting curves in, 16
lip and jaw sync, 156
main stage, converting to symbols, 55
model and color sheets, 81-82
mouths, 74-75, 151-155
noses, 72
phonemes, 156-157
poses, 79-80, 96
preparing for viewing on television, 215
profiles, 77-78
replaying, 184-185
run cycles, 144
sound. *See* sound
straight-ahead animation, 129
tweening. *See* tweening animations
walk cycles, 138-144
Yogi Bear, 69
anime, 134
anticipation in motion, 129-130
arcs, movement in, 123-128
arms
  length of, 72
  swing of, 142
Arney, Doug, 218
Arrow tool, 18-19
artifacting, 210
AtomFilms, 6, 217-218
attributer, 26
Audio Technica AT804 cardioid, 89
audio. *See* sound

B

backgrounds
  choosing for scenes, 166
  fitting into movie boundaries, 30
  separating from foregrounds, 5-6, 166-168
balance, animated characters, 79-80

balloon, as sound effect, 89-90
balls, adding stretch and squash to, 114-115
bandwidth profiler, 212-215
bandwidth, Flash animations, 7-8
Barbera, Joseph "Joe", 4, 133
Beals, Ed, 6, 144, 220
bending curves, 22-23
Bézier curves, creating, 36-38
bidirectional microphones, 88
bitmaps
  backgrounds as, 166
  breaking apart, 103
  building animated characters in Flash,
    80-81
  converting to fills, 31-36
  described, 12
  exporting movies as series of, 213
  importing, 31
  JPG compression, 209, 210
  optimizing movies created with, 214
  PNG compression, 210
  setting sizes of, 30
  size reports, 210
black mattes, creating for animatics, 104-105
blank frames, looping through, 193-195
Blockbuster, 217
boosting sound bands, 92
Bopsey models, 133-138, 145-148
brainstorming sessions, 43-47
Bravo, Johnny, 156
breakdown drawings, 122
breaking
  animations into frames, 122-128
  groups, 128
  lines and curves, 23
  scanned bitmap images, 103
  text, 34
breaks, face outlines when mouths are open,
    74-75
broadcast color, 215
Brown, Treg, 90

ABOUT THE AUTHOR

Mark Clarkson was often in trouble during his brief stint as a software analyst at the Boeing Company, for the cartoons he sketched on the company whiteboards during long program compiles. Sadly, his efforts were universally panned by management, who often felt (however unfairly) that they were the intended butt of his jokes.

After much grave discussion, both parties agreed that Mark should leave Boeing and pursue other interests.

Since that time twelve years ago, he's worked as a freelance writer for the computer industry and as a computer artist. He has written a project-oriented book on how to use Microsoft's graphical programming software to create artificial life, entitled *Windows Hothouse: Creating Artificial Life with Visual C++* (Reading, MA: Addison-Wesley, 1993), and articles on everything from molecular computers and genetic algorithms to online gaming and girls' software. Although he's primarily a writer, Mark's 3D renderings have appeared online, in print magazines, and on the cover of *Desktop Engineering*. You can see his Flash cartooning running right now on AtomFilms (`www.atomfilms.com`).

Mark has been using computers to make himself laugh since the days of the Radio Shack TRS-80 and can honestly say he's been using — and writing about — Macromedia Flash for as long as anyone has. Mark is currently working on a short CGI film in 3D and several Flash cartoons — including the Penguin & Rat series he's producing with his home-schooled daughter, Pamela.

COLOPHON

Acquisitions Editor: Michael Roney
Project Editors: Marti Paul, Ken Brown
Technical Editor: Ibis Fernandez
Copy Editors: Cindy Lai, Nancy Rapoport, Julie Moss
Proof Editor: Patsy Owens
Project Coordinator: Louigene Santos
Graphics and Production Specialists: Robert Bihlmayer, Jude Levinson, Michael Lewis, Marcos Vergara
Quality Control Technician: Dina F Quan
Permissions Editor: Carmen Krikorian
Media Development Specialist: Brock Bigard
Media Development Coordinator: Marisa Pearman
Book Designers: Margery Cantor, Kurt Krames
Proofreading and Indexing: York Production Services
Cover Design: Anthony Bunyan
Front Cover Art
      Top Left: Wish Tank Studios
      Top Left: Vaughn Anderson
      Top Left: The Joe Cartoon Co.
Back Cover Art
      Left: Wish Tank Studios
      Middle: Alen Puaca
      Left: Dave Jones

HUNGRY MINDS, INC.
END-USER LICENSE AGREEMENT

READ THIS. You should carefully read these terms and conditions before opening the software packet(s) included with this book ("Book"). This is a license agreement ("Agreement") between you and Hungry Minds, Inc. ("HMI"). By opening the accompanying software packet(s), you acknowledge that you have read and accept the following terms and conditions. If you do not agree and do not want to be bound by such terms and conditions, promptly return the Book and the unopened software packet(s) to the place you obtained them for a full refund.

1. **License Grant.** HMI grants to you (either an individual or entity) a nonexclusive license to use one copy of the enclosed software program(s) (collectively, the "Software") solely for your own personal or business purposes on a single computer (whether a standard computer or a workstation component of a multiuser network). The Software is in use on a computer when it is loaded into temporary memory (RAM) or installed into permanent memory (hard disk, CD-ROM, or other storage device). HMI reserves all rights not expressly granted herein.

2. **Ownership.** HMI is the owner of all right, title, and interest, including copyright, in and to the compilation of the Software recorded on the disk(s) or CD-ROM ("Software Media"). Copyright to the individual programs recorded on the Software Media is owned by the author or other authorized copyright owner of each program. Ownership of the Software and all proprietary rights relating thereto remain with HMI and its licensers.

3. **Restrictions On Use and Transfer.**
 (a) You may only (i) make one copy of the Software for backup or archival purposes, or (ii) transfer the Software to a single hard disk, provided that you keep the original for backup or archival purposes. You may not (i) rent or lease the Software, (ii) copy or reproduce the Software through a LAN or other network system or through any computer subscriber system or bulletin-board system, or (iii) modify, adapt, or create derivative works based on the Software.
 (b) You may not reverse engineer, decompile, or disassemble the Software. You may transfer the Software and user documentation on a permanent basis, provided that the transferee agrees to accept the terms and conditions of this Agreement and you retain no copies. If the Software is an update or has been updated, any transfer must include the most recent update and all prior versions.

4. **Restrictions on Use of Individual Programs.** You must follow the individual requirements and restrictions detailed for each individual program in the appendix of this Book. These limitations are also contained in the individual license agreements recorded on the Software Media. These limitations may include a requirement that after using the program for a specified period of time, the user must pay a registration

fee or discontinue use. By opening the Software packet(s), you will be agreeing to abide by the licenses and restrictions for these individual programs that are detailed in the appendix and on the Software Media. None of the material on this Software Media or listed in this Book may ever be redistributed, in original or modified form, for commercial purposes.

5. Limited Warranty.

(a) HMI warrants that the Software and Software Media are free from defects in materials and workmanship under normal use for a period of sixty (60) days from the date of purchase of this Book. If HMI receives notification within the warranty period of defects in materials or workmanship, HMI will replace the defective Software Media.

(b) **HMI AND THE AUTHOR OF THE BOOK DISCLAIM ALL OTHER WARRANTIES, EXPRESS OR IMPLIED, INCLUDING WITHOUT LIMITATION IMPLIED WARRANTIES OF MERCHANTABILITY AND FITNESS FOR A PARTICULAR PURPOSE, WITH RESPECT TO THE SOFTWARE, THE PROGRAMS, THE SOURCE CODE CONTAINED THEREIN, AND/OR THE TECHNIQUES DESCRIBED IN THIS BOOK. HMI DOES NOT WARRANT THAT THE FUNCTIONS CONTAINED IN THE SOFTWARE WILL MEET YOUR REQUIREMENTS OR THAT THE OPERATION OF THE SOFTWARE WILL BE ERROR FREE.**

(c) This limited warranty gives you specific legal rights, and you may have other rights that vary from jurisdiction to jurisdiction.

6. Remedies.

(a) HMI's entire liability and your exclusive remedy for defects in materials and workmanship shall be limited to replacement of the Software Media, which may be returned to HMI with a copy of your receipt at the following address: Software Media Fulfillment Department, Attn.: *Flash 5 Cartooning*, Hungry Minds, Inc., 10475 Crosspointe Blvd., Indianapolis, IN 46256, or call 1-800-762-2974. Please allow three to four weeks for delivery. This Limited Warranty is void if failure of the Software Media has resulted from accident, abuse, or misapplication. Any replacement Software Media will be warranted for the remainder of the original warranty period or thirty (30) days, whichever is longer.

(b) In no event shall HMI or the author be liable for any damages whatsoever (including without limitation damages for loss of business profits, business interruption, loss of business information, or any other pecuniary loss) arising from the use of or inability to use the Book or the Software, even if HMI has been advised of the possibility of such damages.

(c) Because some jurisdictions do not allow the exclusion or limitation of liability for consequential or incidental damages, the above limitation or exclusion may not apply to you.

7. U.S. Government Restricted Rights. Use, duplication, or disclosure of the Software by the U.S. Government is subject to restrictions stated in paragraph (c)(1)(ii) of the Rights in Technical Data and Computer Software clause of DFARS 252.227-7013, and in subparagraphs (a) through (d) of the Commercial Computer — Restricted Rights clause at FAR 52.227-19, and in similar clauses in the NASA FAR supplement, when applicable.

8. General. This Agreement constitutes the entire understanding of the parties and revokes and supersedes all prior agreements, oral or written, between them and may not be modified or amended except in a writing signed by both parties hereto that specifically refers to this Agreement. This Agreement shall take precedence over any other documents that may be in conflict herewith. If any one or more provisions contained in this Agreement are held by any court or tribunal to be invalid, illegal, or otherwise unen-

CD-ROM INSTALLATION INSTRUCTIONS

Insert the CD into your CD-ROM drive. On the Mac, a CD icon appears on your desktop. Under Windows, you probably need to double-click the My Computer icon on your desktop to find the CD icon.

Double-click the icon to open the CD-ROM. Depending on your platform, you will see one of two independent partitions, one for the Mac and the other for the PC. If you own Virtual PC on the Mac, you can check out the PC half of the CD from inside Windows.

The most important thing you'll find on the CD is the Chapter Files folder. Within this folder are the folders for each chapter. For example, you'll find the example files for Chapter 13 within the folder called Chapter 13. If some folders seem to be missing, don't worry: not all chapters have supporting files. While it isn't strictly necessary, you'll probably want to copy the Chapter Files folder to your hard drive. It makes the folders easier to work with.

The coolest items on the CD are the animated movies. You'll find them, appropriately enough, in the "Movies" folder of the CD. You'll find a wide variety of work to inspire you: some short, some long, some interactive, some funny, some beautiful, some indescribably bizarre. You'll surely find something that blows your feathers back. Enjoy.

The CD holds a complete digital version of this book, rendered in Adobe Acrobat format, in the folder called Flash 5 Cartooning PDF. You'll need to install Acrobat to access this copy of the book. You'll find installation instructions in the Adobe Acrobat folder.

You'll also find free and demonstration software from a variety of vendors, including a trial version of Macromedia Flash 5.